STAR WARS®

VECTOR

VOLUME TWO

REBELLION VOLUME 4   LEGACY VOLUME 6

PAST > > > > > > PRESENT > > > > > > FUTURE

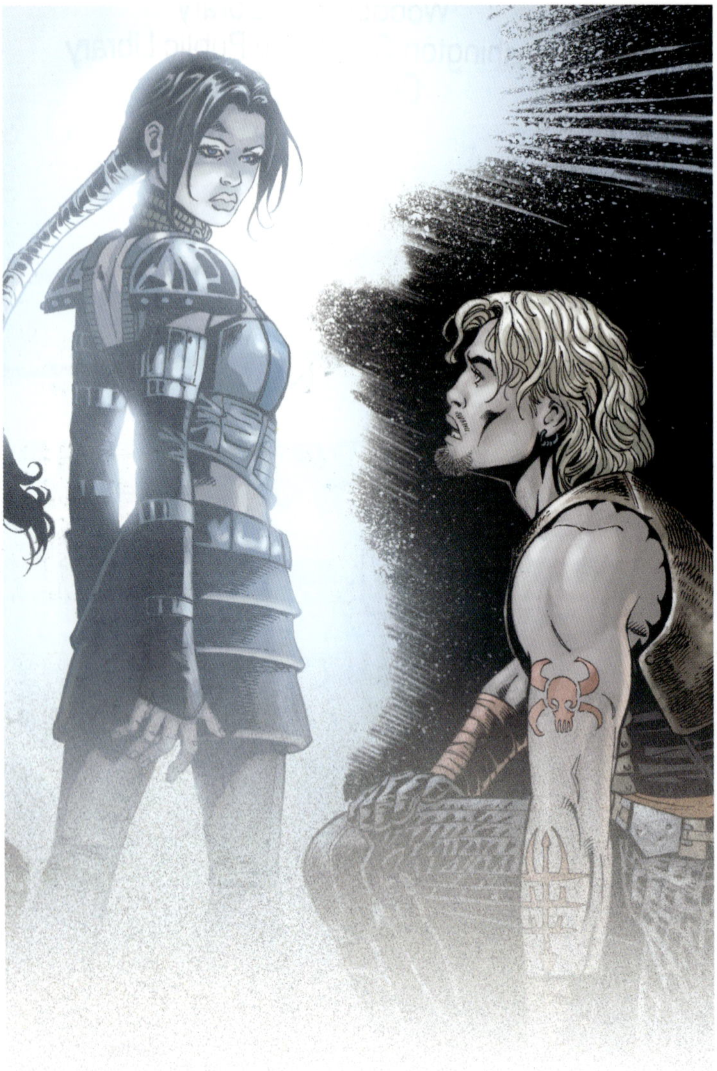

REBELLION

(From the Battle of Yavin to five years after)

Open resistance begins to spread across the galaxy in protest of the Empire's tyranny. Rebel groups unite, and the Galactic Civil War begins. This era begins with the Rebel victory that secured the Death Star plans, and ends a year after the death of the Emperor high over the forest moon of Endor. This is the era in which the events in *A New Hope*, *The Empire Strikes Back*, and *Return of the Jedi* take place.

The events in this story take place approximately nine months after the Battle of Yavin.

LEGACY

(Forty years after the Battle of Yavin and beyond)

As this era began, Luke Skywalker had unified the Jedi Order into a cohesive group of powerful Jedi Knights. It was a time a relative peace, yet darkness approached on the horizon. Now, Skywalker's descendants face new and resurgent threats to the galaxy, and to the balance of the Force.

The events in this story begin approximately 137 years after the Battle of Yavin.

PAST > > > > > > > PRESENT > > > > > > > FUTURE

STAR WARS®

VECTOR

VOLUME TWO

CHAPTER THREE

REBELLION VOLUME 4

Script
ROB WILLIAMS

Art
DUSTIN WEAVER

Colors
WIL GLASS

Lettering
MICHAEL HEISLER

CHAPTER FOUR

LEGACY VOLUME 6

Story
JOHN OSTRANDER
JAN DUURSEMA

Script
JOHN OSTRANDER

Pencils
JAN DUURSEMA

Inks
DAN PARSONS

Colors
BRAD ANDERSON

Lettering
MICHAEL HEISLER

Front Cover Art TRAVIS CHAREST Back Cover Art JAN DUURSEMA

KNIGHTS OF THE OLD REPUBLIC > > > DARK TIMES > > > REBELLION > > > LEGACY

DARK HORSE BOOKS®

Publisher MIKE RICHARDSON Collection Designer JOSH ELLIOTT Art Director LIA RIBACCHI Editor RANDY STRADLEY
Associate Editor DAVE MARSHALL Assistant Editor FREDDYE LINS

Special thanks to Elaine Mederer, Jann Moorhead, David Anderman, Leland Chee, Sue Rostoni, and Carol Roeder at Lucas Licensing

STAR WARS VECTOR Volume Two
STAR WARS REBELLION Volume Four
STAR WARS LEGACY Volume Six

This volume collects issues fifteen and sixteen of the Dark Horse Comics series
Star Wars: Rebellion, and issues twenty-eight through thirty-one of the Dark
Horse Comics series *Star Wars: Legacy*.

Published by
DARK HORSE BOOKS
A division of Dark Horse Comics, Inc.
10956 SE Main Street
Milwaukie, OR 97222

darkhorse.com
starwars.com

To find a comics shop in your area, call the Comic Shop Locator Service
toll-free at 1-888-266-4226

First edition: June 2009
ISBN 978-1-59582-227-7

1 2 3 4 5 6 7 8 9 10   Printed in China

PAST > > > > > PRESENT > > > > > FUTURE

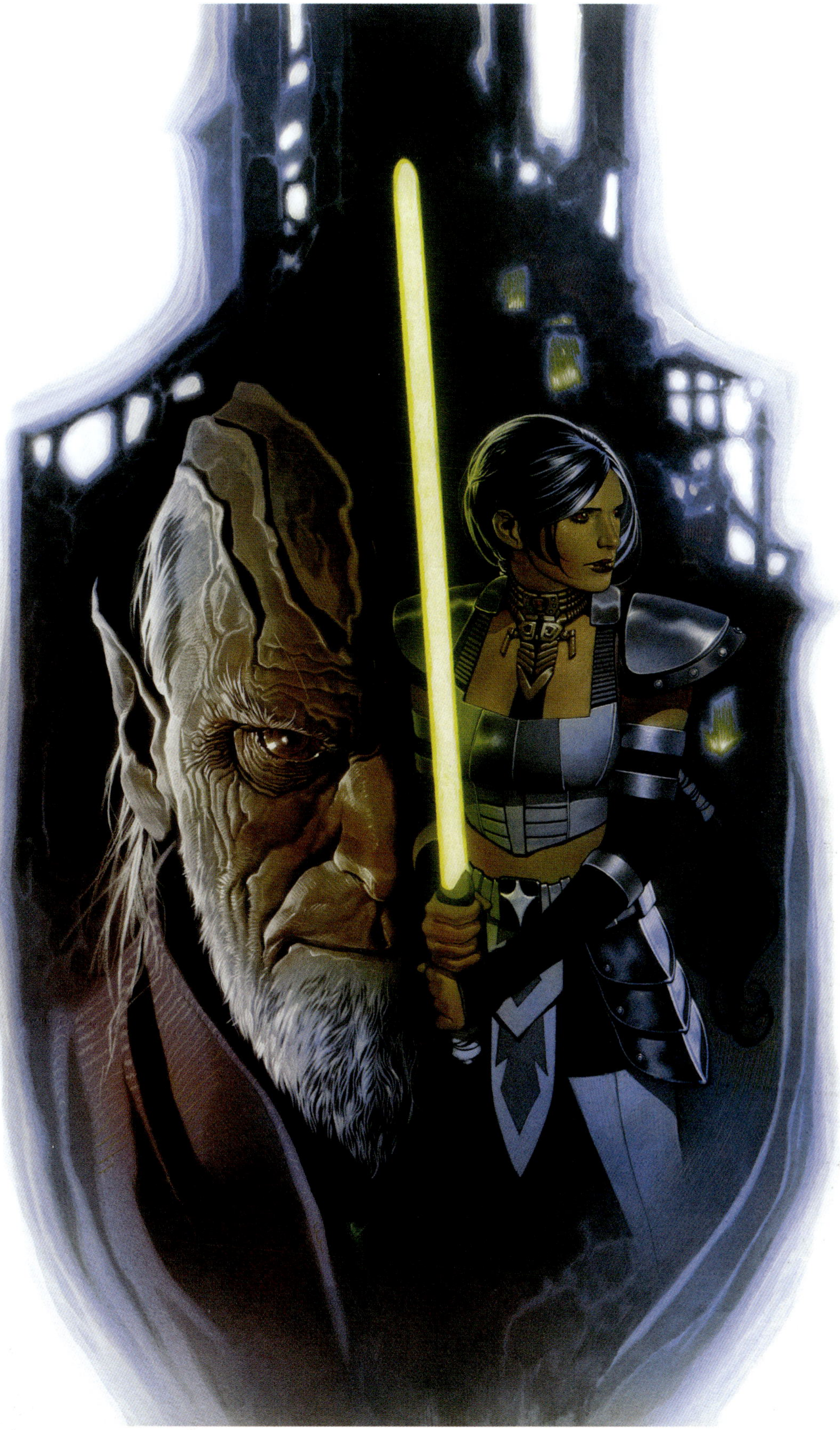

Illustration by **TRAVIS CHAREST**

PAST > > > > > > > PRESENT > > > > > > > FUTURE

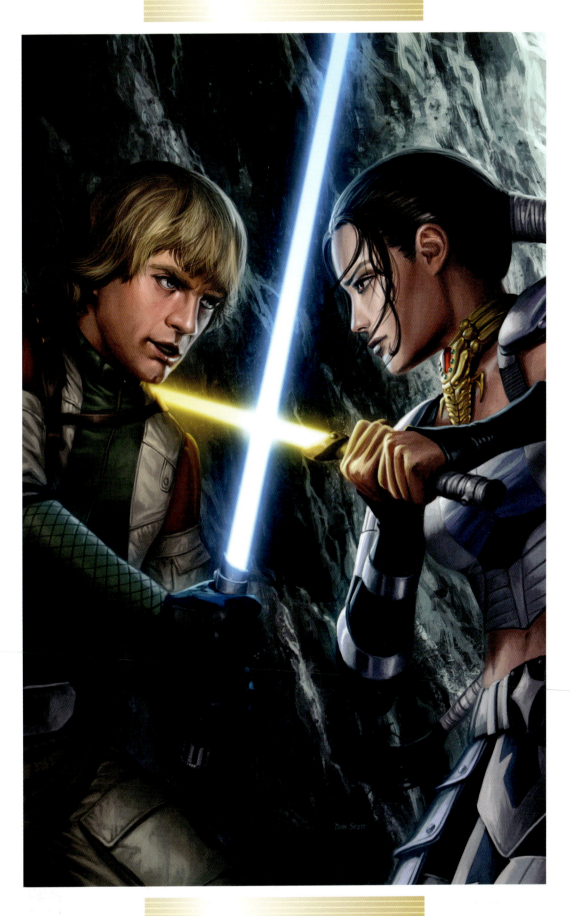

Illustration by **DAN SCOTT**

REBELLION

VOLUME 4 Nearly 4,000 years ago, Jedi Master Celeste Morne was possessed by an ancient Sith artifact called the Muur Talisman. Cursed with the power to create and control an army of Rakghoul monsters, Morne allowed herself to be sealed within a Sith stasis casket until a way could be found to destroy the Talisman.

Thousands of years later, Darth Vader found the casket and woke Morne. She was able to resist his call to Sith apprenticeship, but Vader left her stranded on a desolate moon with only the whispering Sith spirit for company.

Twenty years have passed. The Rebellion has begun: Luke Skywalker, Princess Leia, Han Solo, and many others fight to overthrow the Empire. Seeking a weapon with which to crush the rebels, Darth Vader recalls Celeste Morne . . .

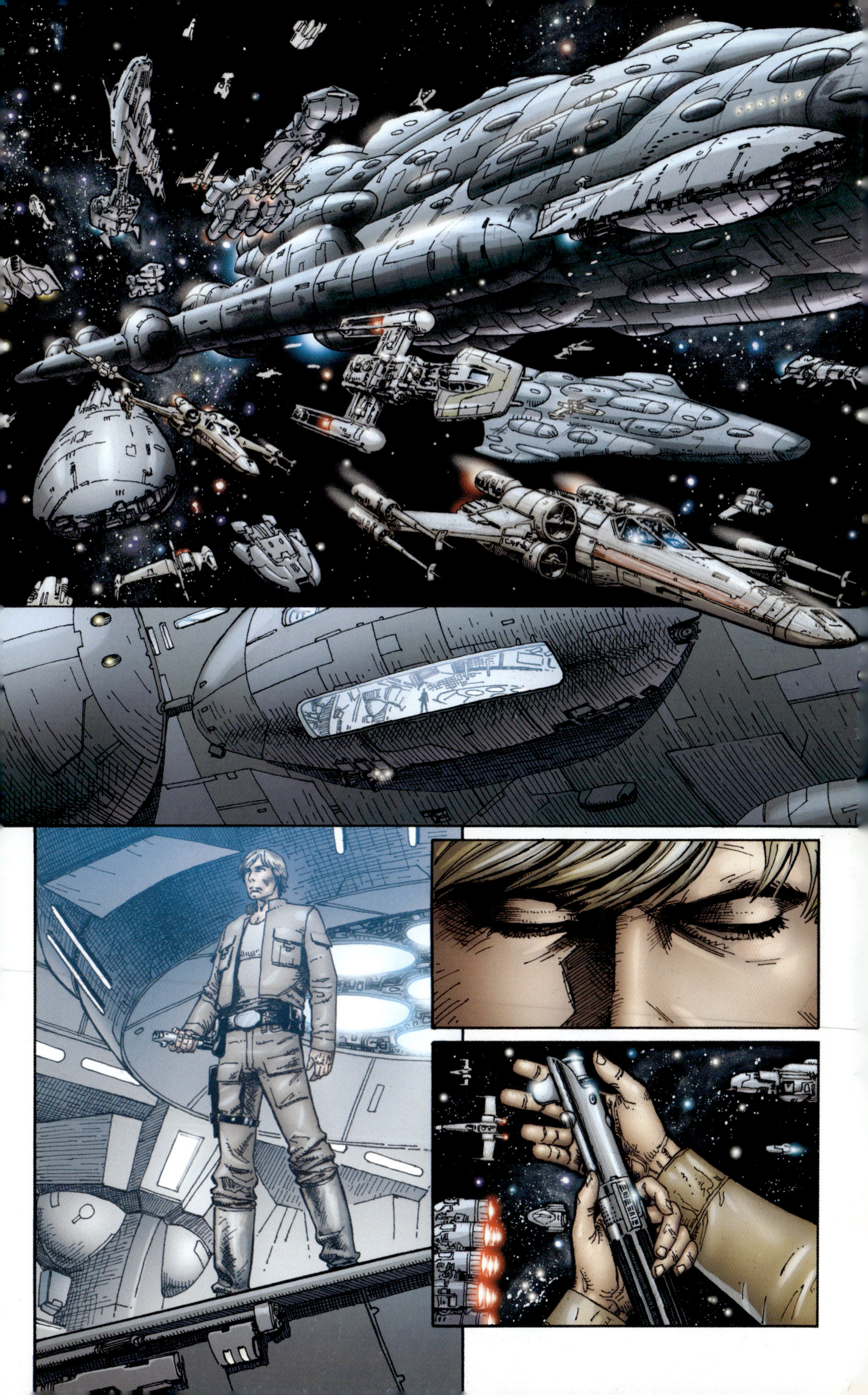

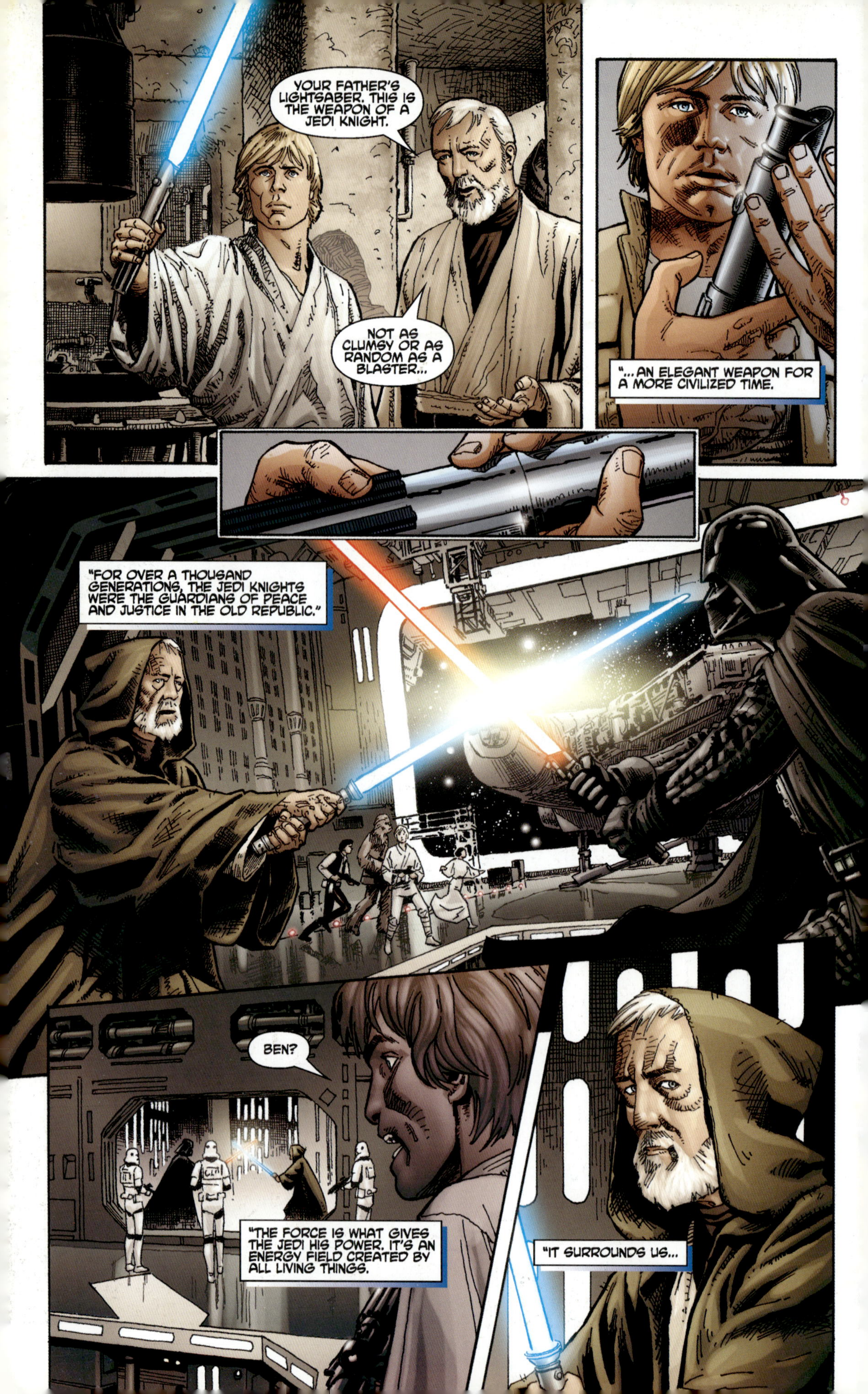
YOUR FATHER'S LIGHTSABER. THIS IS THE WEAPON OF A JEDI KNIGHT.
NOT AS CLUMSY OR AS RANDOM AS A BLASTER...
"...AN ELEGANT WEAPON FOR A MORE CIVILIZED TIME.
"FOR OVER A THOUSAND GENERATIONS, THE JEDI KNIGHTS WERE THE GUARDIANS OF PEACE AND JUSTICE IN THE OLD REPUBLIC."
BEN?
"THE FORCE IS WHAT GIVES THE JEDI HIS POWER. IT'S AN ENERGY FIELD CREATED BY ALL LIVING THINGS.
"IT SURROUNDS US...

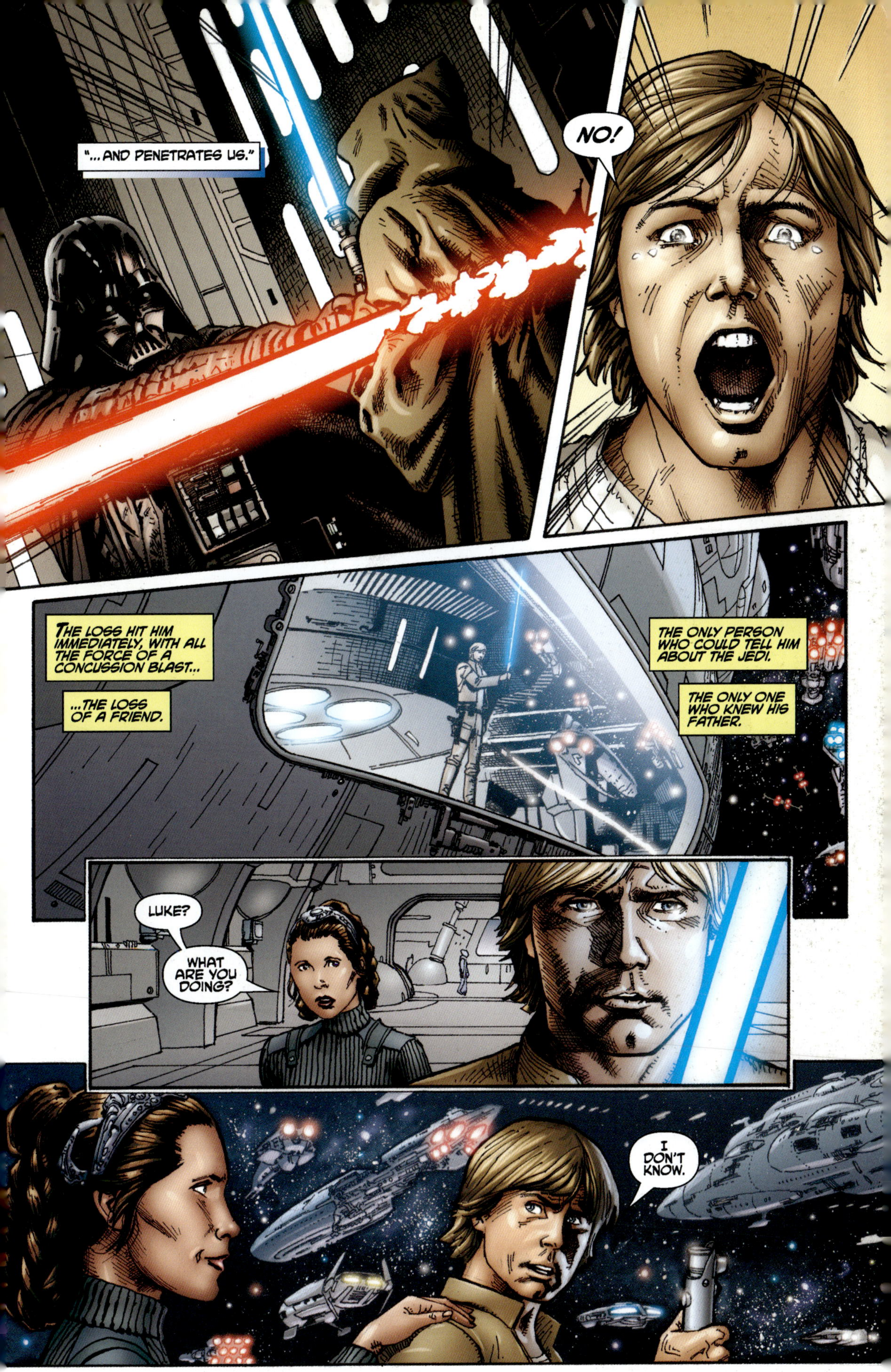
"...AND PENETRATES US."
NO!
THE LOSS HIT HIM IMMEDIATELY, WITH ALL THE FORCE OF A CONCUSSION BLAST...
...THE LOSS OF A FRIEND.
THE ONLY PERSON WHO COULD TELL HIM ABOUT THE JEDI.
THE ONLY ONE WHO KNEW HIS FATHER.
LUKE?
WHAT ARE YOU DOING?
I DON'T KNOW.

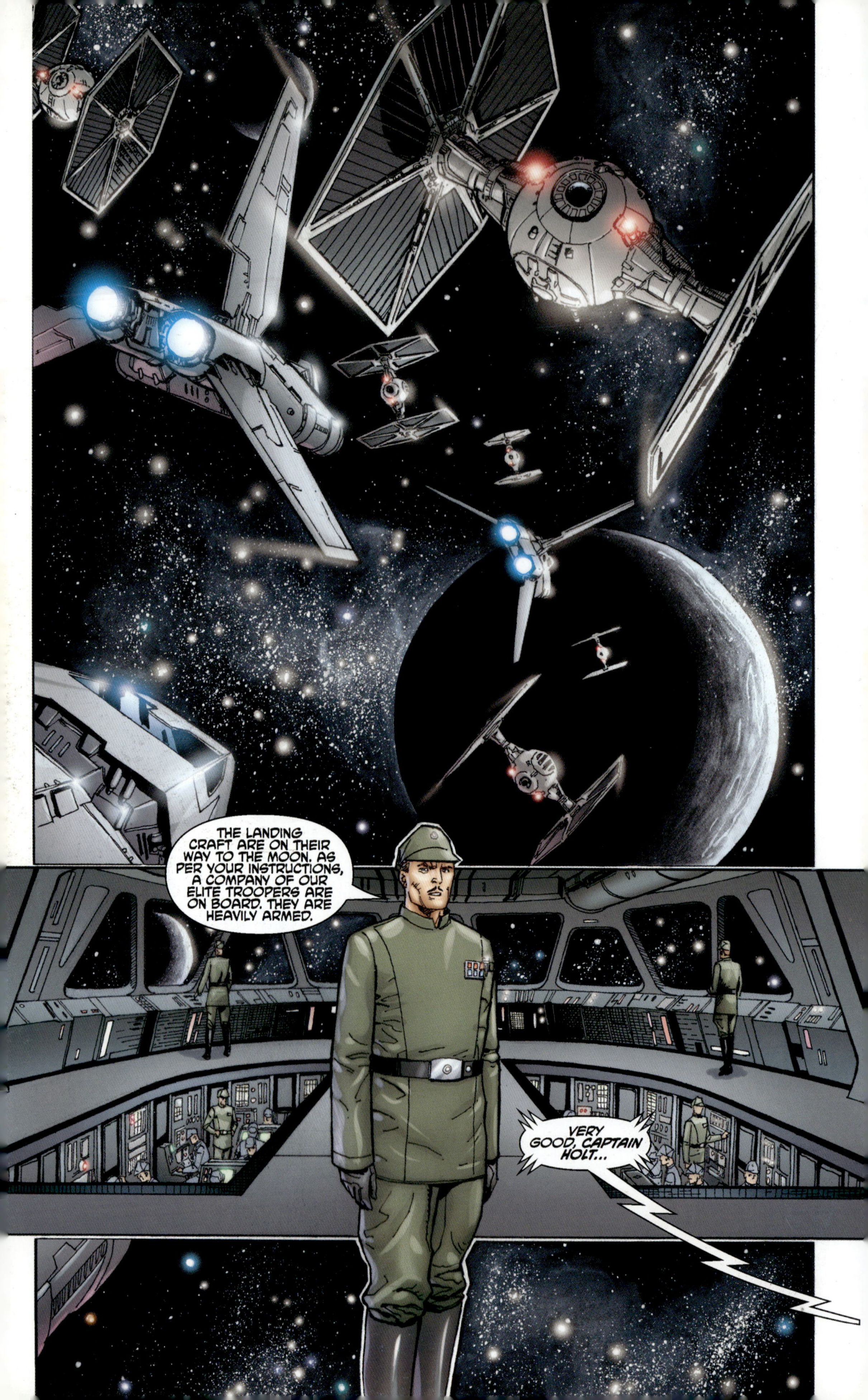
THE LANDING CRAFT ARE ON THEIR WAY TO THE MOON. AS PER YOUR INSTRUCTIONS, A COMPANY OF OUR ELITE TROOPERS ARE ON BOARD. THEY ARE HEAVILY ARMED.
VERY GOOD, CAPTAIN HOLT...

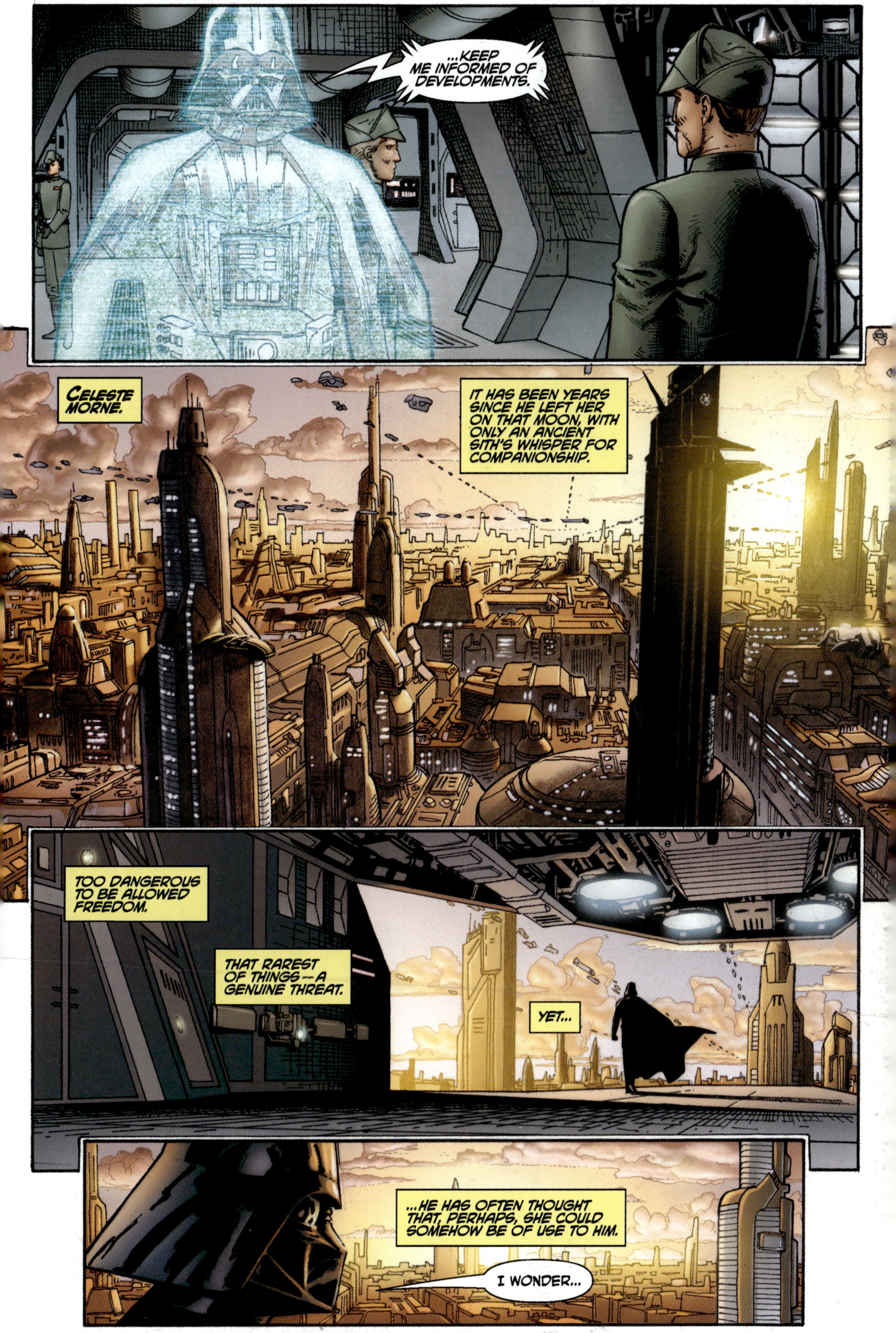
...KEEP ME INFORMED OF DEVELOPMENTS.
CELESTE MORNE.
IT HAS BEEN YEARS SINCE HE LEFT HER ON THAT MOON, WITH ONLY AN ANCIENT SITH'S WHISPER FOR COMPANIONSHIP.
TOO DANGEROUS TO BE ALLOWED FREEDOM.
THAT RAREST OF THINGS -- A GENUINE THREAT.
YET...
...HE HAS OFTEN THOUGHT THAT, PERHAPS, SHE COULD SOMEHOW BE OF USE TO HIM.
I WONDER...

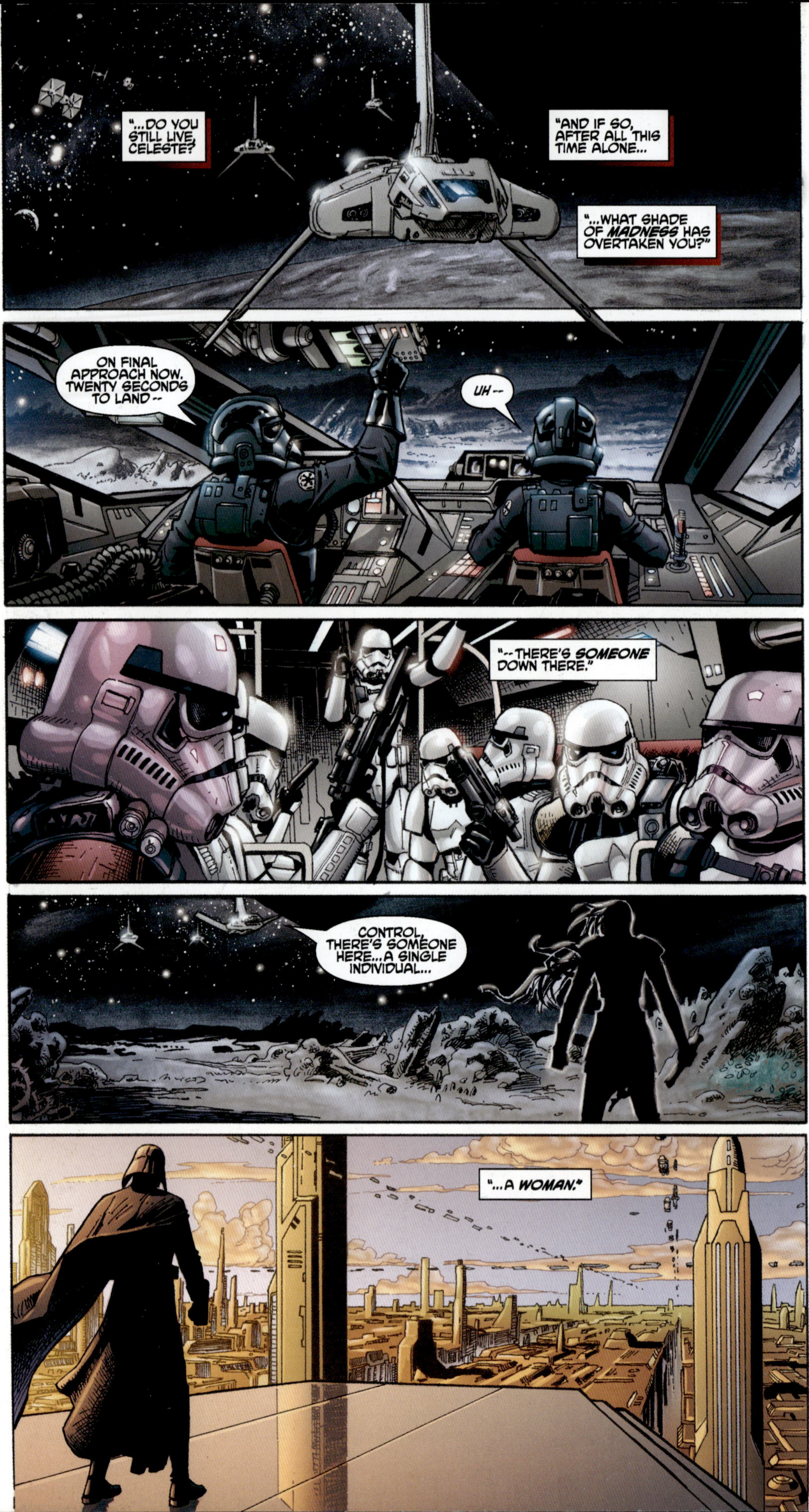
"...DO YOU STILL LIVE, CELESTE?
"AND IF SO, AFTER ALL THIS TIME ALONE...
"...WHAT SHADE OF *MADNESS* HAS OVERTAKEN YOU?"
ON FINAL APPROACH NOW. TWENTY SECONDS TO LAND--
UH--
"--THERE'S *SOMEONE* DOWN THERE."
CONTROL, THERE'S SOMEONE HERE...A SINGLE INDIVIDUAL...
"...A *WOMAN*."

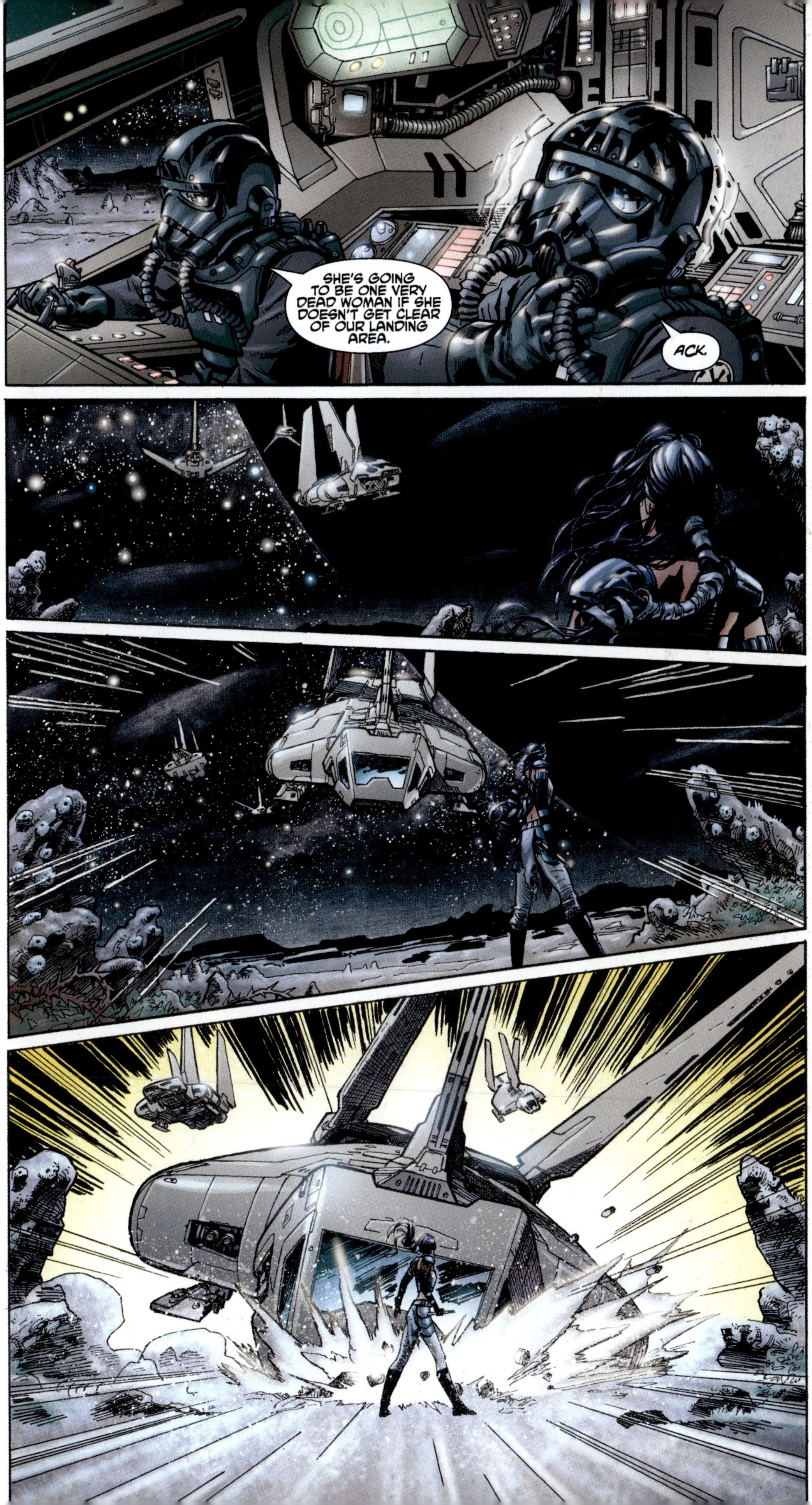
SHE'S GOING TO BE ONE VERY DEAD WOMAN IF SHE DOESN'T GET CLEAR OF OUR LANDING AREA.
ACK.

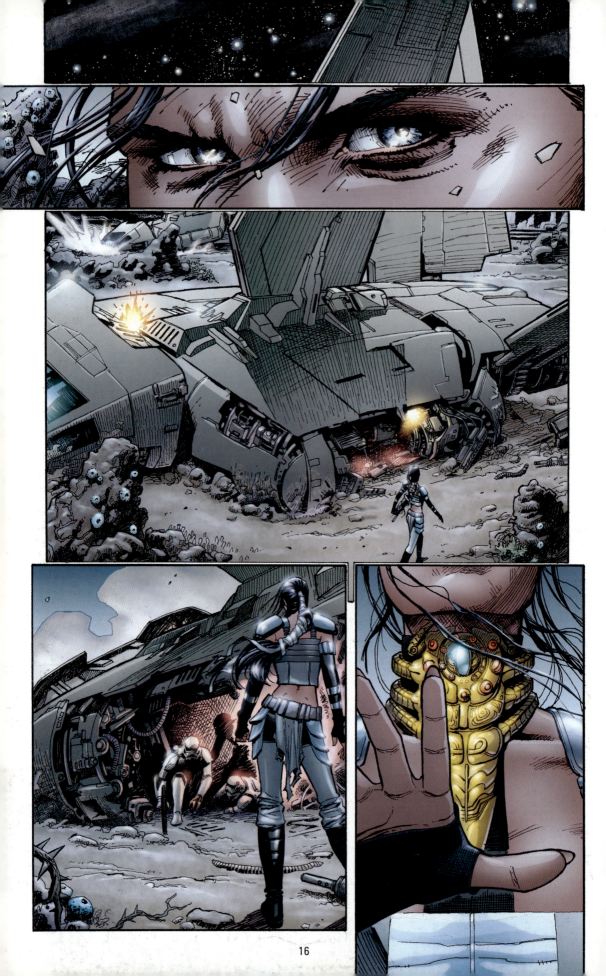

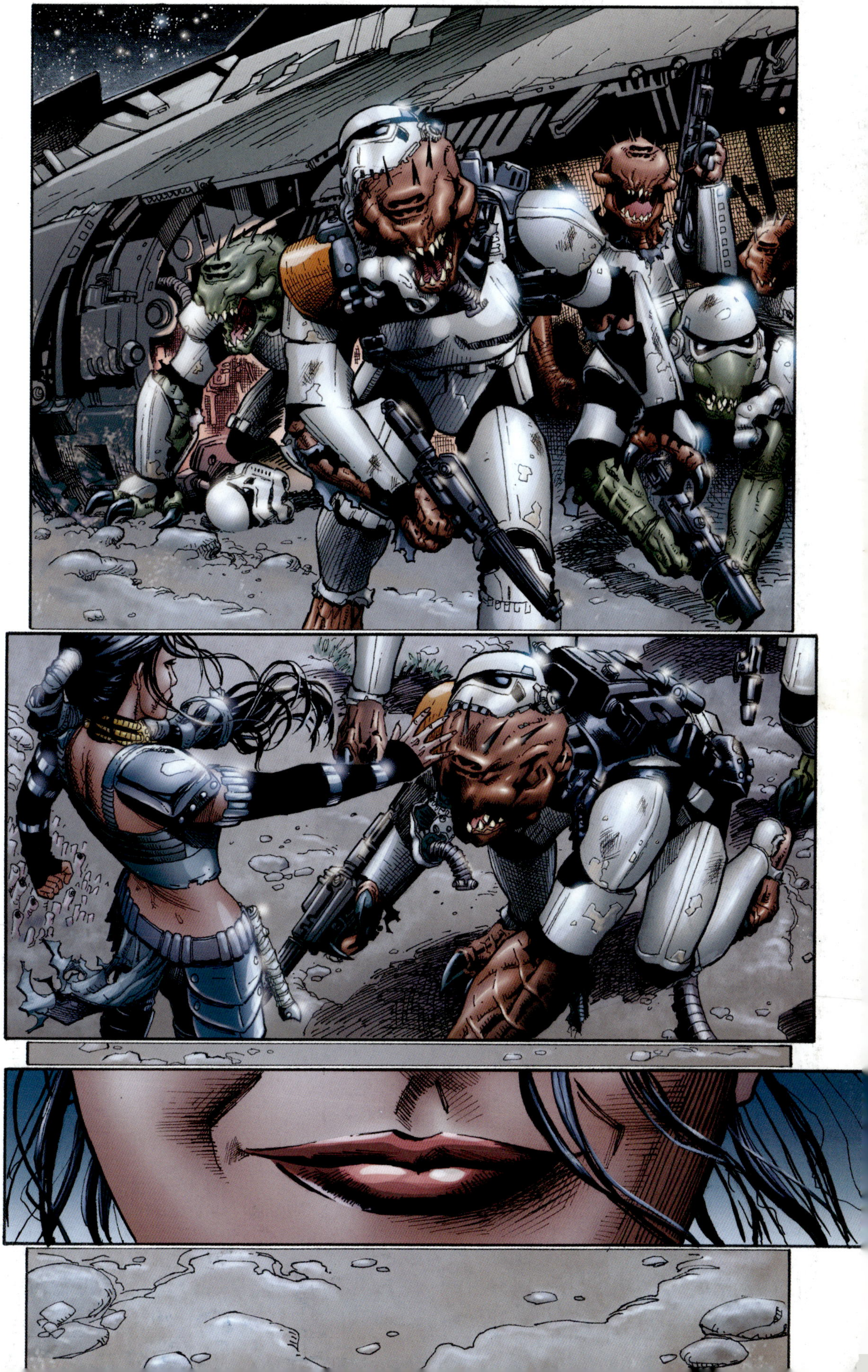

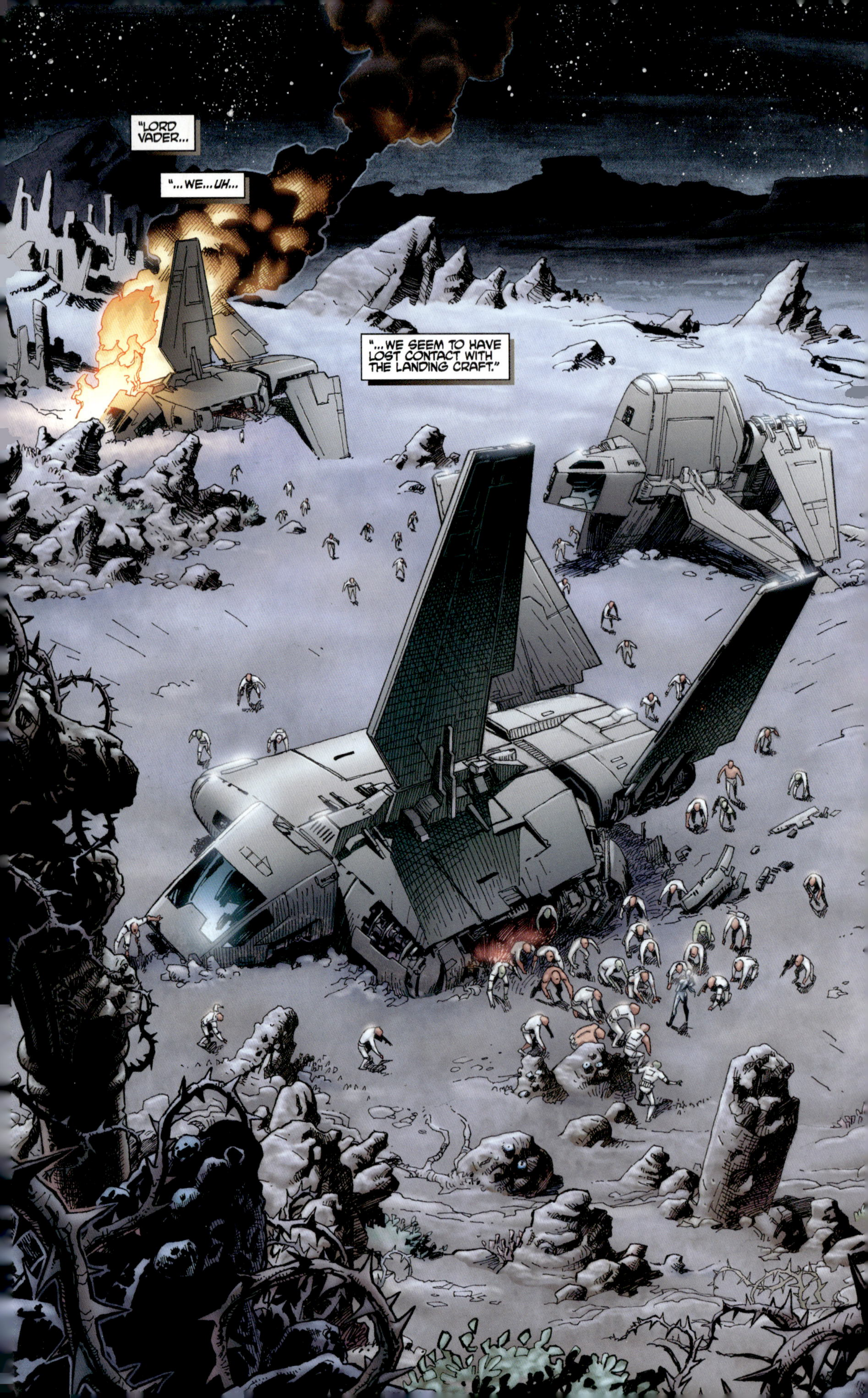
"LORD VADER...
"...WE...UH...
"...WE SEEM TO HAVE LOST CONTACT WITH THE LANDING CRAFT."

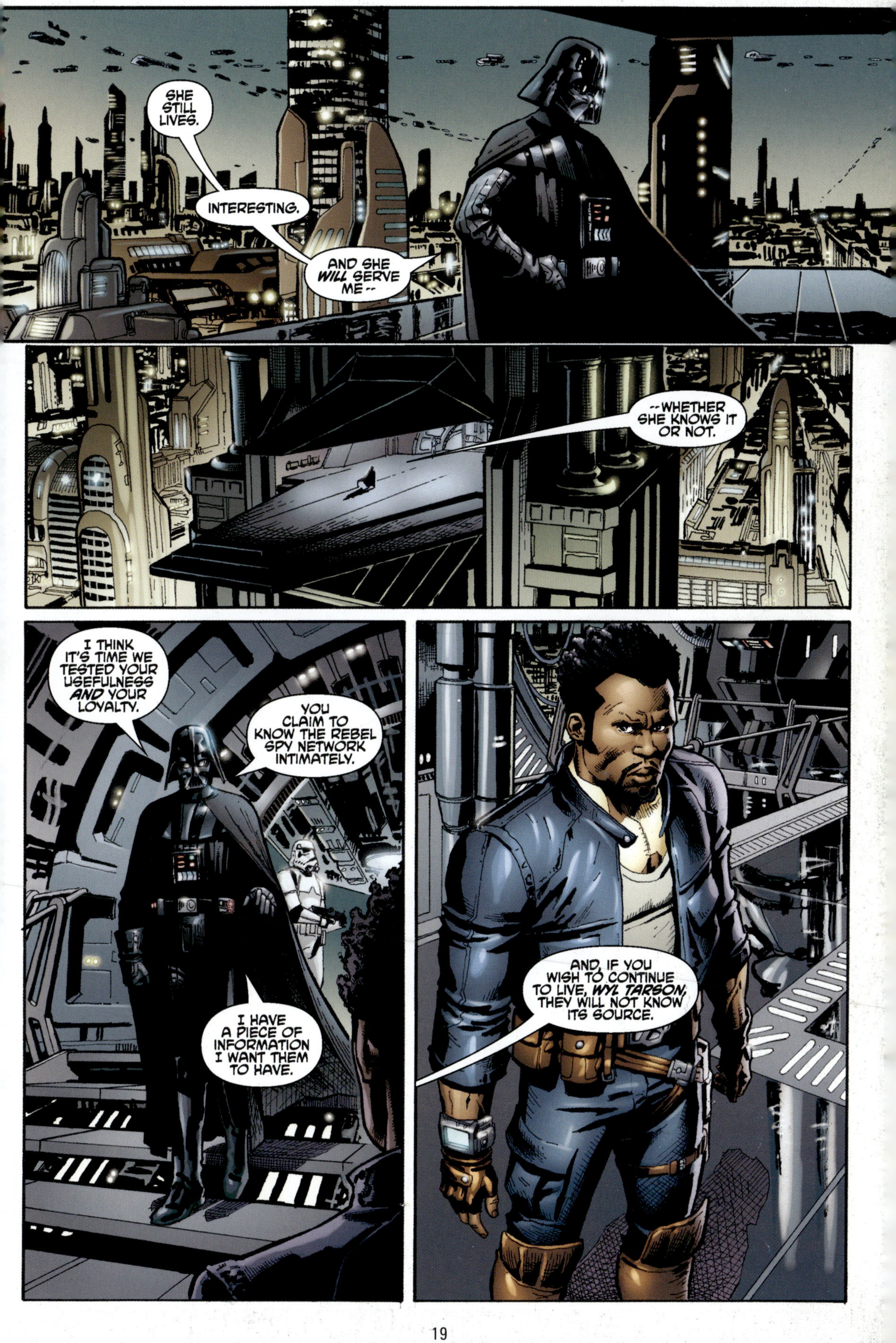
SHE STILL LIVES.
INTERESTING.
AND SHE *WILL* SERVE ME --
--WHETHER SHE KNOWS IT OR NOT.
I THINK IT'S TIME WE TESTED YOUR USEFULNESS *AND* YOUR LOYALTY.
YOU CLAIM TO KNOW THE REBEL SPY NETWORK INTIMATELY.
I HAVE A PIECE OF INFORMATION I WANT THEM TO HAVE.
AND, IF YOU WISH TO CONTINUE TO LIVE, *WYL TARSON*, THEY WILL NOT KNOW ITS SOURCE.

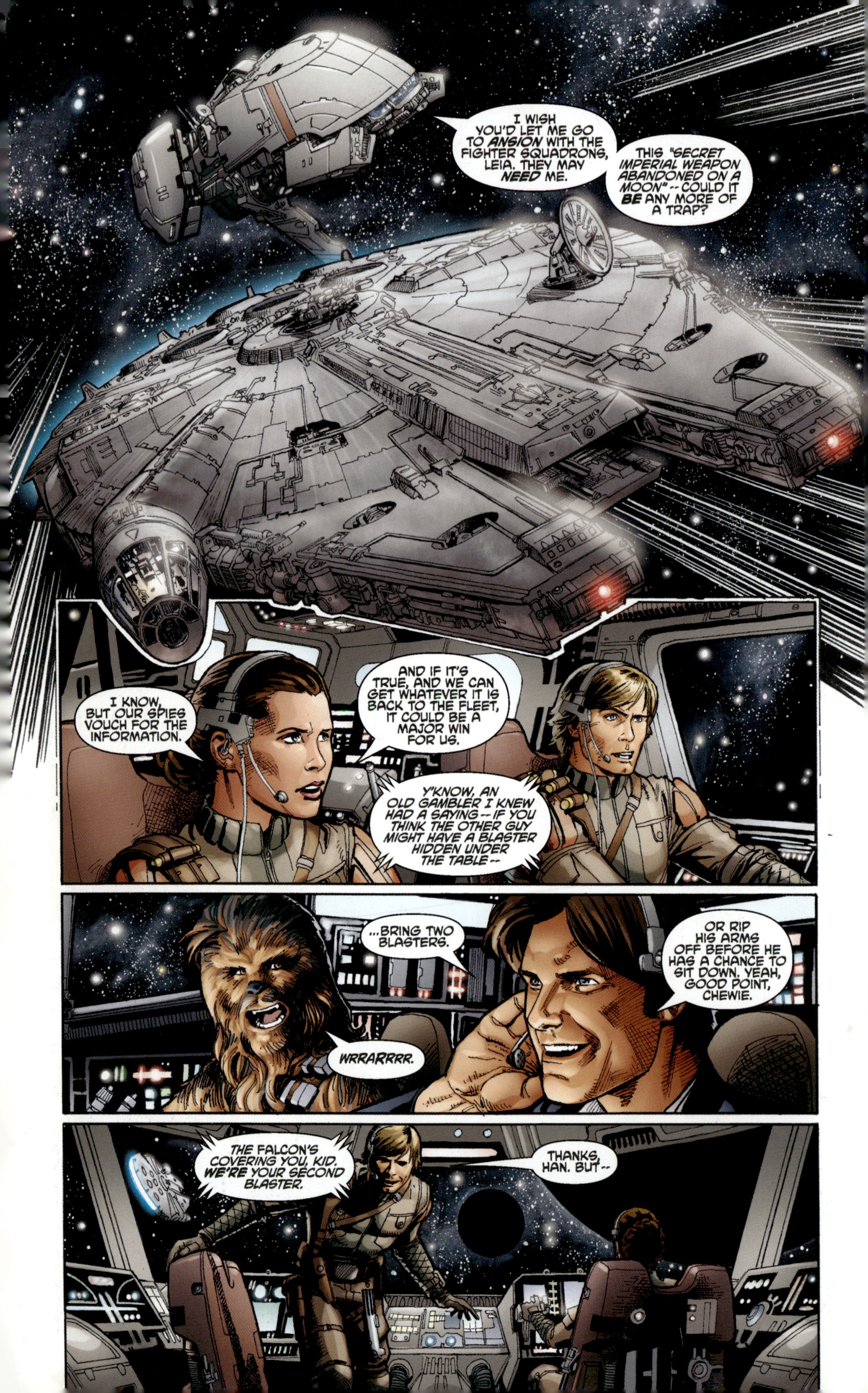
I WISH YOU'D LET ME GO TO *ANSION* WITH THE FIGHTER SQUADRONS, LEIA. THEY MAY *NEED* ME.
THIS *"SECRET IMPERIAL WEAPON ABANDONED ON A MOON"* -- COULD IT *BE* ANY MORE OF A TRAP?
I KNOW, BUT OUR SPIES VOUCH FOR THE INFORMATION.
AND IF IT'S TRUE, AND WE CAN GET WHATEVER IT IS BACK TO THE FLEET, IT COULD BE A MAJOR WIN FOR US.
Y'KNOW, AN OLD GAMBLER I KNEW HAD A SAYING -- IF YOU THINK THE OTHER GUY MIGHT HAVE A BLASTER HIDDEN UNDER THE TABLE --
...BRING TWO BLASTERS.
WRRARRRR.
OR RIP HIS ARMS OFF BEFORE HE HAS A CHANCE TO SIT DOWN. YEAH, GOOD POINT, CHEWIE.
THE FALCON'S COVERING YOU, KID. WE'RE YOUR SECOND BLASTER.
THANKS, HAN. BUT --

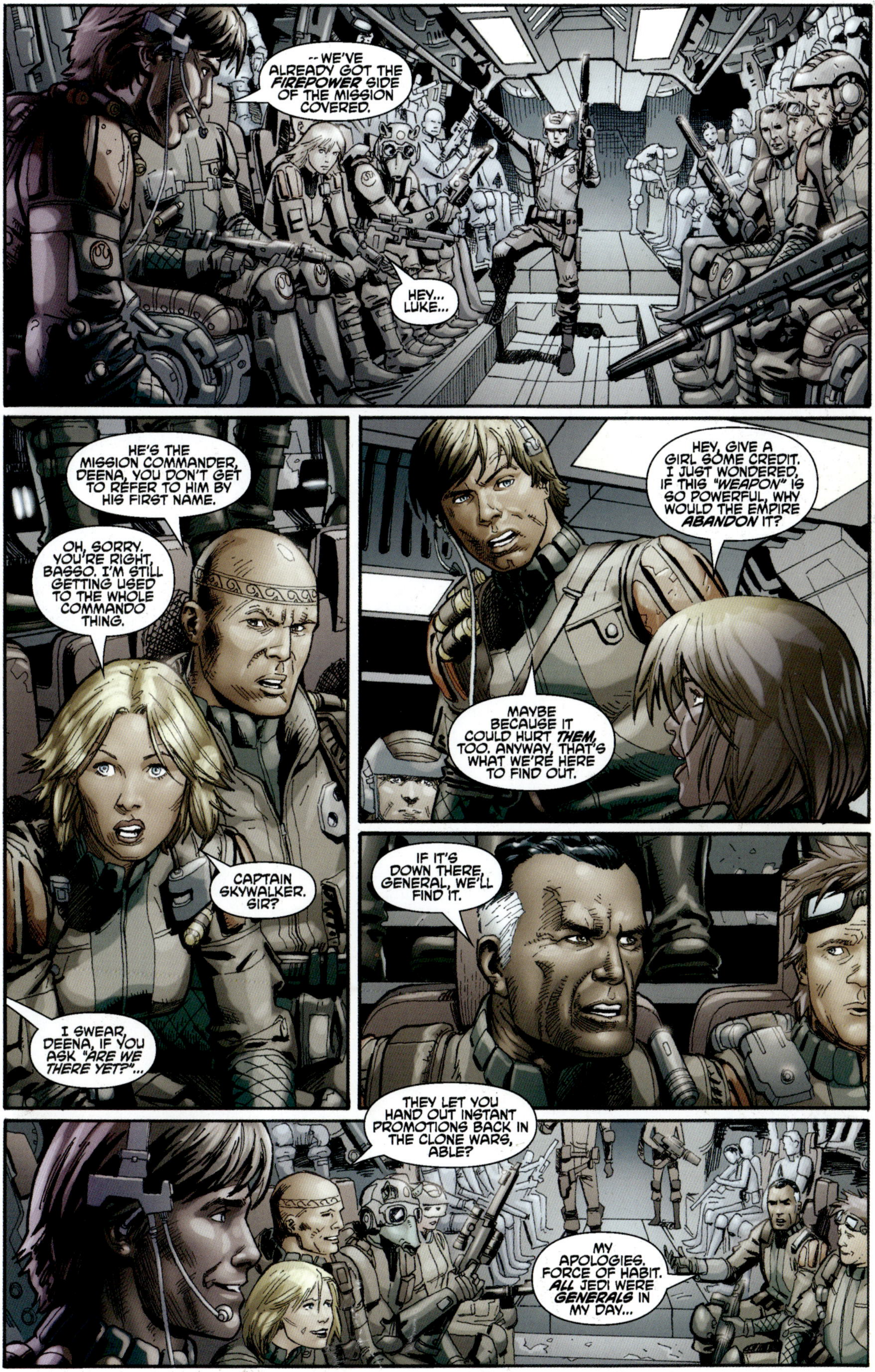
--WE'VE ALREADY GOT THE *FIREPOWER* SIDE OF THE MISSION COVERED.
HEY... LUKE...
HE'S THE MISSION COMMANDER, DEENA. YOU DON'T GET TO REFER TO HIM BY HIS FIRST NAME.
OH, SORRY. YOU'RE RIGHT, BASSO. I'M STILL GETTING USED TO THE WHOLE COMMANDO THING.
CAPTAIN SKYWALKER. SIR?
I SWEAR, DEENA, IF YOU ASK *"ARE WE THERE YET?"*...
HEY, GIVE A GIRL SOME CREDIT. I JUST WONDERED, IF THIS *"WEAPON"* IS SO POWERFUL, WHY WOULD THE EMPIRE *ABANDON* IT?
MAYBE BECAUSE IT COULD HURT *THEM*, TOO. ANYWAY, THAT'S WHAT WE'RE HERE TO FIND OUT.
IF IT'S DOWN THERE, GENERAL, WE'LL FIND IT.
THEY LET YOU HAND OUT INSTANT PROMOTIONS BACK IN THE CLONE WARS, ABLE?
MY APOLOGIES. FORCE OF HABIT. *ALL* JEDI WERE *GENERALS* IN MY DAY...

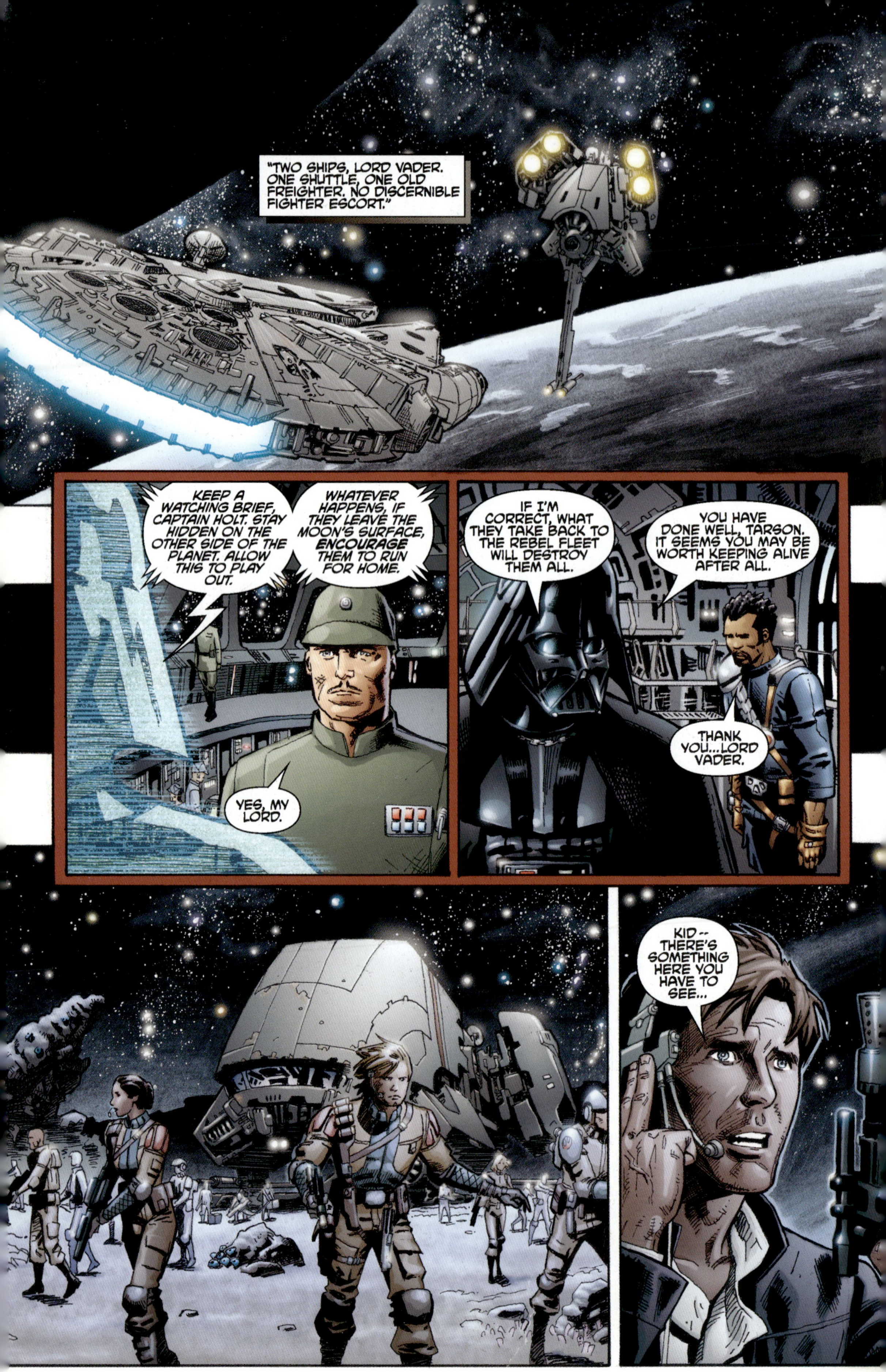
"TWO SHIPS, LORD VADER. ONE SHUTTLE, ONE OLD FREIGHTER. NO DISCERNIBLE FIGHTER ESCORT."
KEEP A WATCHING BRIEF, CAPTAIN HOLT. STAY HIDDEN ON THE OTHER SIDE OF THE PLANET. ALLOW THIS TO PLAY OUT.
WHATEVER HAPPENS, IF THEY LEAVE THE MOON'S SURFACE, ENCOURAGE THEM TO RUN FOR HOME.
YES, MY LORD.
IF I'M CORRECT, WHAT THEY TAKE BACK TO THE REBEL FLEET WILL DESTROY THEM ALL.
YOU HAVE DONE WELL, TARSON. IT SEEMS YOU MAY BE WORTH KEEPING ALIVE AFTER ALL.
THANK YOU...LORD VADER.
KID -- THERE'S SOMETHING HERE YOU HAVE TO SEE...

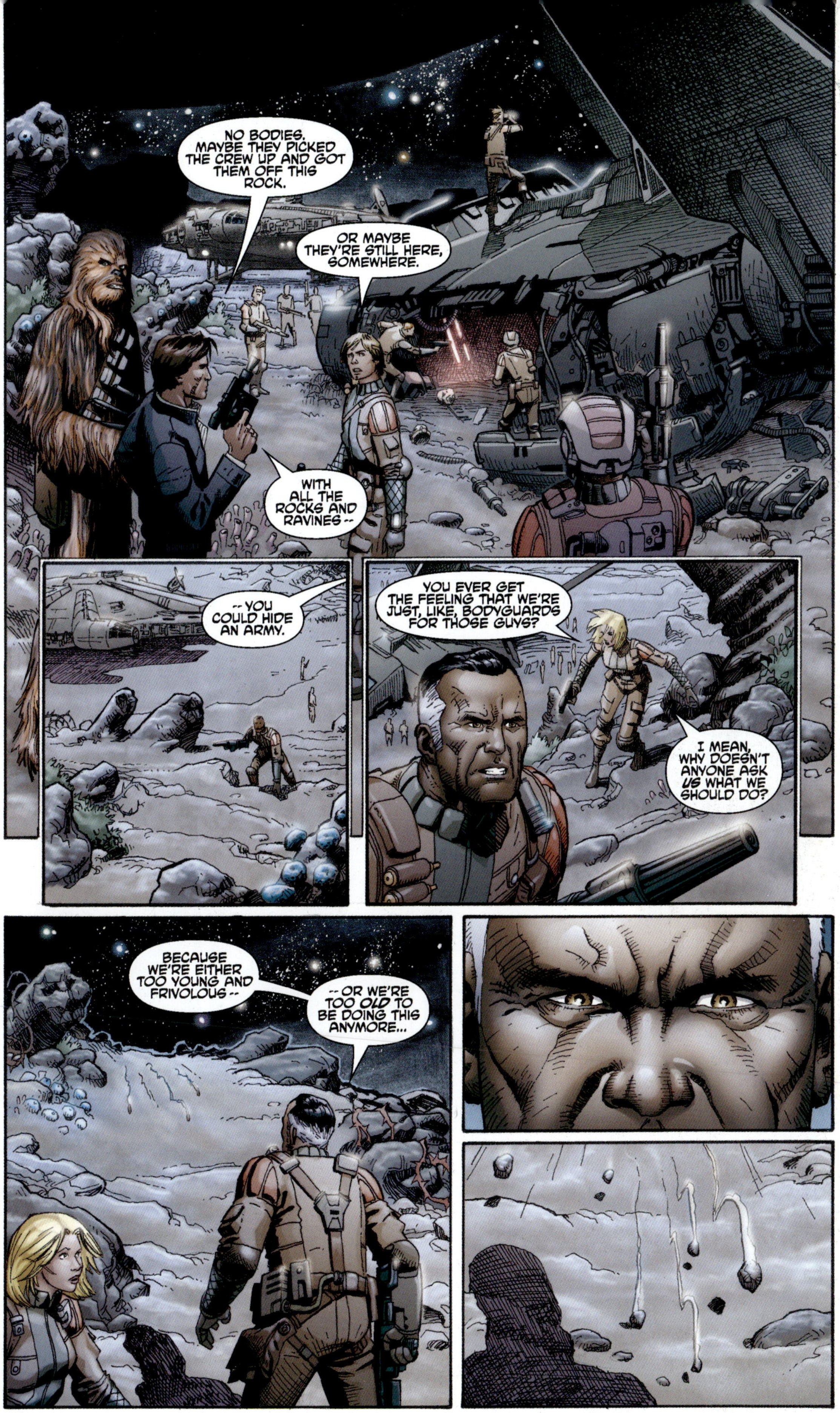
NO BODIES. MAYBE THEY PICKED THE CREW UP AND GOT THEM OFF THIS ROCK.
OR MAYBE THEY'RE STILL HERE, SOMEWHERE.
WITH ALL THE ROCKS AND RAVINES --
-- YOU COULD HIDE AN ARMY.
YOU EVER GET THE FEELING THAT WE'RE JUST, LIKE, BODYGUARDS FOR THOSE GUYS?
I MEAN, WHY DOESN'T ANYONE ASK *US* WHAT WE SHOULD DO?
BECAUSE WE'RE EITHER TOO YOUNG AND FRIVOLOUS --
-- OR WE'RE TOO *OLD* TO BE DOING THIS ANYMORE...

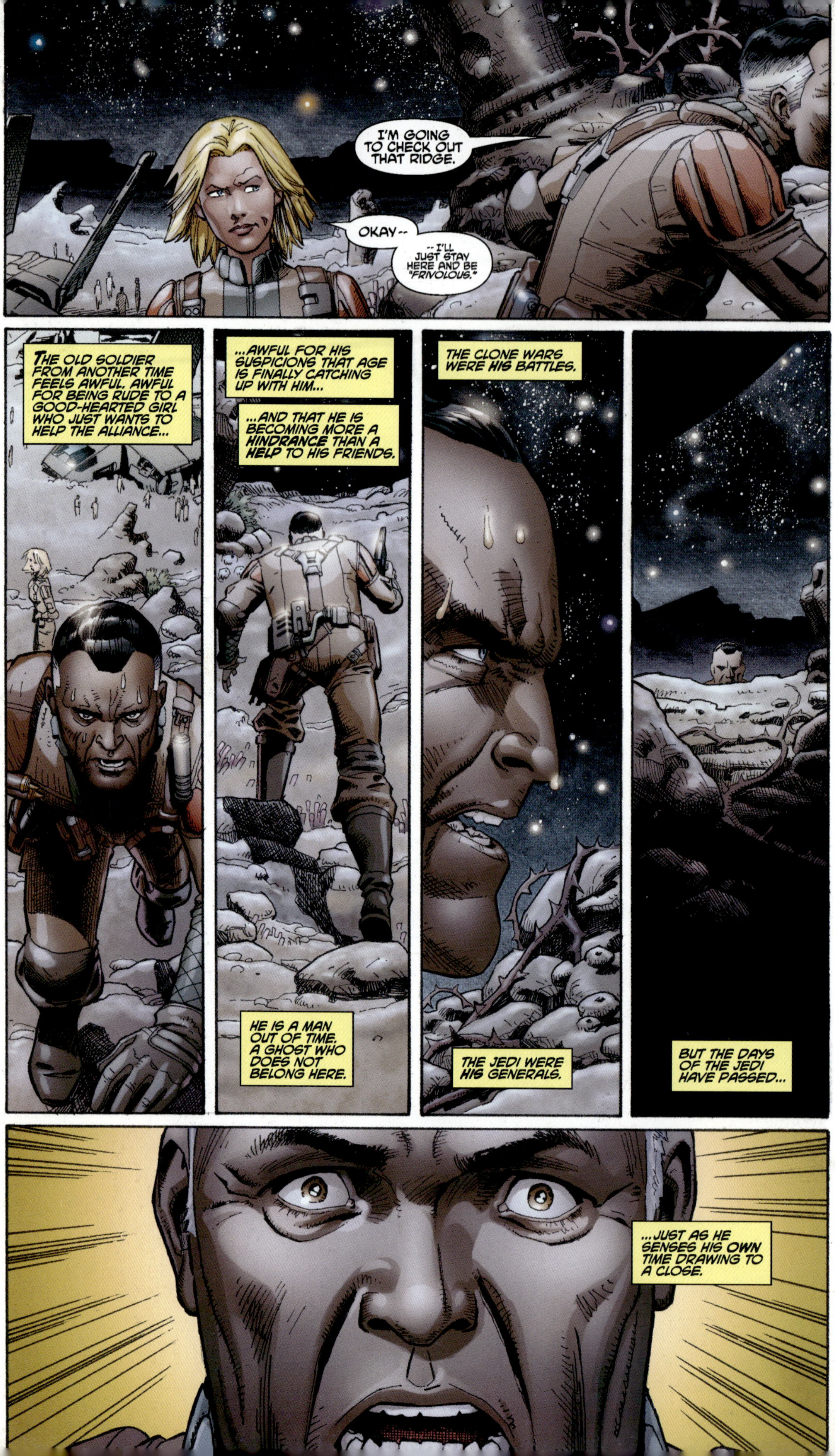
I'M GOING TO CHECK OUT THAT RIDGE.
OKAY--
--I'LL JUST STAY HERE AND BE "FRIVOLOUS."
THE OLD SOLDIER FROM ANOTHER TIME FEELS AWFUL. AWFUL FOR BEING RUDE TO A GOOD-HEARTED GIRL WHO JUST WANTS TO HELP THE ALLIANCE...
...AWFUL FOR HIS SUSPICIONS THAT AGE IS FINALLY CATCHING UP WITH HIM...
...AND THAT HE IS BECOMING MORE A HINDRANCE THAN A HELP TO HIS FRIENDS.
HE IS A MAN OUT OF TIME. A GHOST WHO DOES NOT BELONG HERE.
THE CLONE WARS WERE HIS BATTLES.
THE JEDI WERE HIS GENERALS.
BUT THE DAYS OF THE JEDI HAVE PASSED...
...JUST AS HE SENSES HIS OWN TIME DRAWING TO A CLOSE.

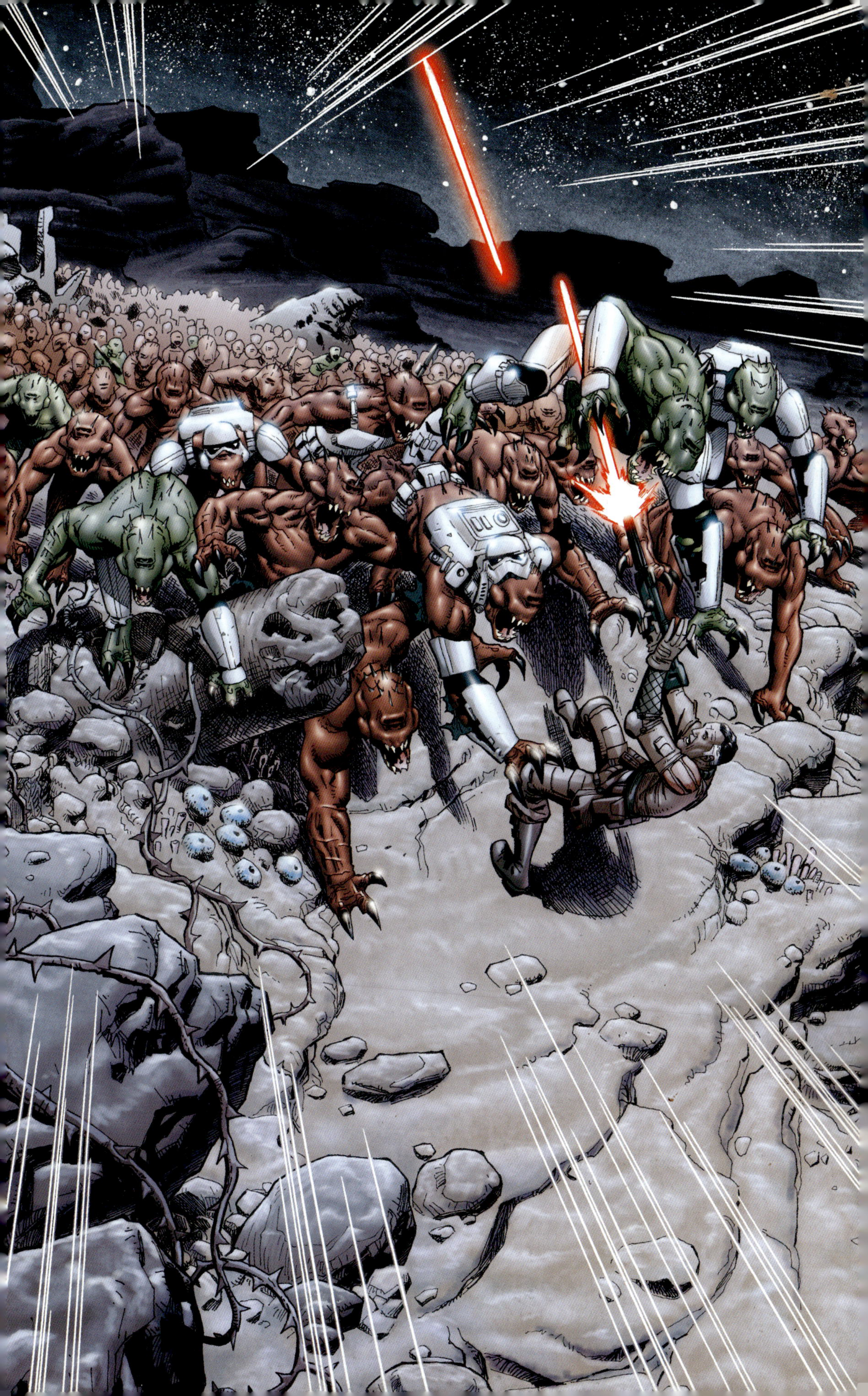

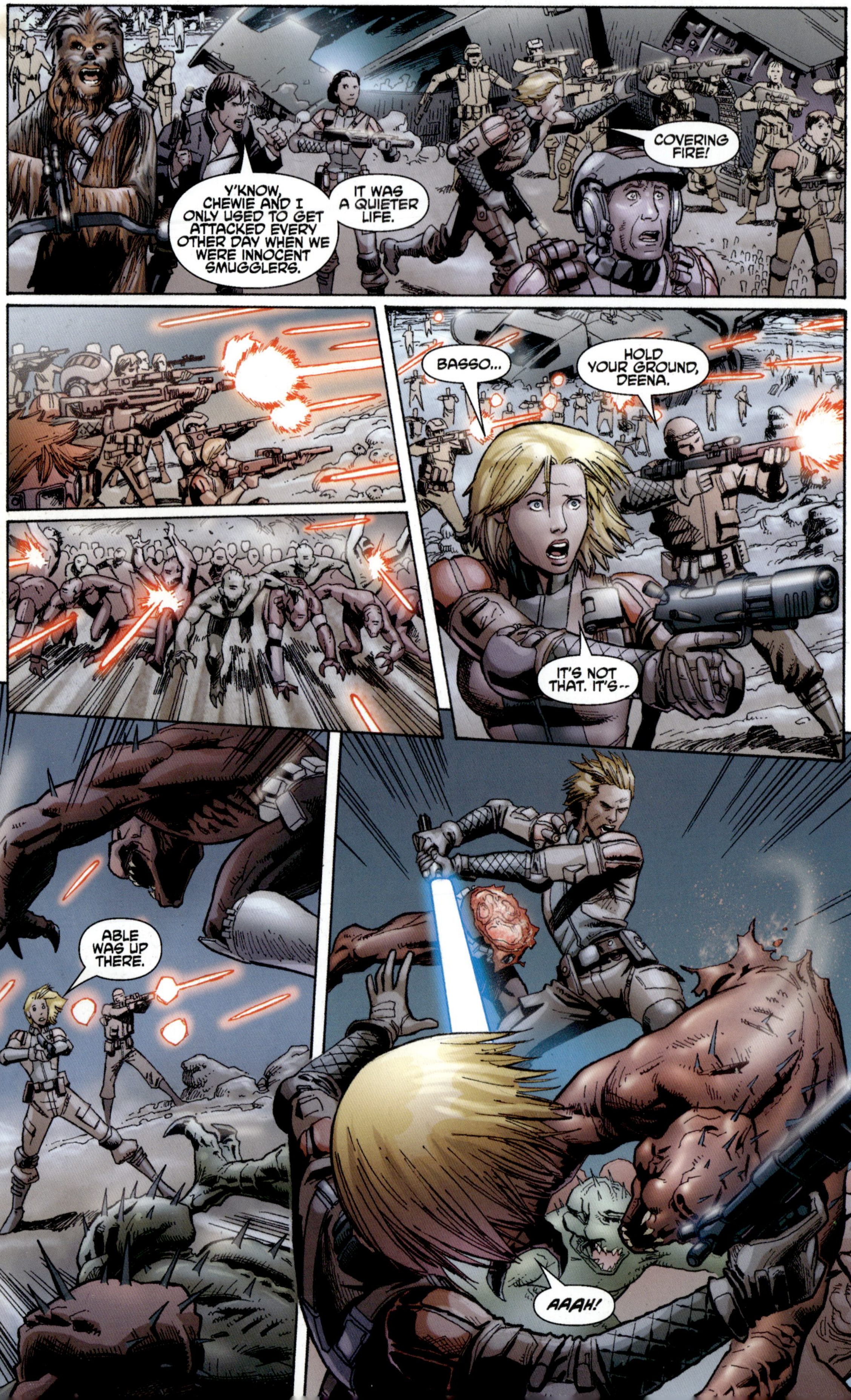
Y'KNOW, CHEWIE AND I ONLY USED TO GET ATTACKED EVERY OTHER DAY WHEN WE WERE INNOCENT SMUGGLERS.
IT WAS A QUIETER LIFE.
COVERING FIRE!
BASSO...
HOLD YOUR GROUND, DEENA.
IT'S NOT THAT. IT'S--
ABLE WAS UP THERE.
AAAH!

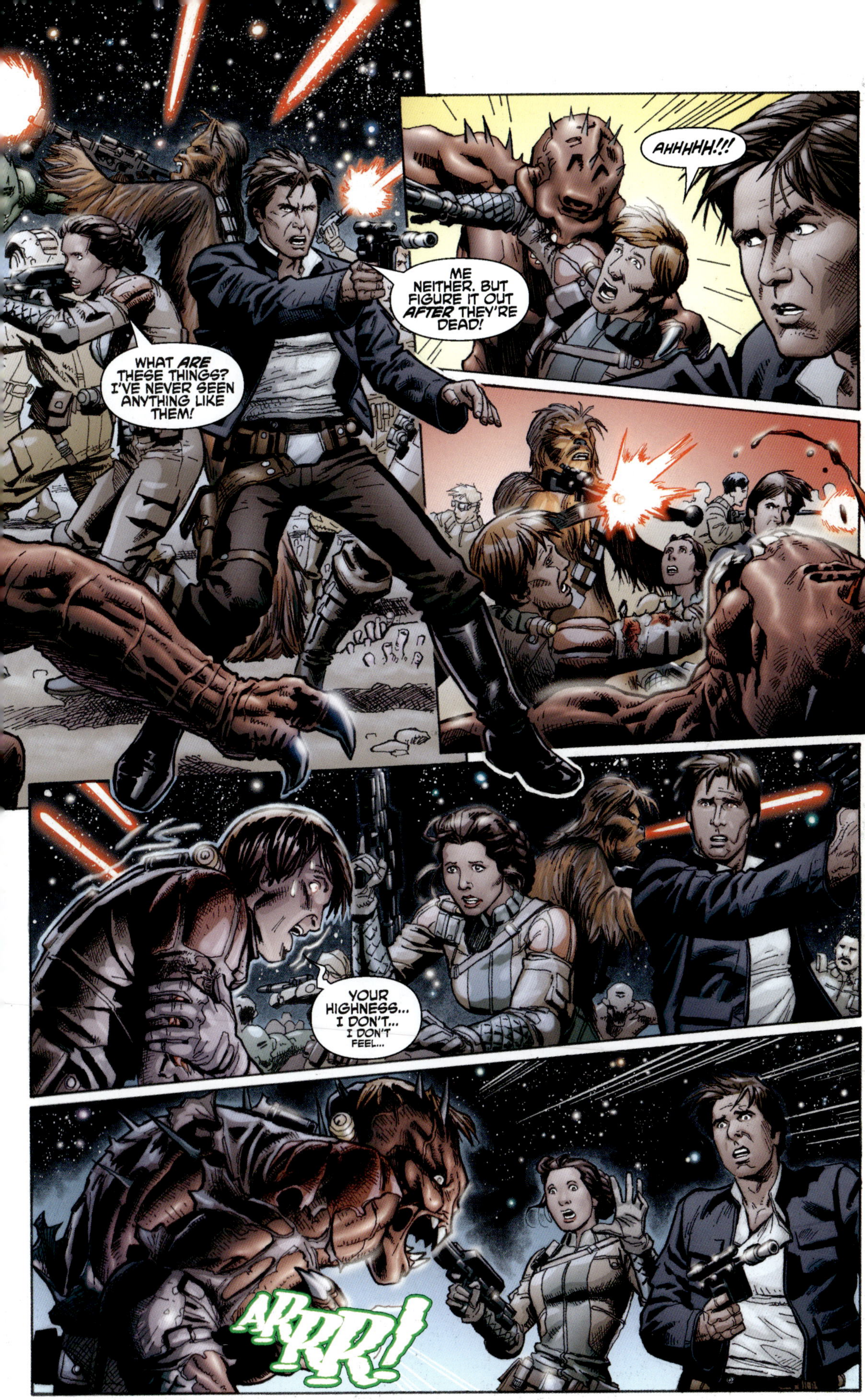
WHAT *ARE* THESE THINGS? I'VE NEVER SEEN ANYTHING LIKE THEM!
ME NEITHER. BUT FIGURE IT OUT *AFTER* THEY'RE DEAD!
AHHHHH!!!
YOUR HIGHNESS... I DON'T... I DON'T FEEL...
AKRRR!

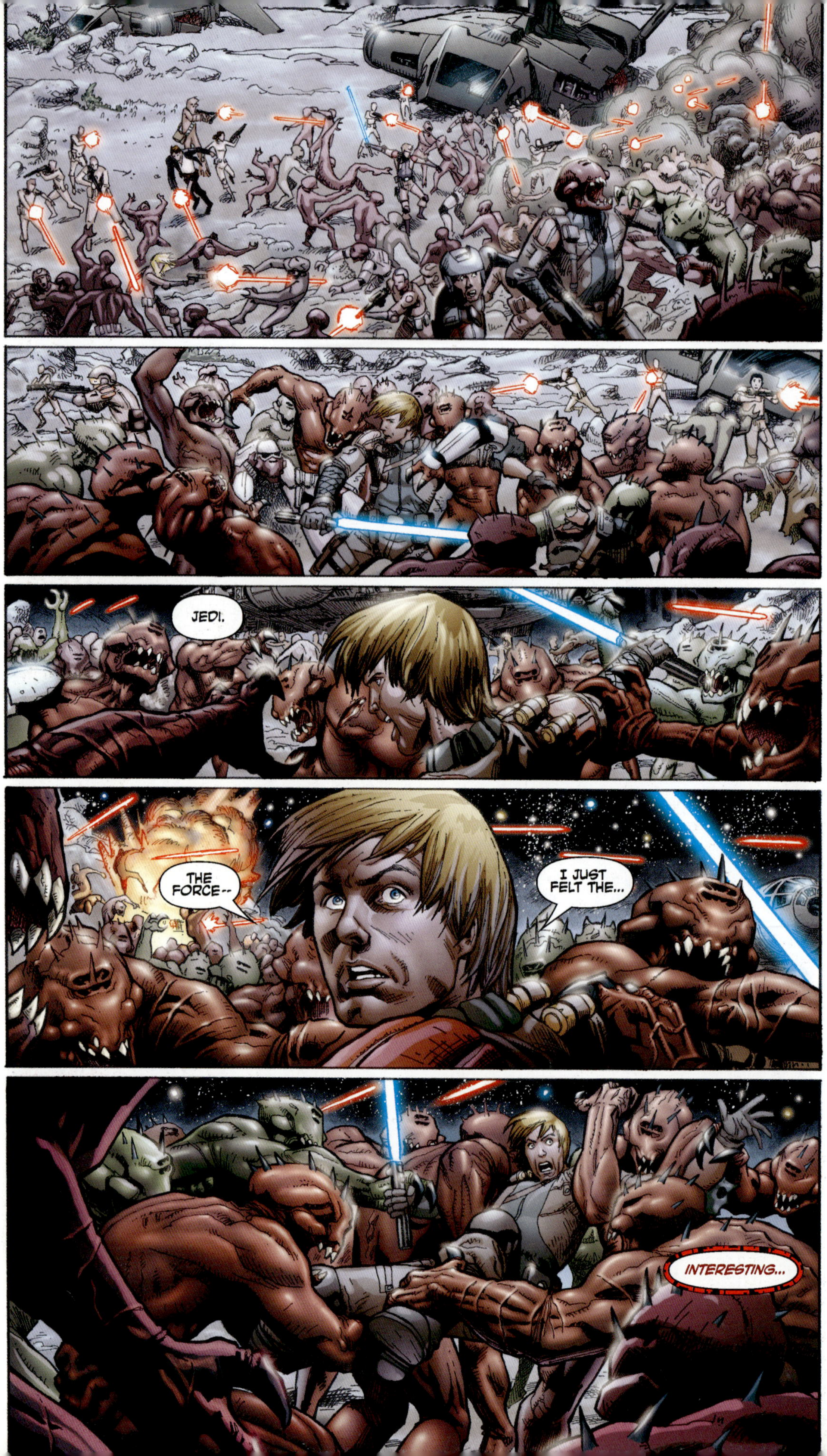
JEDI.
THE FORCE--
I JUST FELT THE...
INTERESTING...

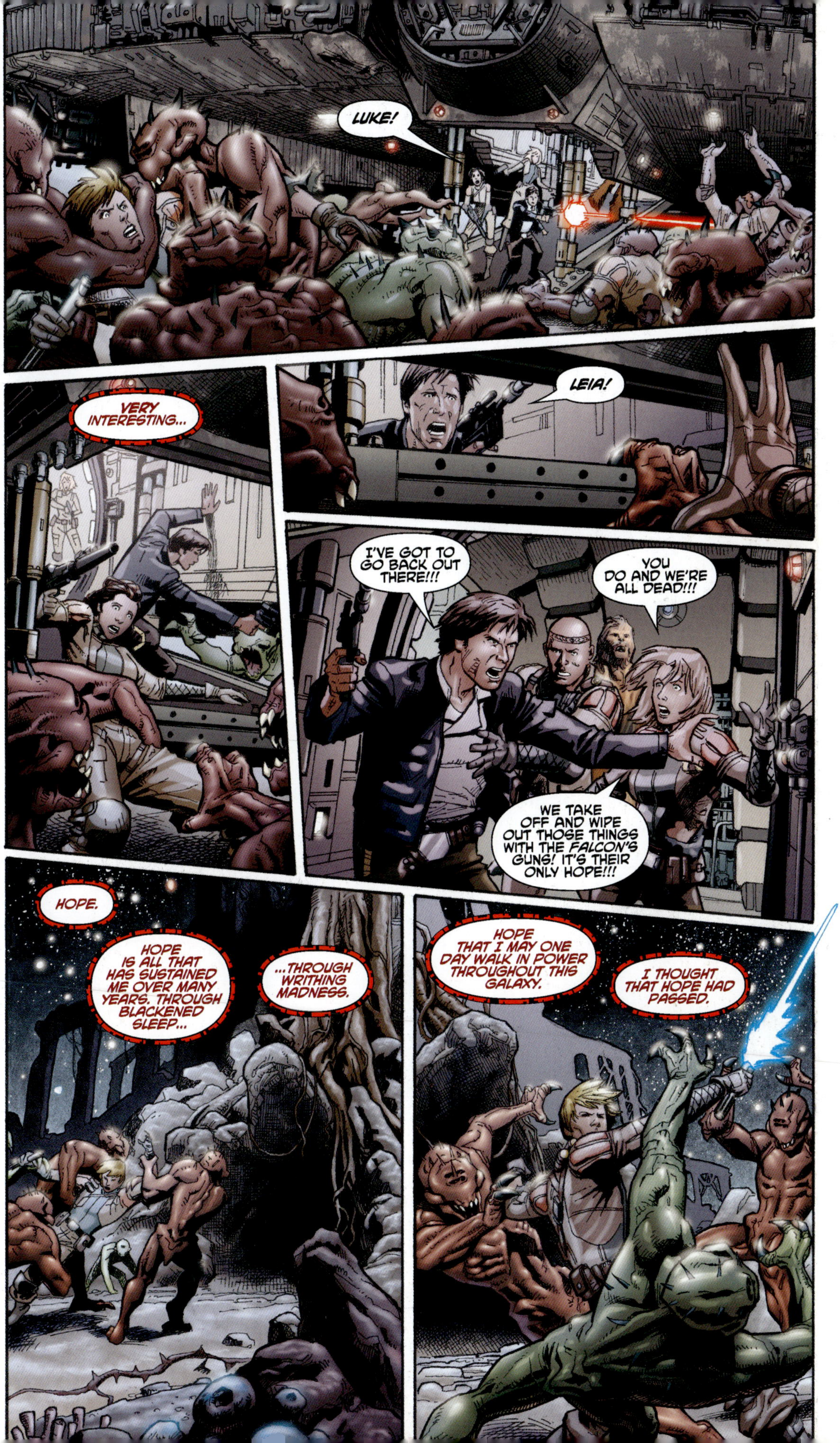
LUKE!
VERY INTERESTING...
LEIA!
I'VE GOT TO GO BACK OUT THERE!!!
YOU DO AND WE'RE ALL DEAD!!!
WE TAKE OFF AND WIPE OUT THOSE THINGS WITH THE FALCON'S GUNS! IT'S THEIR ONLY HOPE!!!
HOPE.
HOPE IS ALL THAT HAS SUSTAINED ME OVER MANY YEARS. THROUGH BLACKENED SLEEP...
...THROUGH WRITHING MADNESS.
HOPE THAT I MAY ONE DAY WALK IN POWER THROUGHOUT THIS GALAXY.
I THOUGHT THAT HOPE HAD PASSED.

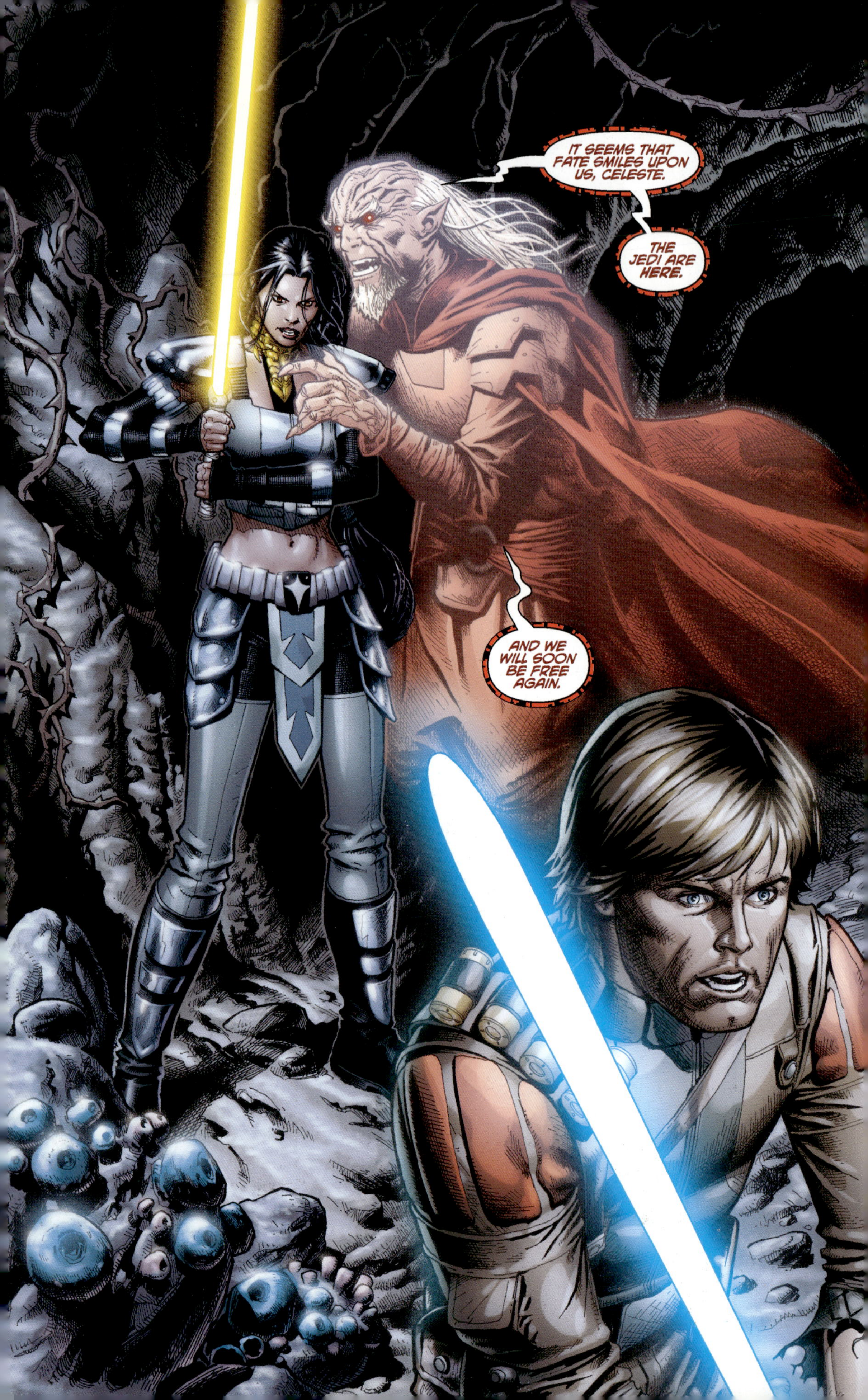
IT SEEMS THAT FATE SMILES UPON US, CELESTE.
THE JEDI ARE HERE.
AND WE WILL SOON BE FREE AGAIN.

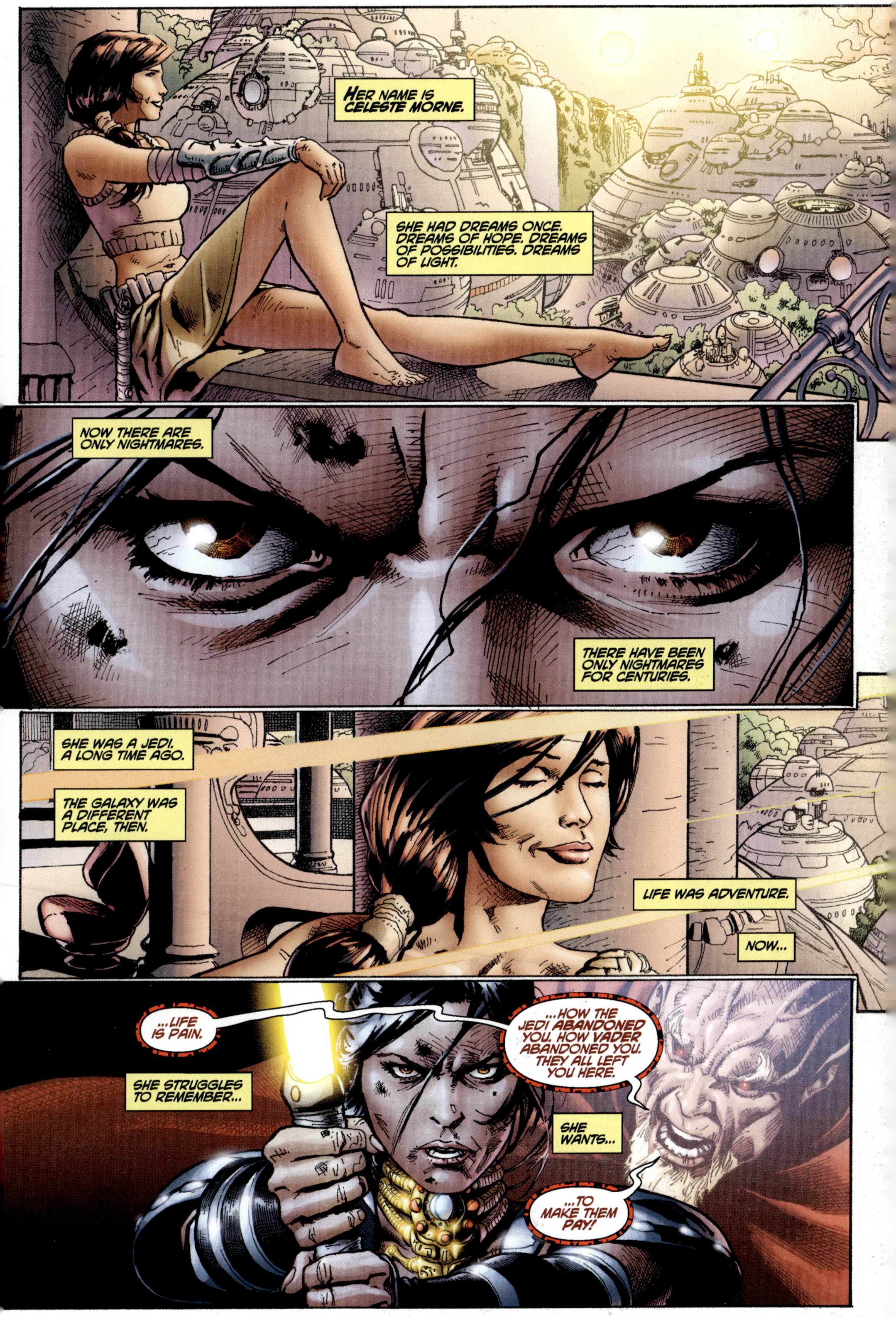
HER NAME IS CELESTE MORNE.
SHE HAD DREAMS ONCE. DREAMS OF HOPE. DREAMS OF POSSIBILITIES. DREAMS OF LIGHT.
NOW THERE ARE ONLY NIGHTMARES.
THERE HAVE BEEN ONLY NIGHTMARES FOR CENTURIES.
SHE WAS A JEDI. A LONG TIME AGO.
THE GALAXY WAS A DIFFERENT PLACE, THEN.
LIFE WAS ADVENTURE.
NOW...
...LIFE IS PAIN.
SHE STRUGGLES TO REMEMBER...
...HOW THE JEDI ABANDONED YOU. HOW VADER ABANDONED YOU. THEY ALL LEFT YOU HERE.
SHE WANTS...
...TO MAKE THEM PAY!

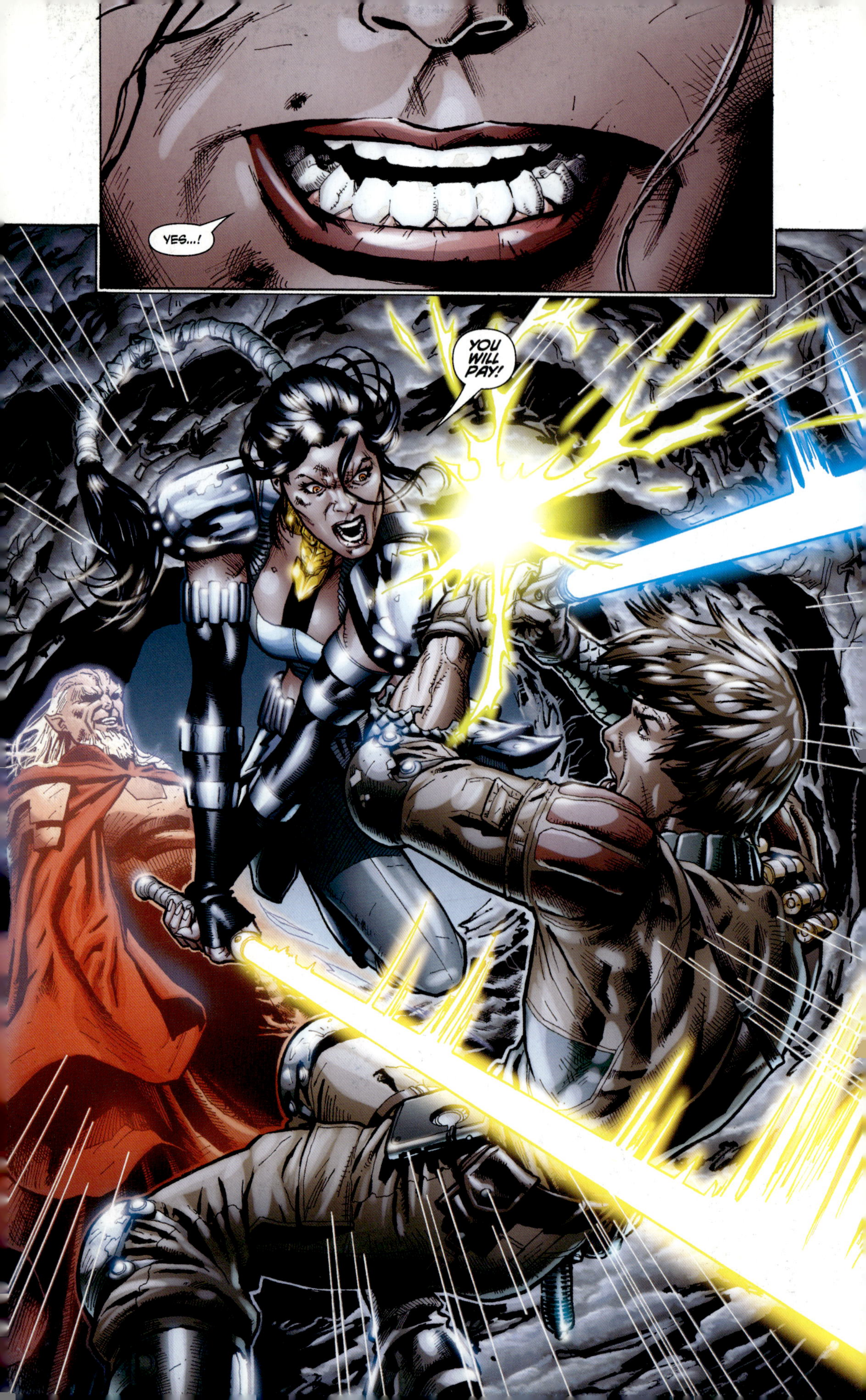
YES...!
YOU WILL PAY!

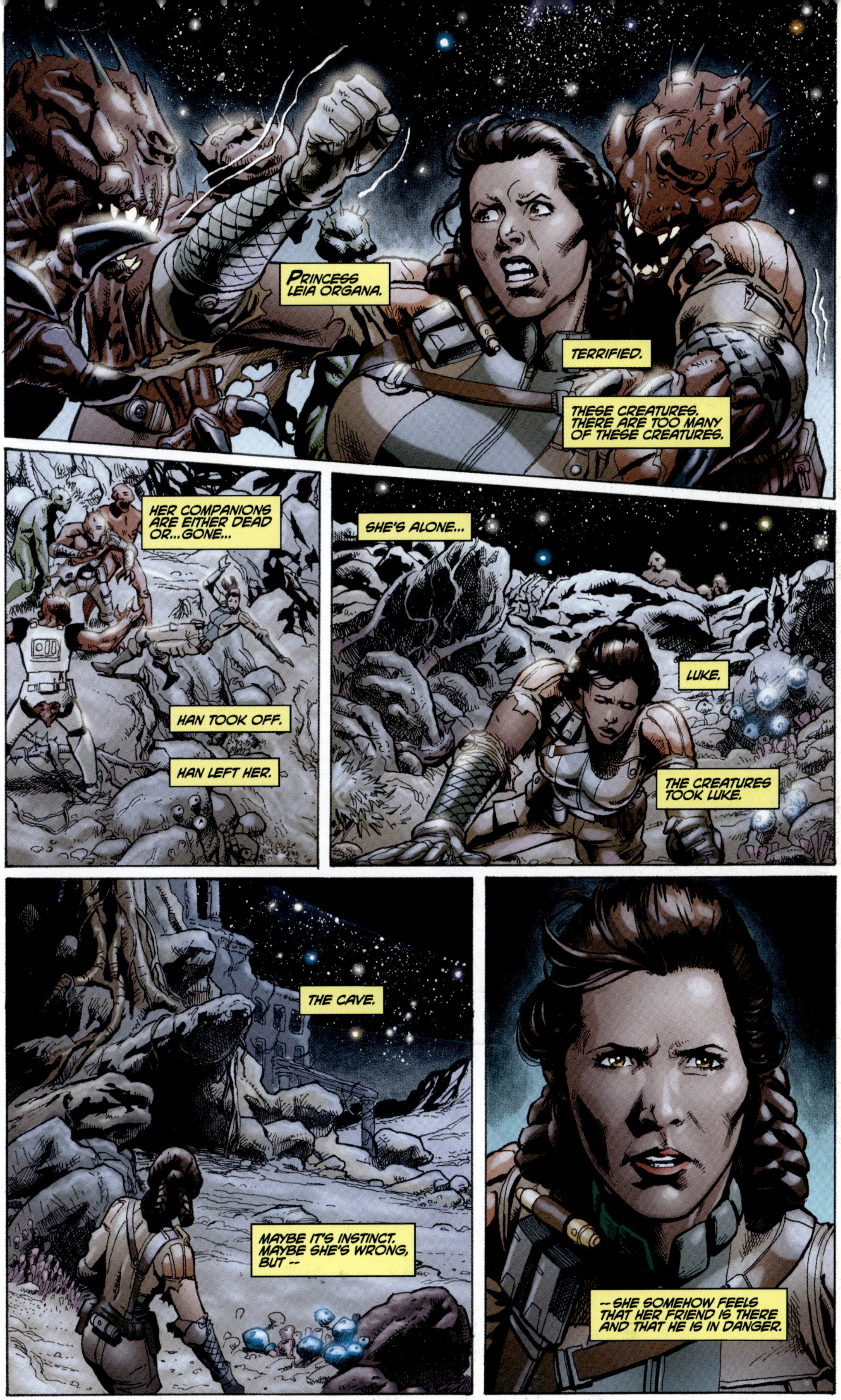

PRINCESS LEIA ORGANA.
TERRIFIED.
THESE CREATURES. THERE ARE TOO MANY OF THESE CREATURES.
HER COMPANIONS ARE EITHER DEAD OR...GONE...
HAN TOOK OFF.
HAN LEFT HER.
SHE'S ALONE...
LUKE.
THE CREATURES TOOK LUKE.
THE CAVE.
MAYBE IT'S INSTINCT. MAYBE SHE'S WRONG, BUT --
-- SHE SOMEHOW FEELS THAT HER FRIEND IS THERE AND THAT HE IS IN DANGER.

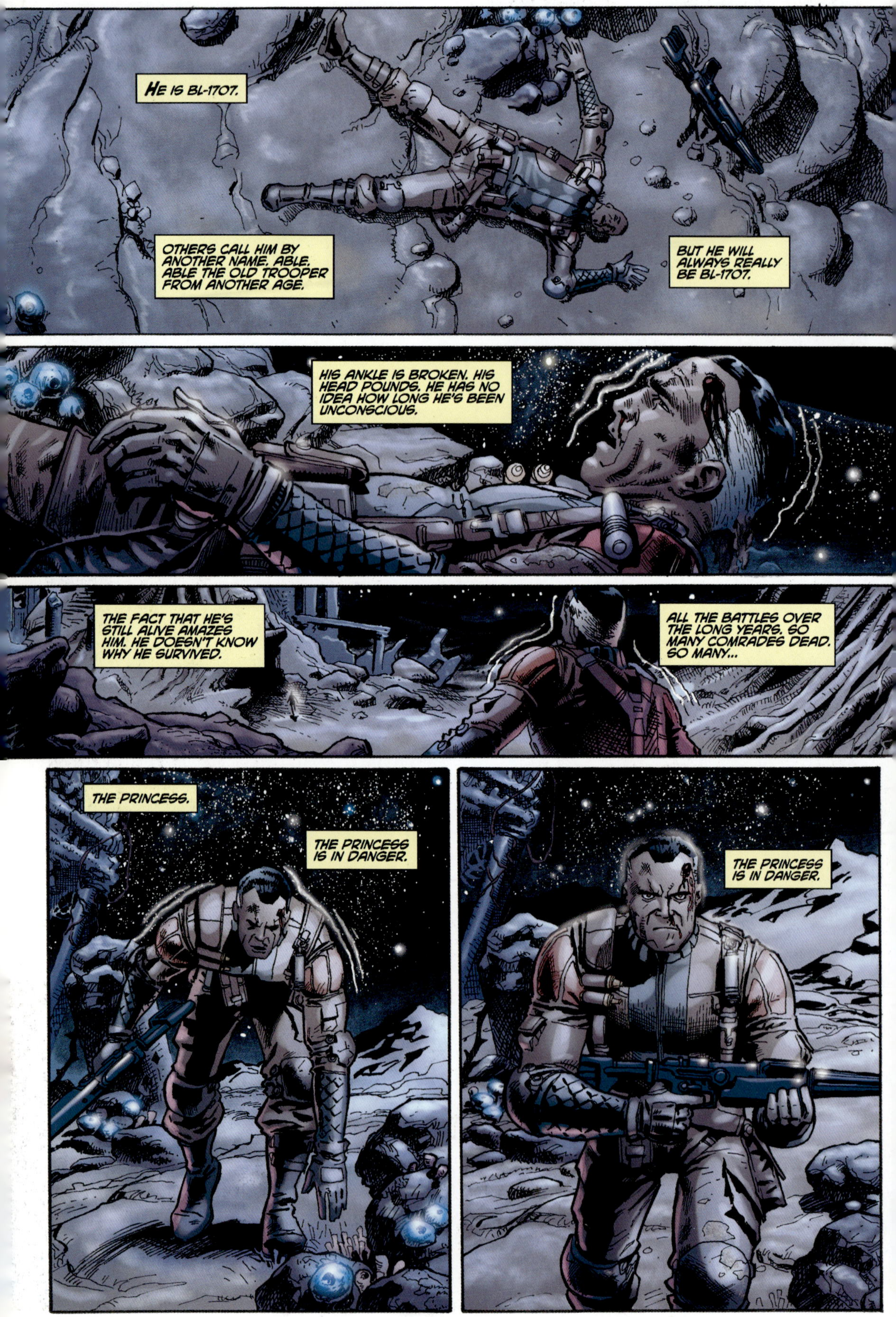
HE IS BL-1707.
OTHERS CALL HIM BY ANOTHER NAME. ABLE. ABLE THE OLD TROOPER FROM ANOTHER AGE.
BUT HE WILL ALWAYS REALLY BE BL-1707.
HIS ANKLE IS BROKEN. HIS HEAD POUNDS. HE HAS NO IDEA HOW LONG HE'S BEEN UNCONSCIOUS.
THE FACT THAT HE'S STILL ALIVE AMAZES HIM. HE DOESN'T KNOW WHY HE SURVIVED.
ALL THE BATTLES OVER THE LONG YEARS. SO MANY COMRADES DEAD. SO MANY...
THE PRINCESS.
THE PRINCESS IS IN DANGER.
THE PRINCESS IS IN DANGER.

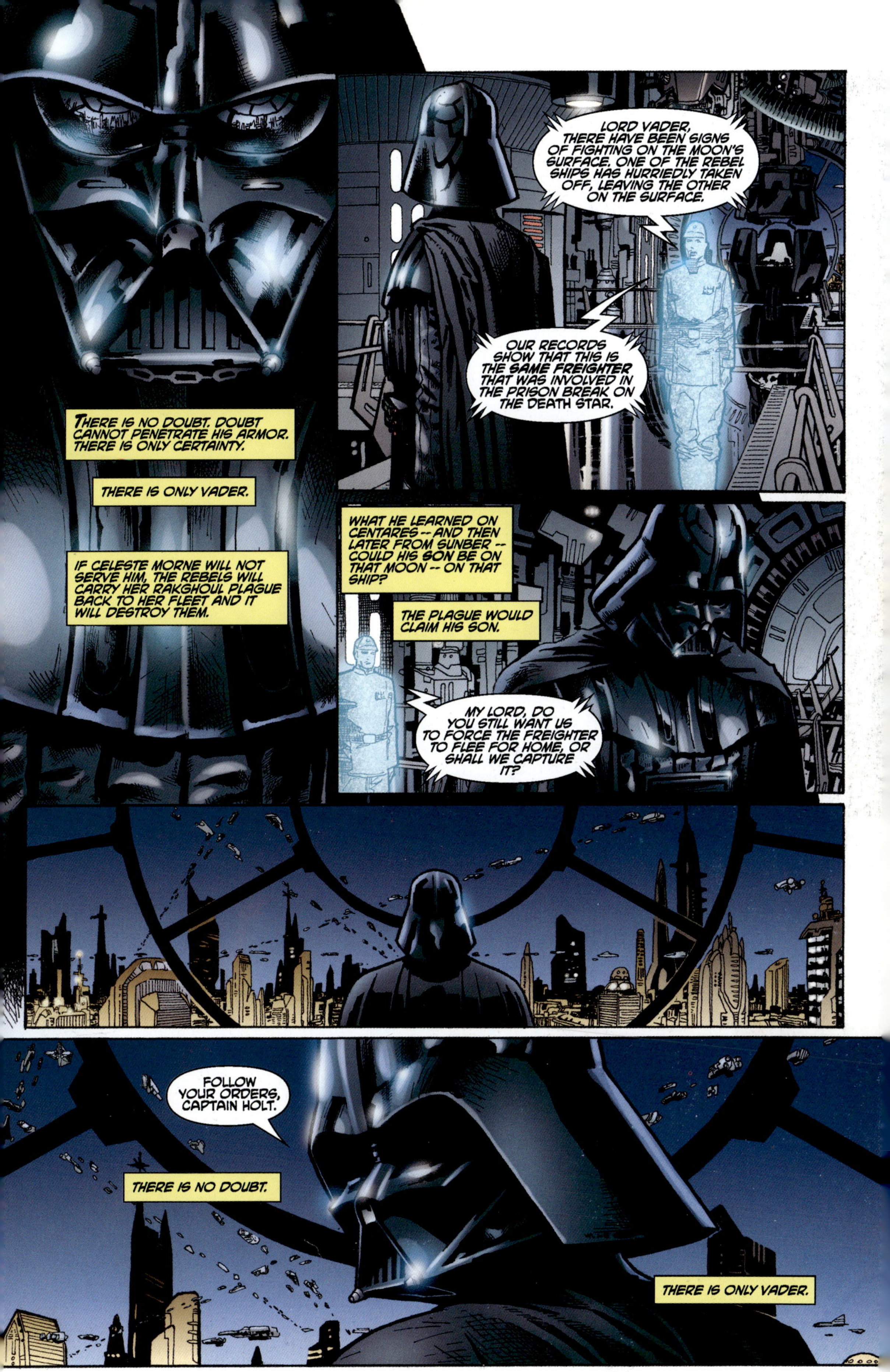

LORD VADER, THERE HAVE BEEN SIGNS OF FIGHTING ON THE MOON'S SURFACE. ONE OF THE REBEL SHIPS HAS HURRIEDLY TAKEN OFF, LEAVING THE OTHER ON THE SURFACE.
OUR RECORDS SHOW THAT THIS IS THE SAME FREIGHTER THAT WAS INVOLVED IN THE PRISON BREAK ON THE DEATH STAR.
THERE IS NO DOUBT. DOUBT CANNOT PENETRATE HIS ARMOR. THERE IS ONLY CERTAINTY.
THERE IS ONLY VADER.
IF CELESTE MORNE WILL NOT SERVE HIM, THE REBELS WILL CARRY HER RAKGHOUL PLAGUE BACK TO HER FLEET AND IT WILL DESTROY THEM.
WHAT HE LEARNED ON CENTARES -- AND THEN LATER FROM SUNBER -- COULD HIS SON BE ON THAT MOON -- ON THAT SHIP?
THE PLAGUE WOULD CLAIM HIS SON.
MY LORD, DO YOU STILL WANT US TO FORCE THE FREIGHTER TO FLEE FOR HOME, OR SHALL WE CAPTURE IT?
FOLLOW YOUR ORDERS, CAPTAIN HOLT.
THERE IS NO DOUBT.
THERE IS ONLY VADER.

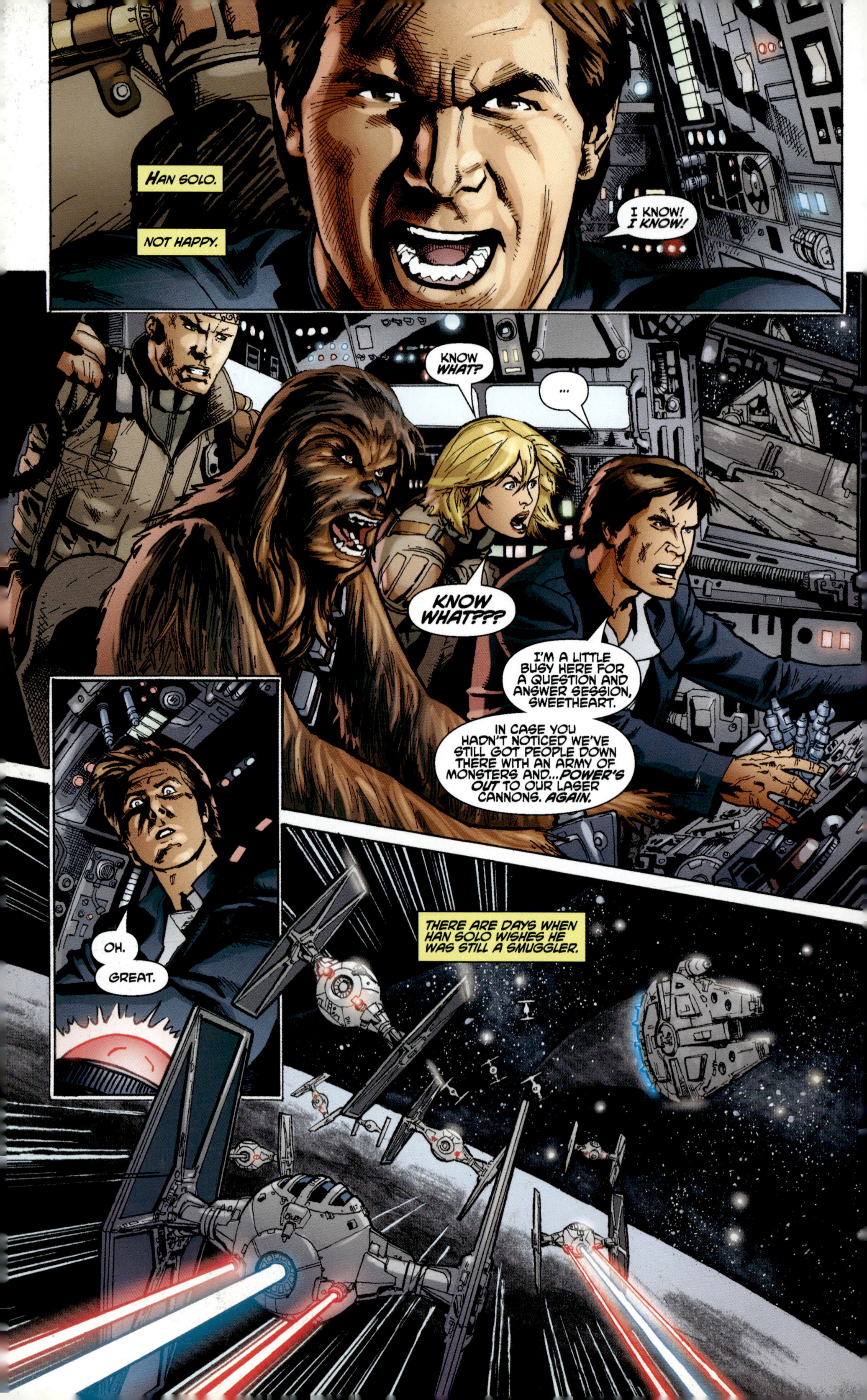
HAN SOLO.
NOT HAPPY.
I KNOW! I KNOW!
KNOW WHAT?
...
KNOW WHAT???
I'M A LITTLE BUSY HERE FOR A QUESTION AND ANSWER SESSION, SWEETHEART.
IN CASE YOU HADN'T NOTICED WE'VE STILL GOT PEOPLE DOWN THERE WITH AN ARMY OF MONSTERS AND...POWER'S OUT TO OUR LASER CANNONS. AGAIN.
OH.
GREAT.
THERE ARE DAYS WHEN HAN SOLO WISHES HE WAS STILL A SMUGGLER.

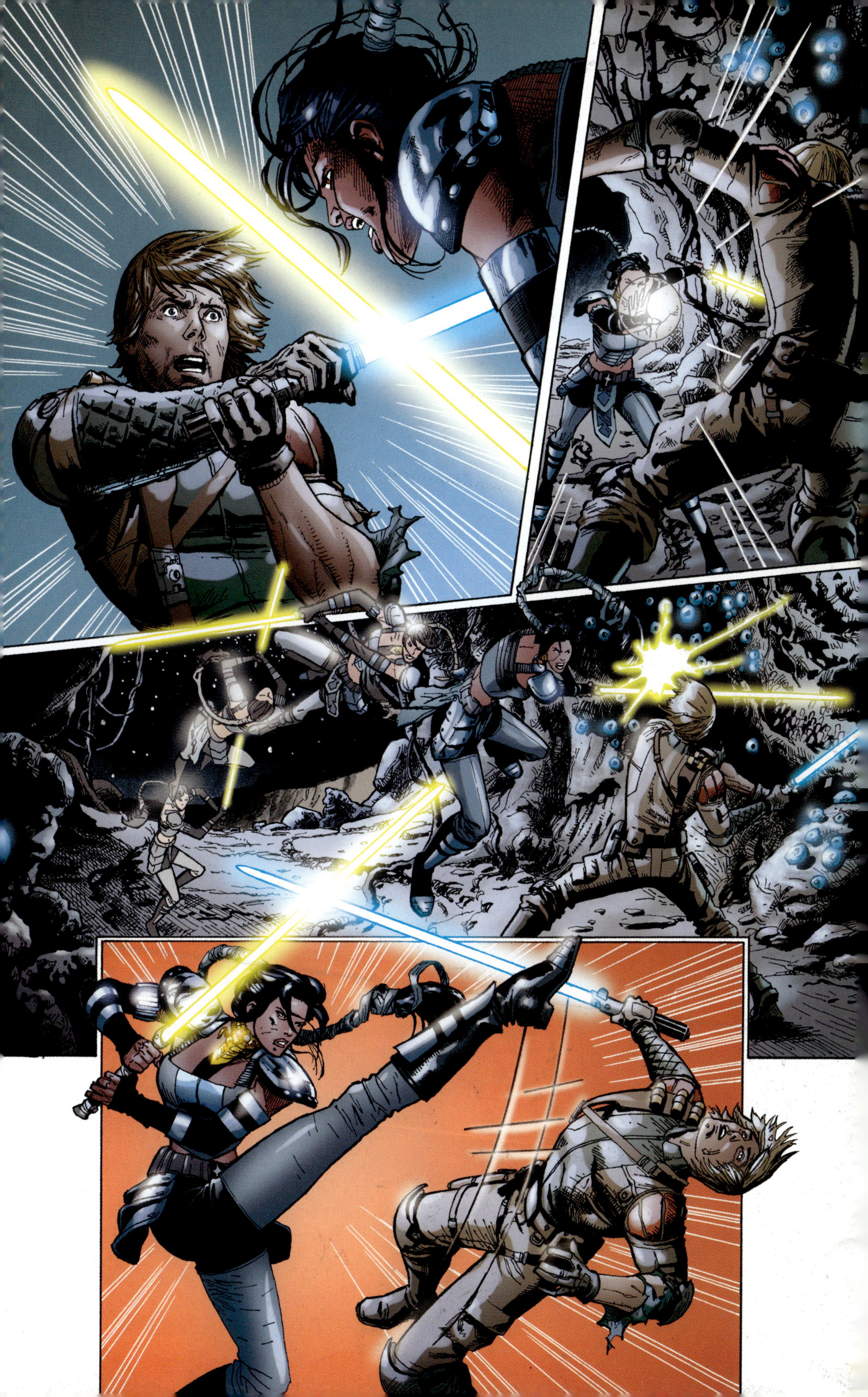

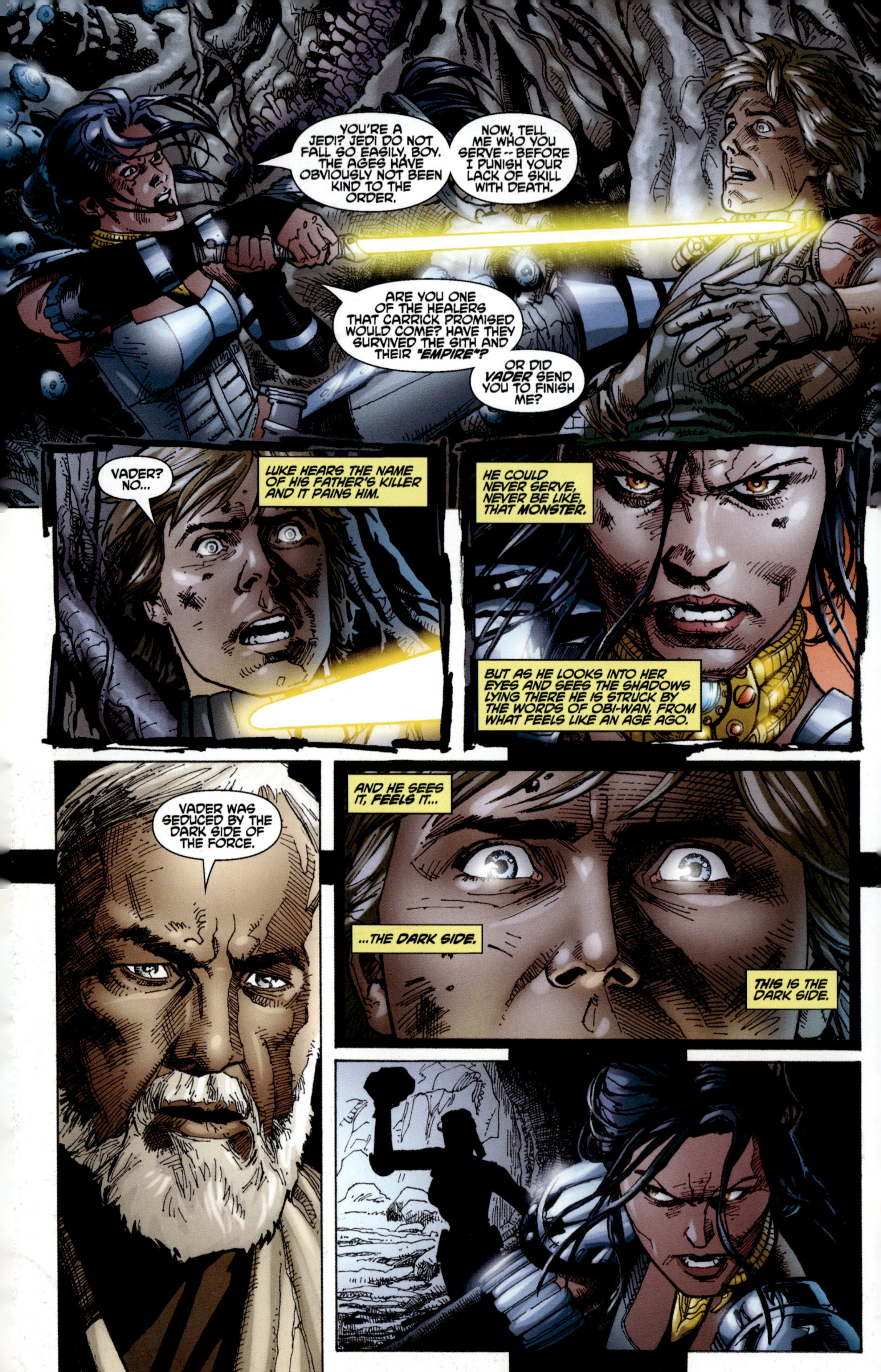
YOU'RE A JEDI? JEDI DO NOT FALL SO EASILY, BOY. THE AGES HAVE OBVIOUSLY NOT BEEN KIND TO THE ORDER.
NOW, TELL ME WHO YOU SERVE -- BEFORE I PUNISH YOUR LACK OF SKILL WITH DEATH.
ARE YOU ONE OF THE HEALERS THAT CARRICK PROMISED WOULD COME? HAVE THEY SURVIVED THE SITH AND THEIR *"EMPIRE"*?
OR DID *VADER* SEND YOU TO FINISH ME?
VADER? NO...
LUKE HEARS THE NAME OF HIS FATHER'S KILLER AND IT PAINS HIM.
HE COULD NEVER SERVE, NEVER BE LIKE, THAT *MONSTER.*
BUT AS HE LOOKS INTO HER EYES AND SEES THE SHADOWS LYING THERE HE IS STRUCK BY THE WORDS OF OBI-WAN, FROM WHAT FEELS LIKE AN AGE AGO.
VADER WAS SEDUCED BY THE DARK SIDE OF THE FORCE.
AND HE SEES IT, *FEELS* IT...
...THE DARK SIDE.
THIS IS THE DARK SIDE.

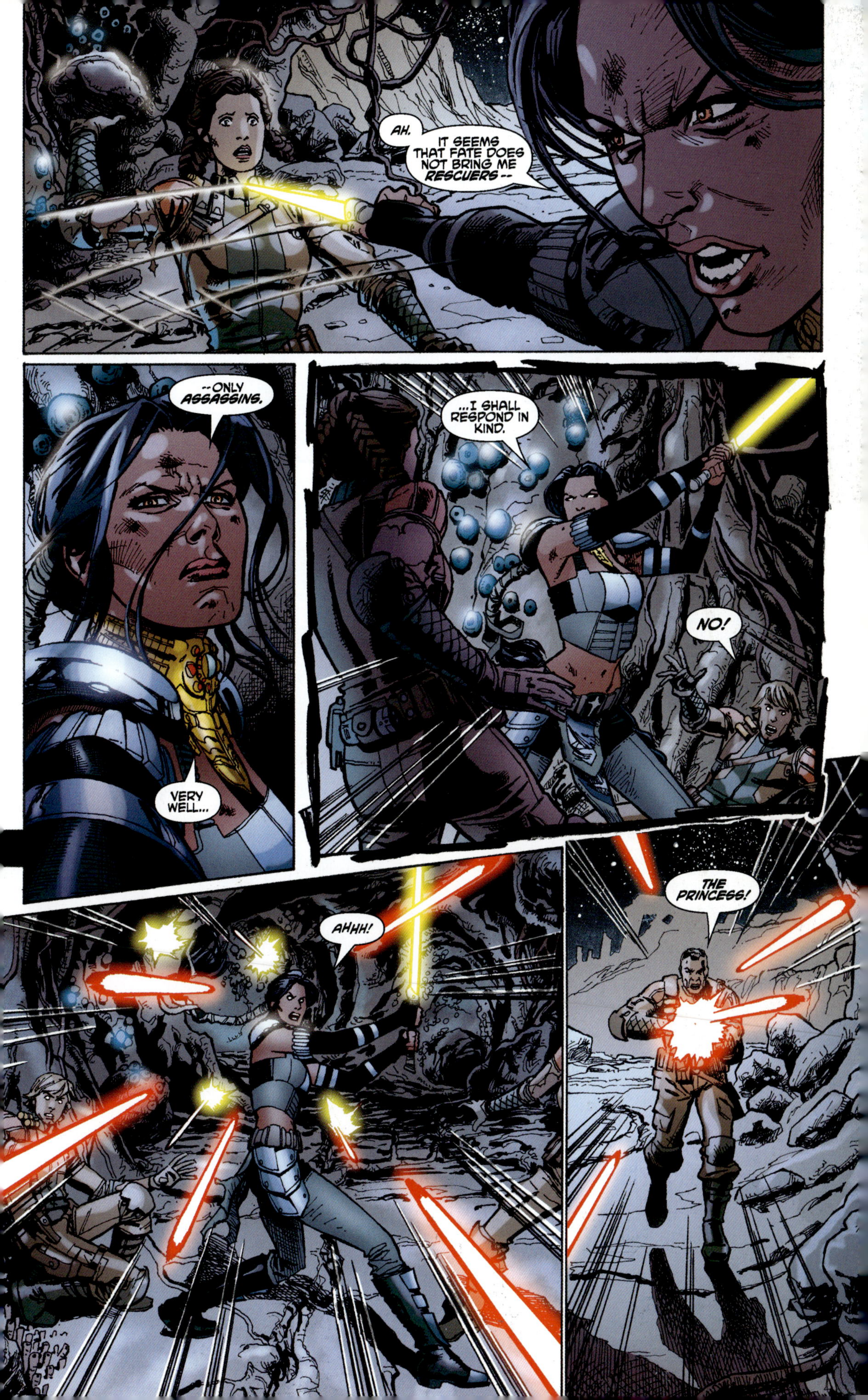
AH.
IT SEEMS THAT FATE DOES NOT BRING ME RESCUERS --
--ONLY ASSASSINS.
VERY WELL...
...I SHALL RESPOND IN KIND.
NO!
AHHH!
THE PRINCESS!

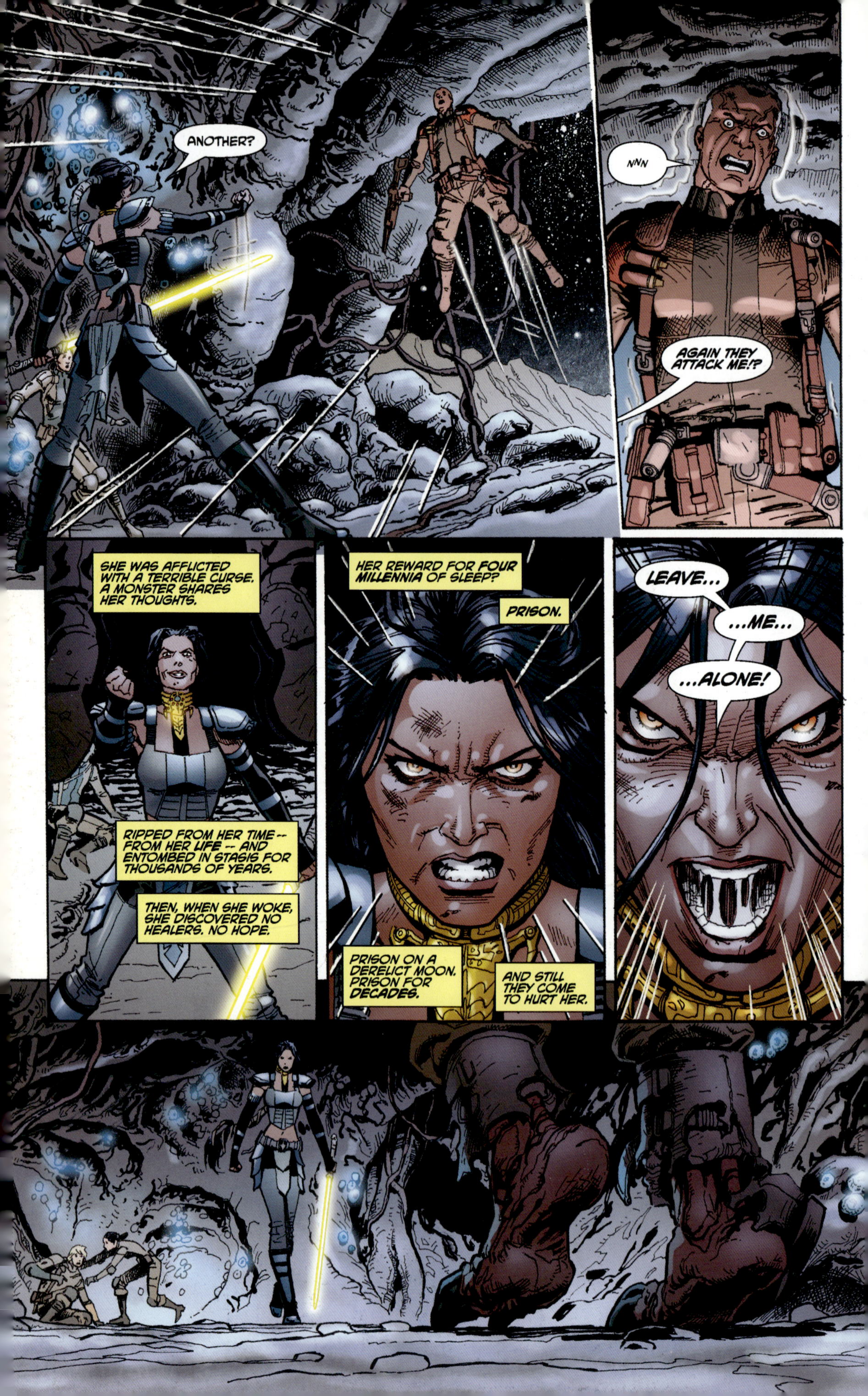
ANOTHER?
NNN
AGAIN THEY ATTACK ME!?
SHE WAS AFFLICTED WITH A TERRIBLE CURSE. A MONSTER SHARES HER THOUGHTS.
RIPPED FROM HER TIME -- FROM HER LIFE -- AND ENTOMBED IN STASIS FOR THOUSANDS OF YEARS.
THEN, WHEN SHE WOKE, SHE DISCOVERED NO HEALERS. NO HOPE.
HER REWARD FOR FOUR MILLENNIA OF SLEEP?
PRISON.
PRISON ON A DERELICT MOON. PRISON FOR DECADES.
AND STILL THEY COME TO HURT HER.
LEAVE...
...ME...
...ALONE!

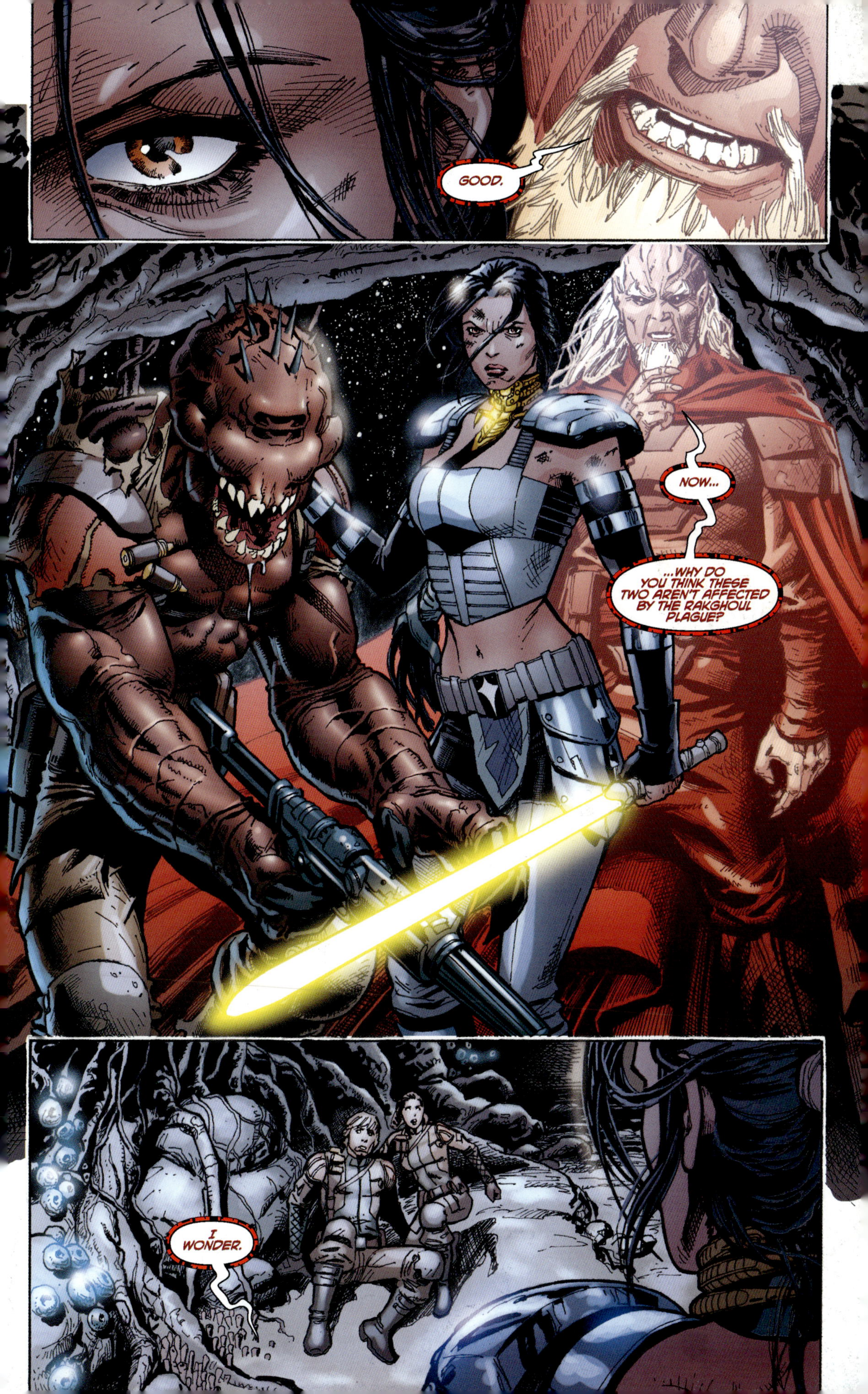
GOOD.
NOW...
...WHY DO YOU THINK THESE TWO AREN'T AFFECTED BY THE RAKGHOUL PLAGUE?
I WONDER.

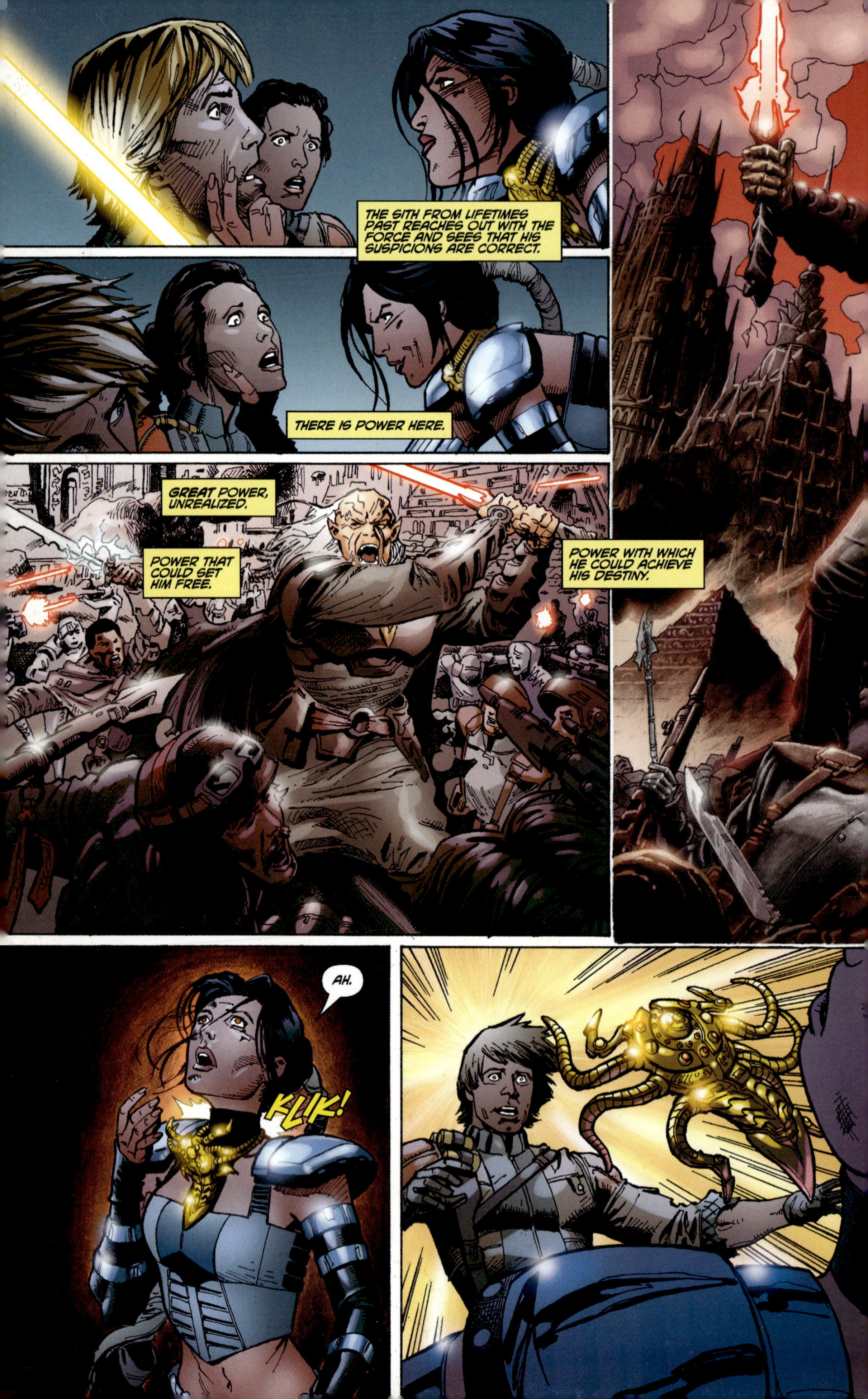
THE SITH FROM LIFETIMES PAST REACHES OUT WITH THE FORCE AND SEES THAT HIS SUSPICIONS ARE CORRECT.
THERE IS POWER HERE.
GREAT POWER, UNREALIZED.
POWER THAT COULD SET HIM FREE.
POWER WITH WHICH HE COULD ACHIEVE HIS DESTINY.
AH.
KLIK!

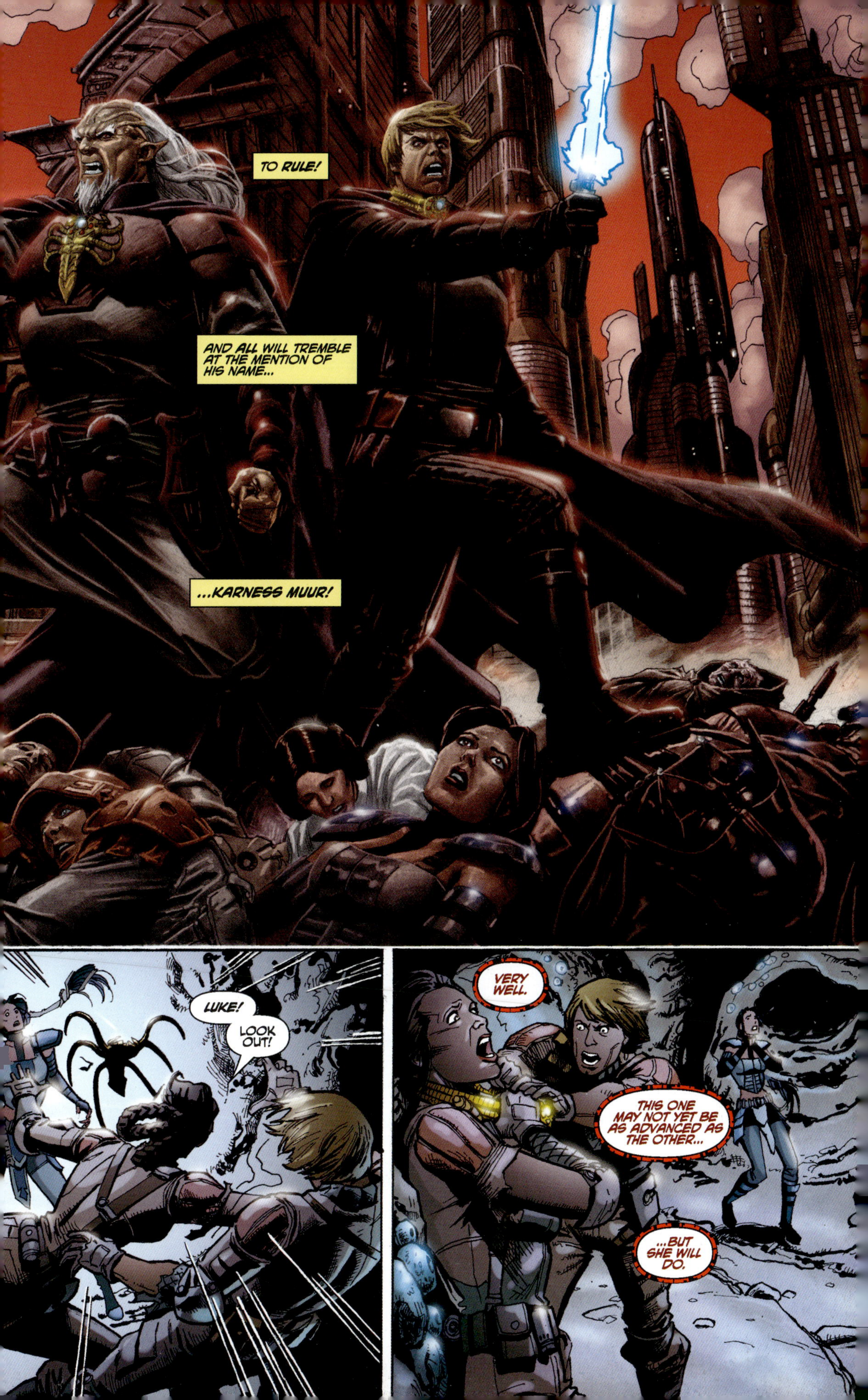
TO RULE!
AND ALL WILL TREMBLE AT THE MENTION OF HIS NAME...
...KARNESS MUUR!
LUKE!
LOOK OUT!
VERY WELL.
THIS ONE MAY NOT YET BE AS ADVANCED AS THE OTHER...
...BUT SHE WILL DO.

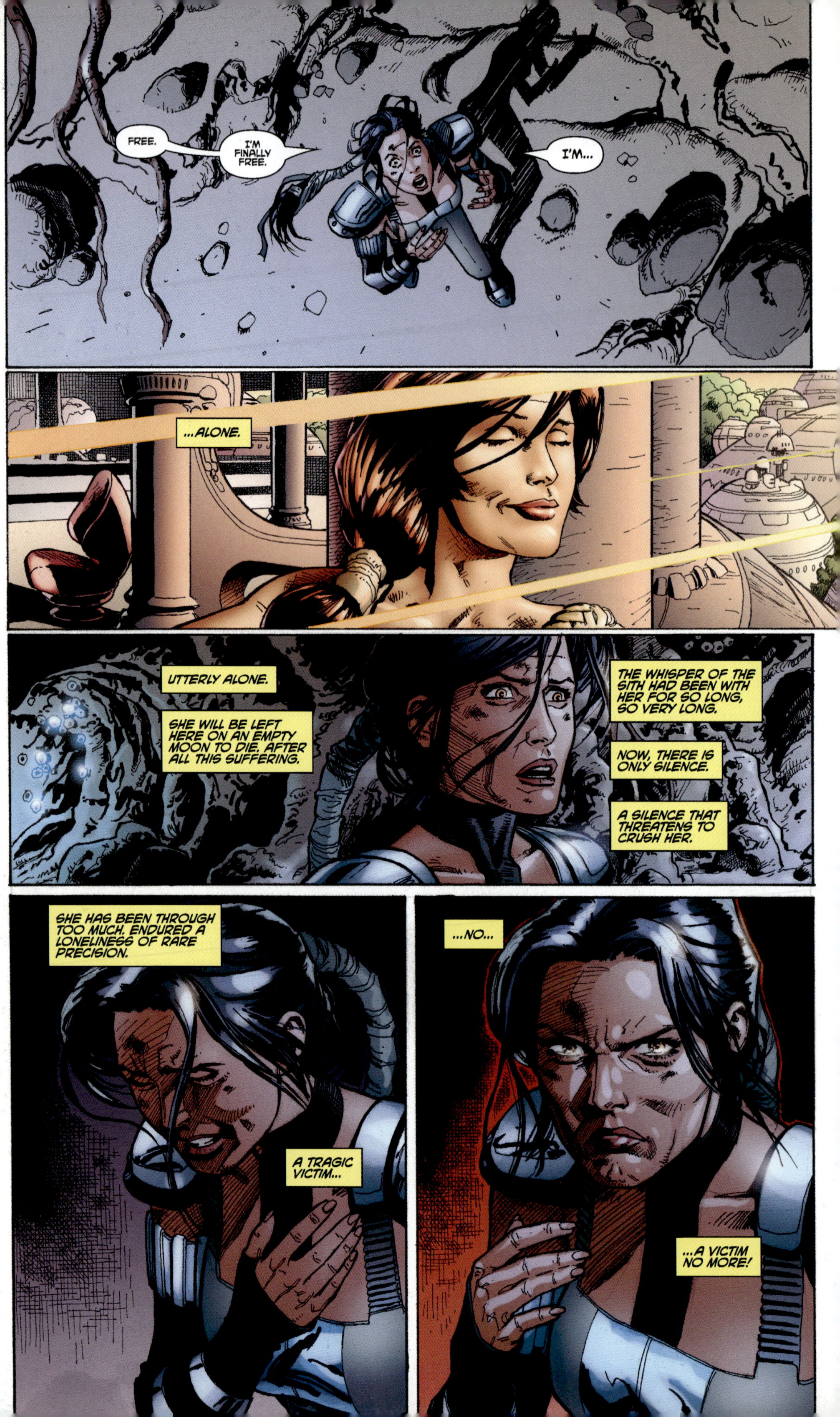
FREE.
I'M FINALLY FREE.
I'M...
...ALONE.
UTTERLY ALONE.
SHE WILL BE LEFT HERE ON AN EMPTY MOON TO DIE. AFTER ALL THIS SUFFERING.
THE WHISPER OF THE SITH HAD BEEN WITH HER FOR SO LONG, SO VERY LONG.
NOW, THERE IS ONLY SILENCE.
A SILENCE THAT THREATENS TO CRUSH HER.
SHE HAS BEEN THROUGH TOO MUCH. ENDURED A LONELINESS OF RARE PRECISION.
A TRAGIC VICTIM...
...NO...
...A VICTIM NO MORE!

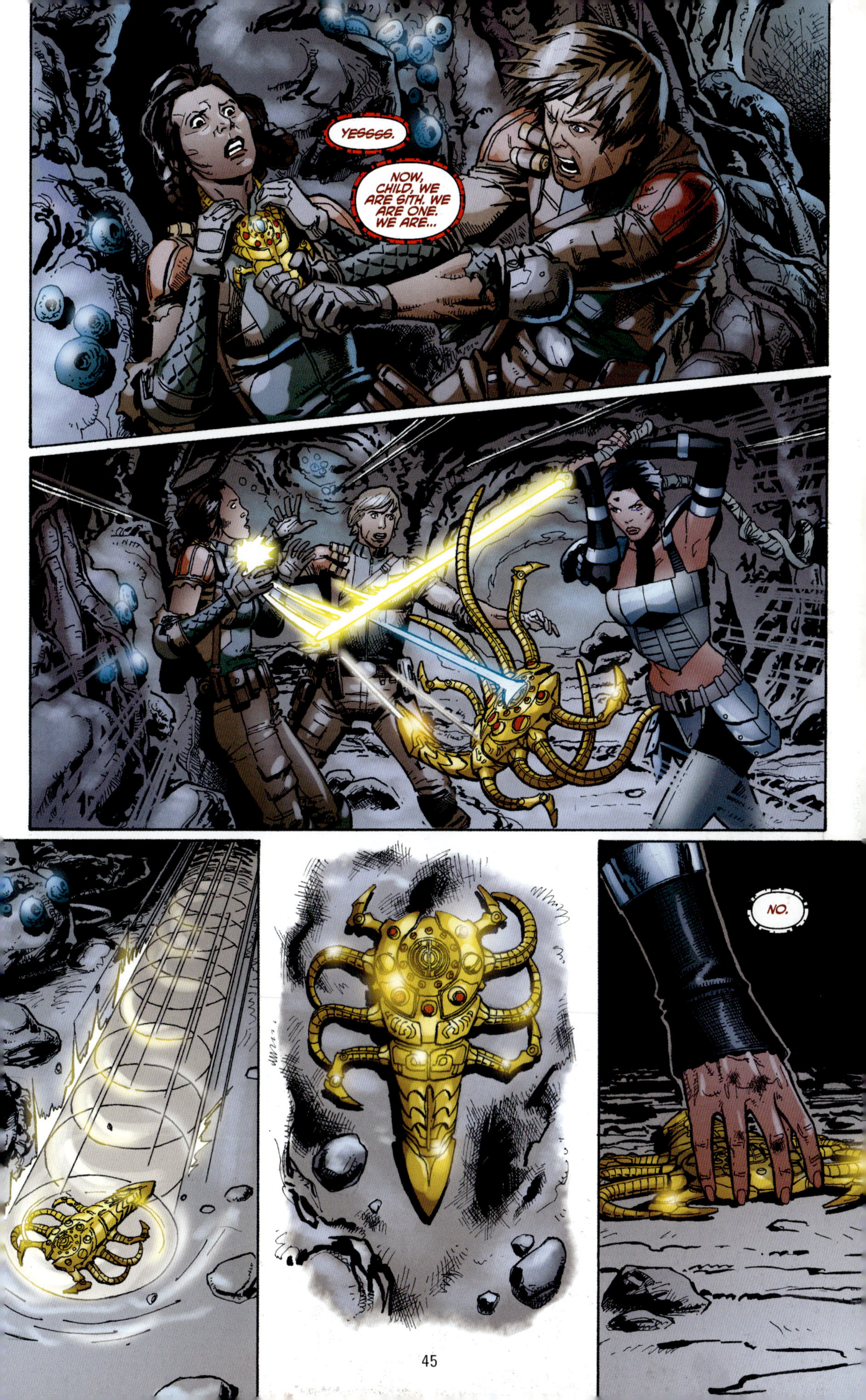
YESSSS.
NOW, CHILD, WE ARE SITH. WE ARE ONE. WE ARE...
NO.

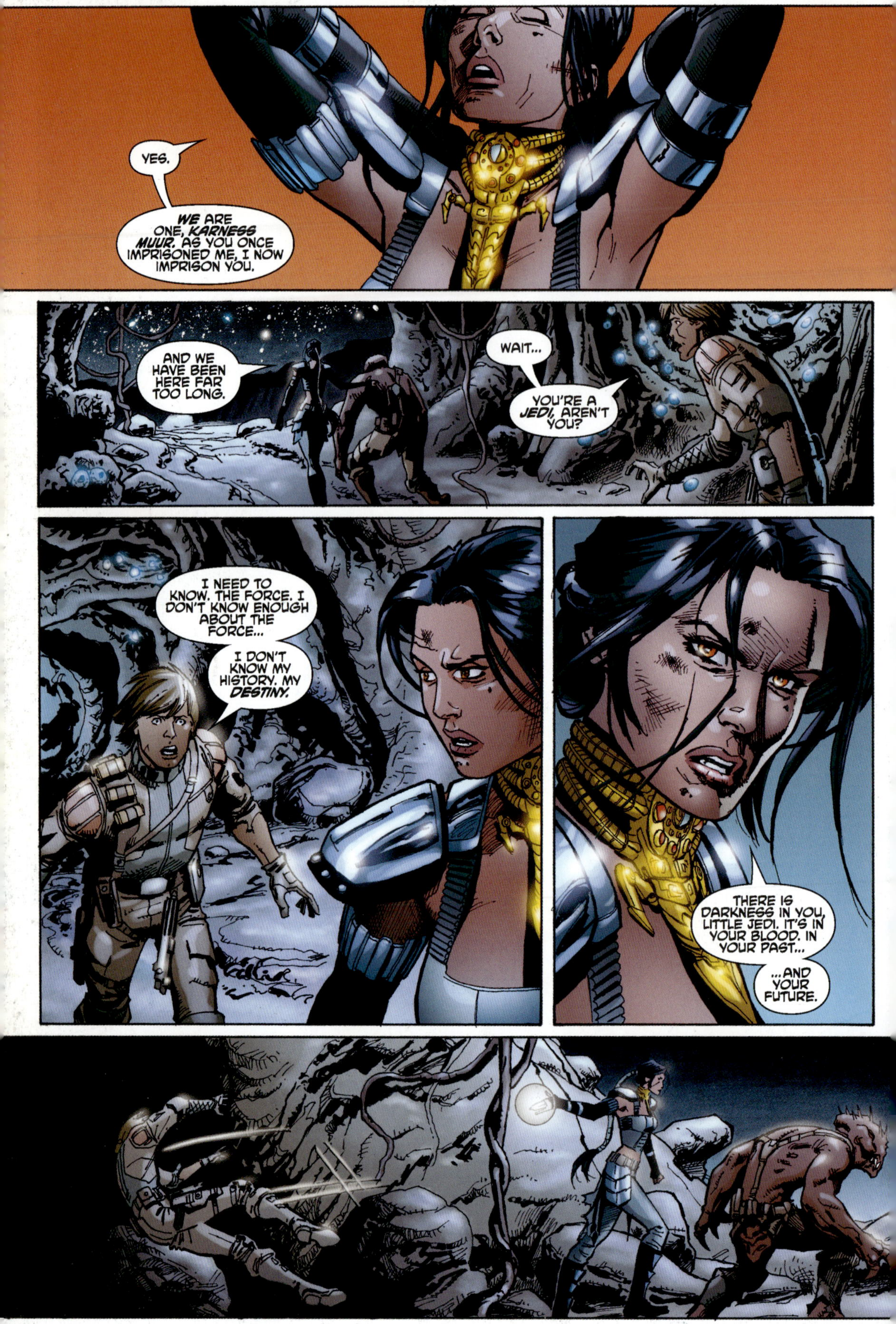
YES.
WE ARE ONE, KARNESS MUUR. AS YOU ONCE IMPRISONED ME, I NOW IMPRISON YOU.
AND WE HAVE BEEN HERE FAR TOO LONG.
WAIT...
YOU'RE A JEDI, AREN'T YOU?
I NEED TO KNOW. THE FORCE. I DON'T KNOW ENOUGH ABOUT THE FORCE...
I DON'T KNOW MY HISTORY. MY DESTINY.
THERE IS DARKNESS IN YOU, LITTLE JEDI. IT'S IN YOUR BLOOD. IN YOUR PAST...
...AND YOUR FUTURE.

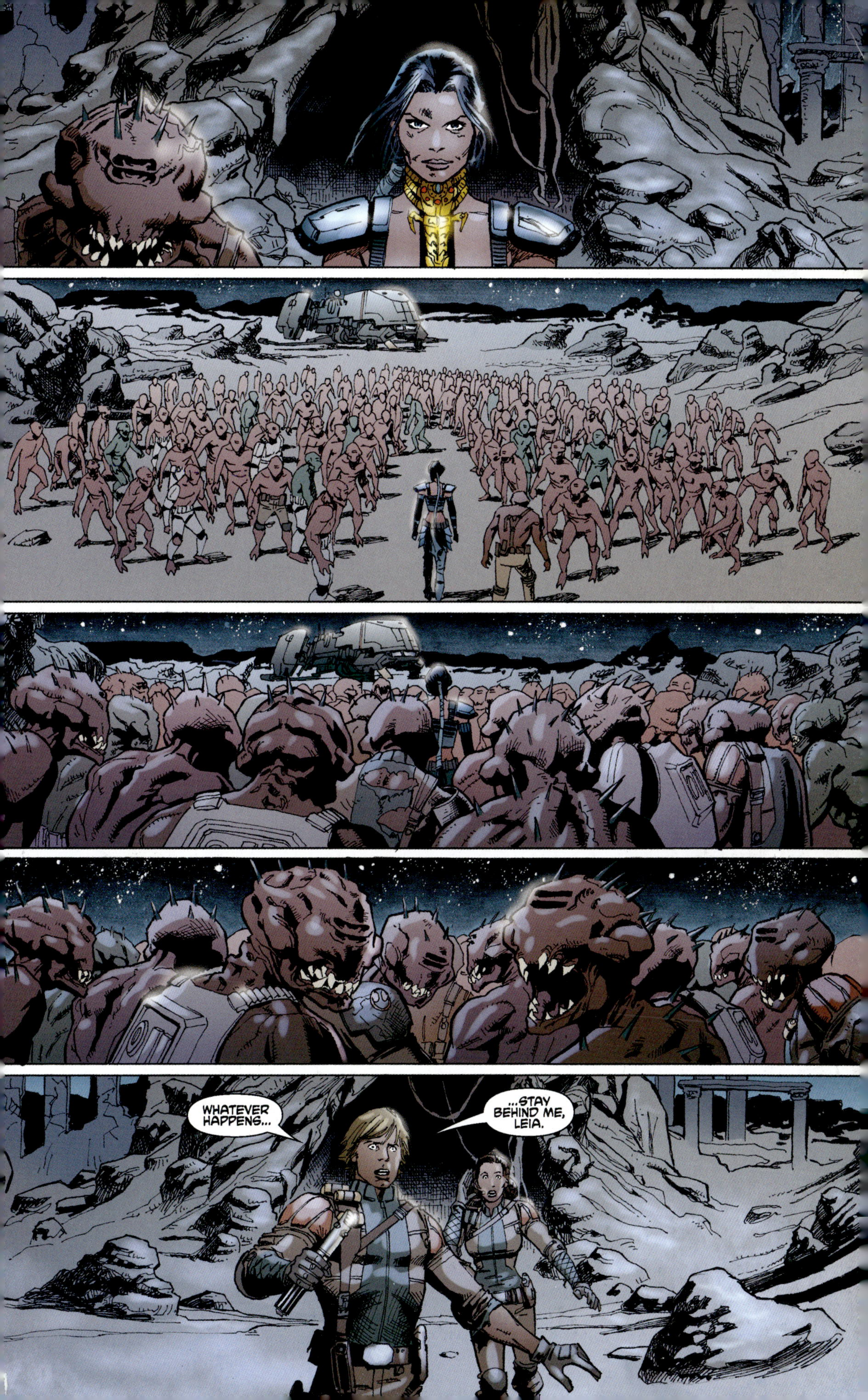
WHATEVER HAPPENS...
...STAY BEHIND ME, LEIA.

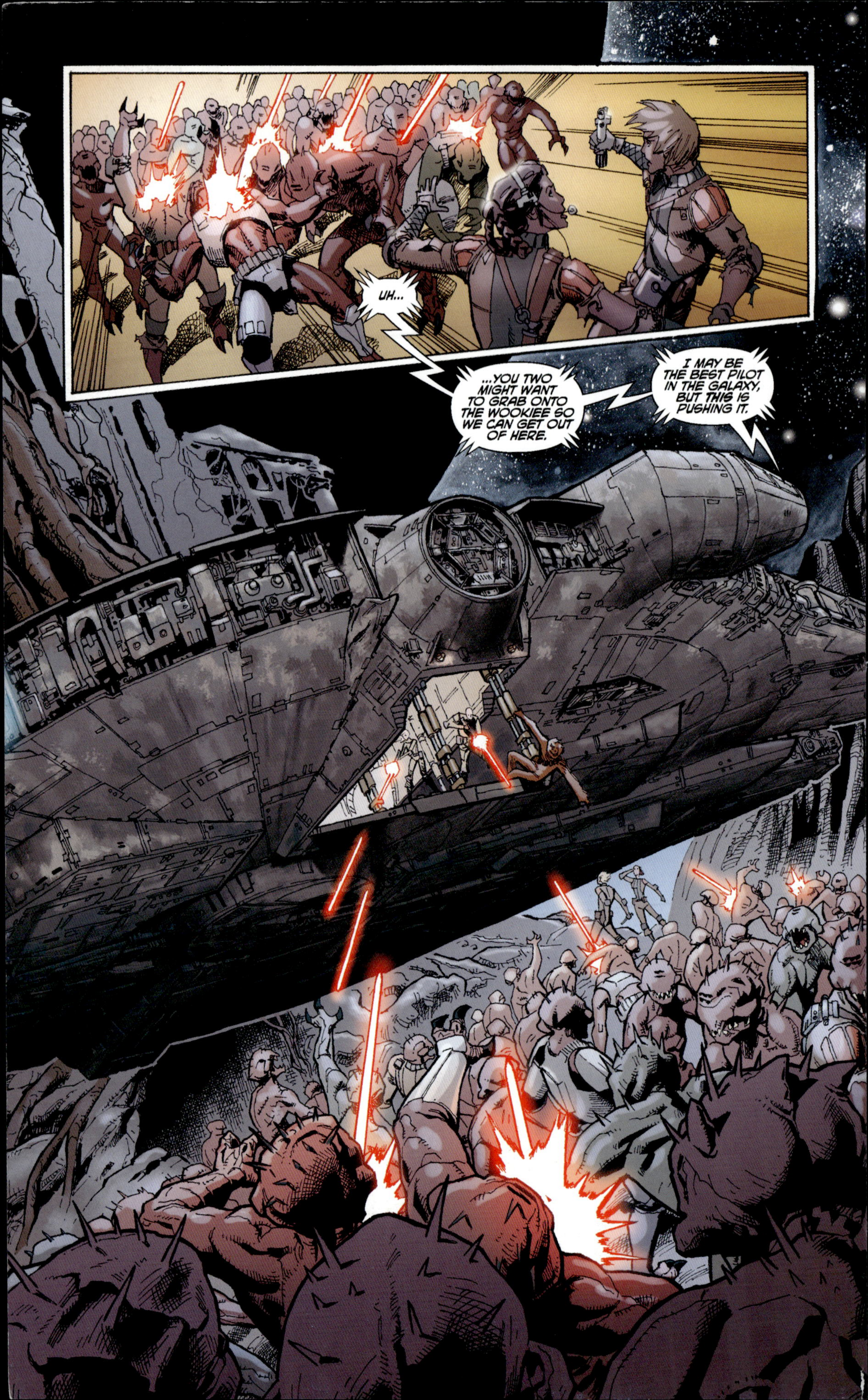
UH...
...YOU TWO MIGHT WANT TO GRAB ONTO THE WOOKIEE SO WE CAN GET OUT OF HERE.
I MAY BE THE BEST PILOT IN THE GALAXY, BUT THIS IS PUSHING IT.

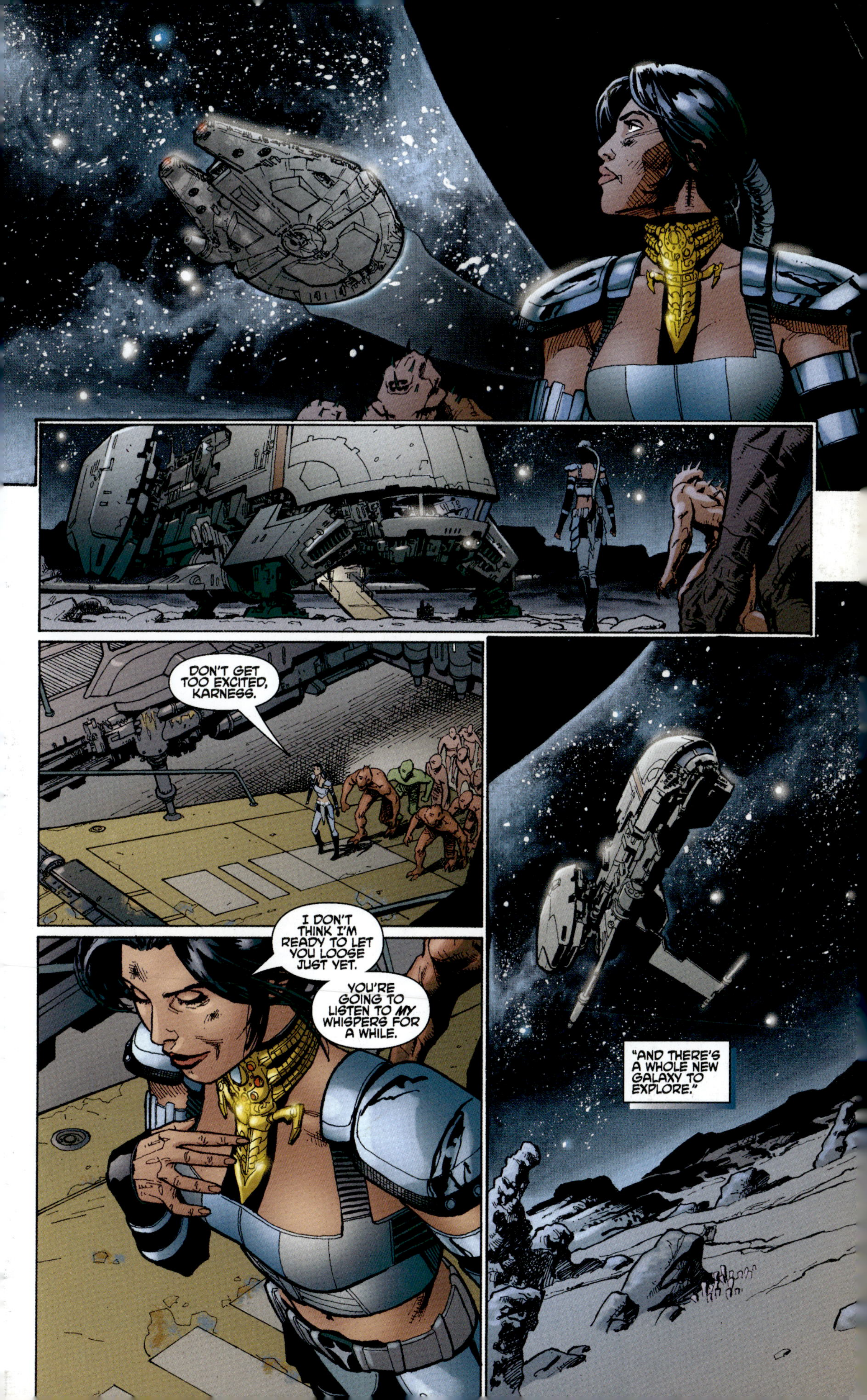
DON'T GET TOO EXCITED, KARNESS.
I DON'T THINK I'M READY TO LET YOU LOOSE JUST YET.
YOU'RE GOING TO LISTEN TO *MY* WHISPERS FOR A WHILE.
"AND THERE'S A WHOLE NEW GALAXY TO EXPLORE."

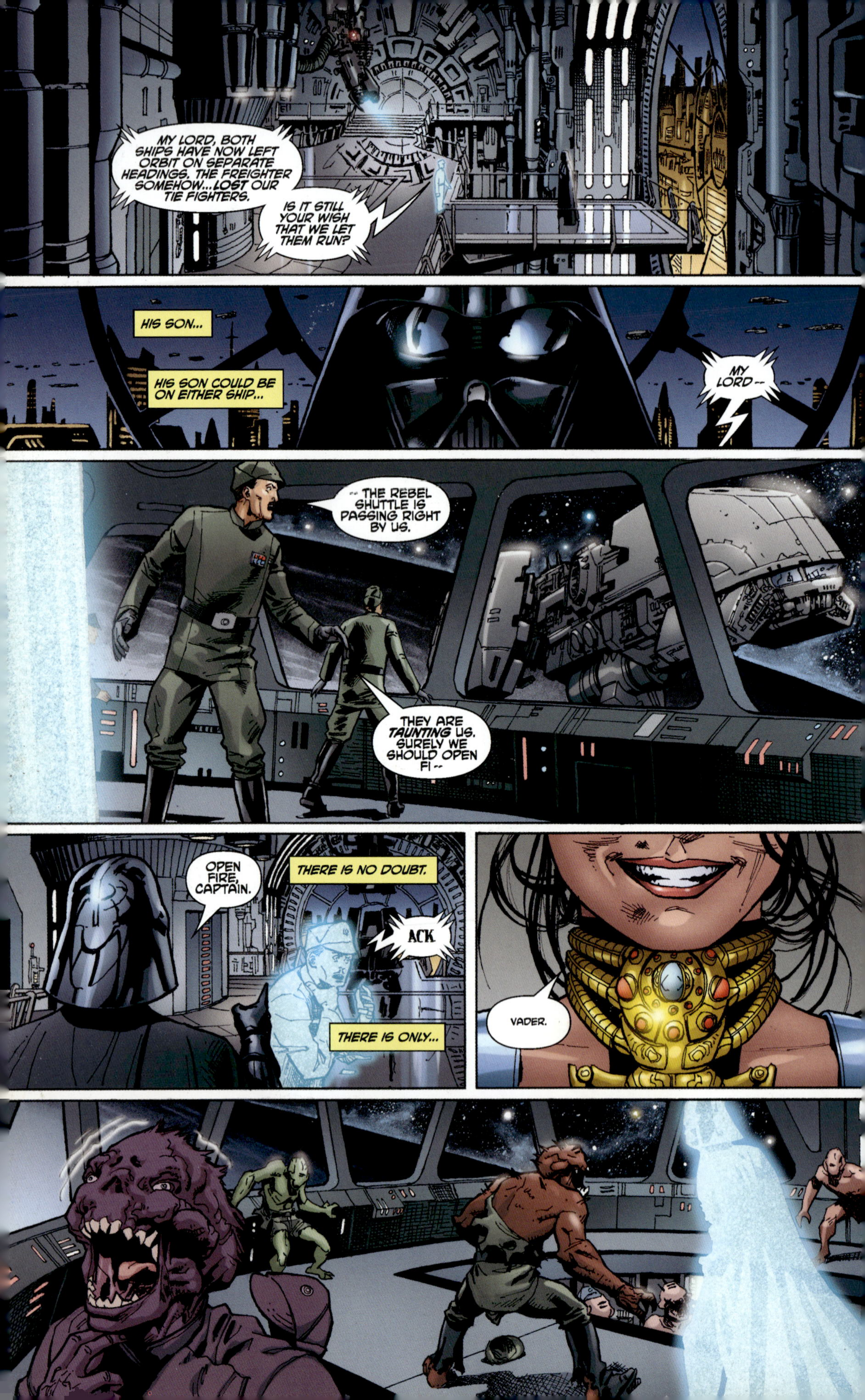
MY LORD, BOTH SHIPS HAVE NOW LEFT ORBIT ON SEPARATE HEADINGS. THE FREIGHTER SOMEHOW... LOST OUR TIE FIGHTERS.
IS IT STILL YOUR WISH THAT WE LET THEM RUN?
HIS SON...
HIS SON COULD BE ON EITHER SHIP...
MY LORD --
-- THE REBEL SHUTTLE IS PASSING RIGHT BY US.
THEY ARE TAUNTING US. SURELY WE SHOULD OPEN FI --
OPEN FIRE, CAPTAIN.
THERE IS NO DOUBT.
ACK
THERE IS ONLY...
VADER.

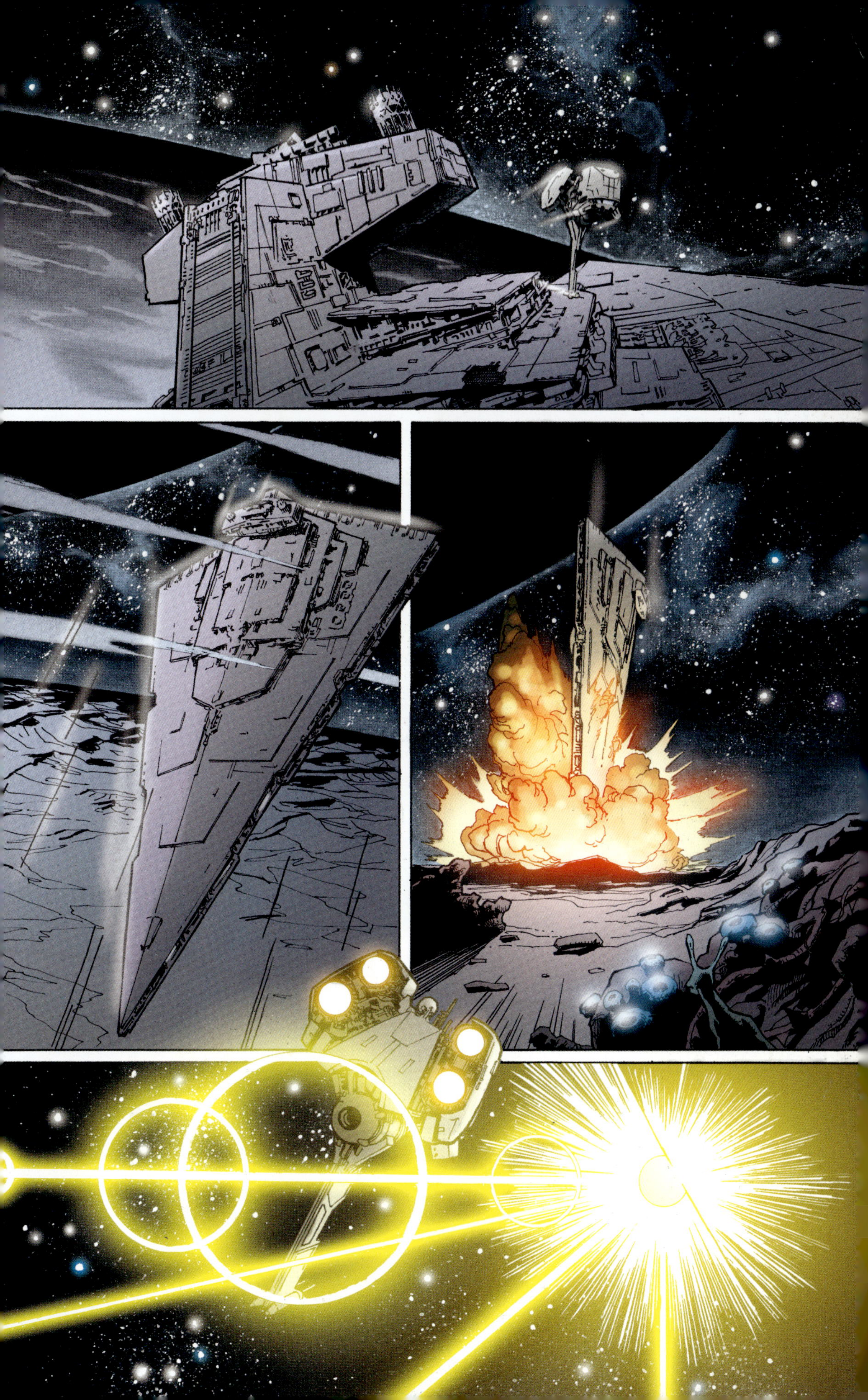

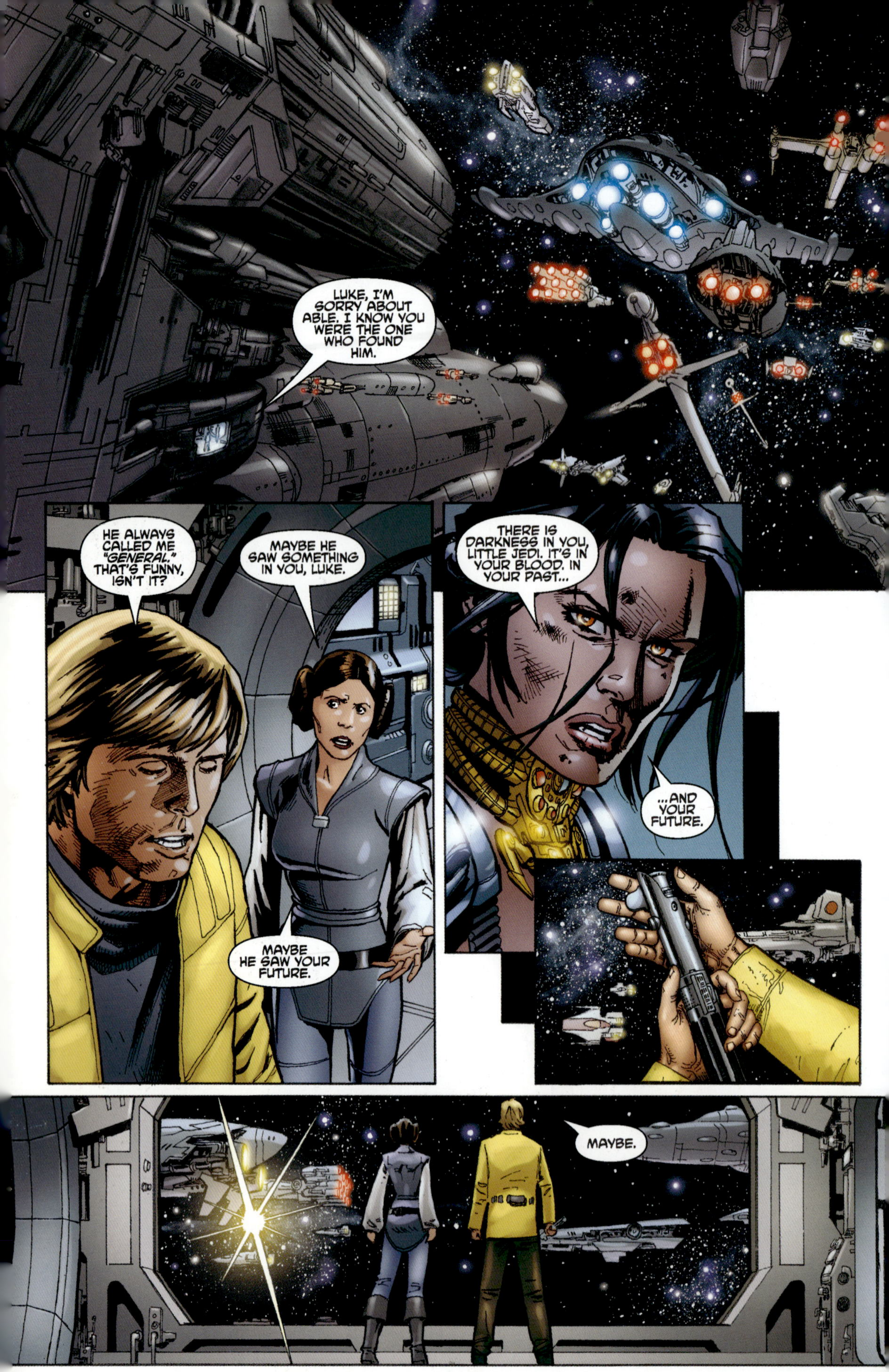
LUKE, I'M SORRY ABOUT ABLE. I KNOW YOU WERE THE ONE WHO FOUND HIM.
HE ALWAYS CALLED ME "GENERAL." THAT'S FUNNY, ISN'T IT?
MAYBE HE SAW SOMETHING IN YOU, LUKE.
MAYBE HE SAW YOUR FUTURE.
THERE IS DARKNESS IN YOU, LITTLE JEDI. IT'S IN YOUR BLOOD. IN YOUR PAST...
...AND YOUR FUTURE.
MAYBE.

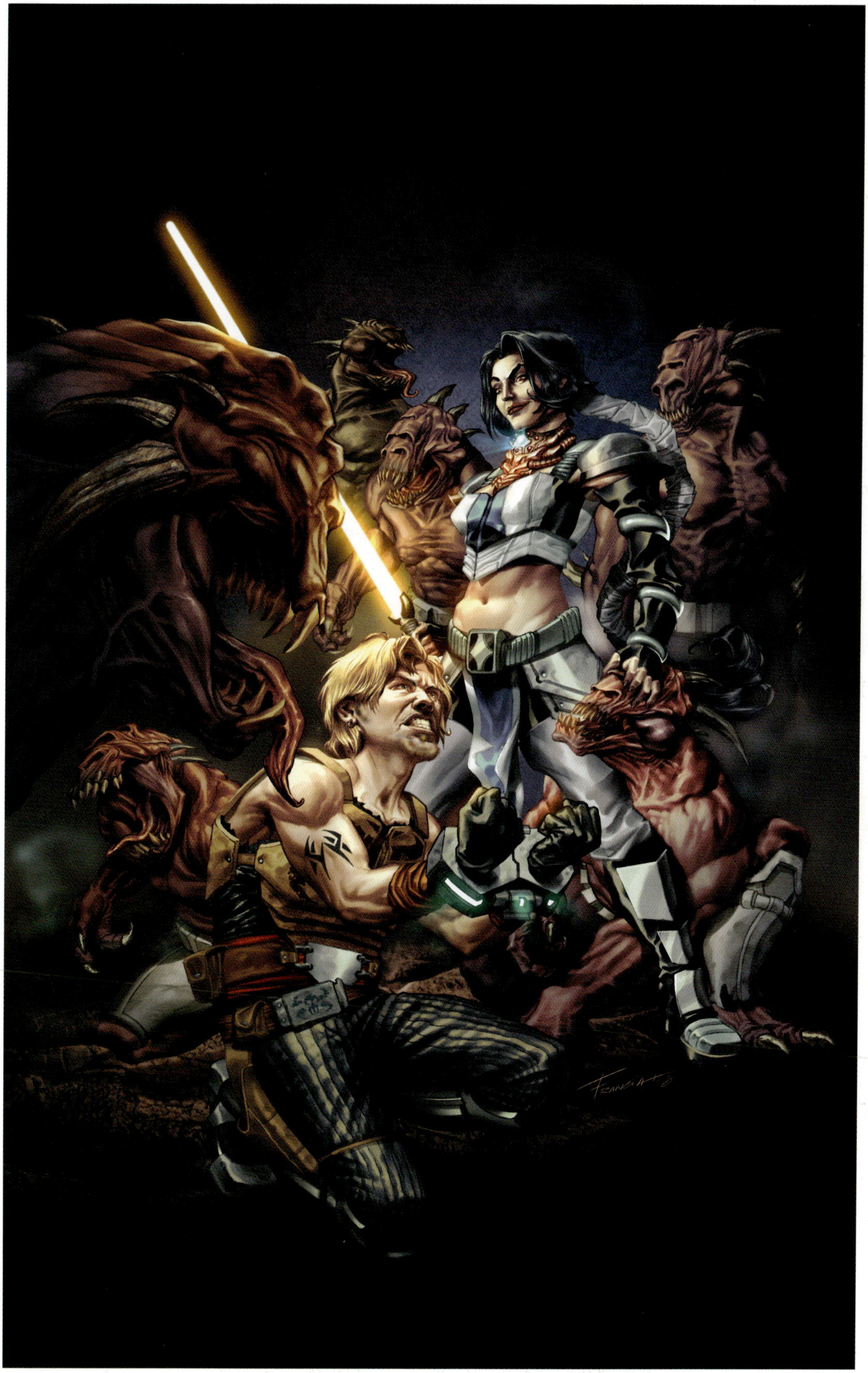

Illustration by **OMAR FRANCIA**

LEGACY

VOLUME 6   The Jedi Council has denied Cade Skywalker's request for assistance in his plot to assassinate Emperor Darth Krayt—but the Council is not Cade's only potential ally.

Cade and his bounty-hunter crew have been joined by three of deposed Emperor Roan Fel's Imperial Knights—one of whom, Azlyn Rae, already shares a past with Cade. Also along for the trip is Jedi Knight Shado Vao, who worries that his friend is another Skywalker coming too close to the dark side.

The *Mynock* and its crew and passengers journey into the galaxy's Deep Core to prepare the downfall of the Emperor, expecting nothing but empty space . . .

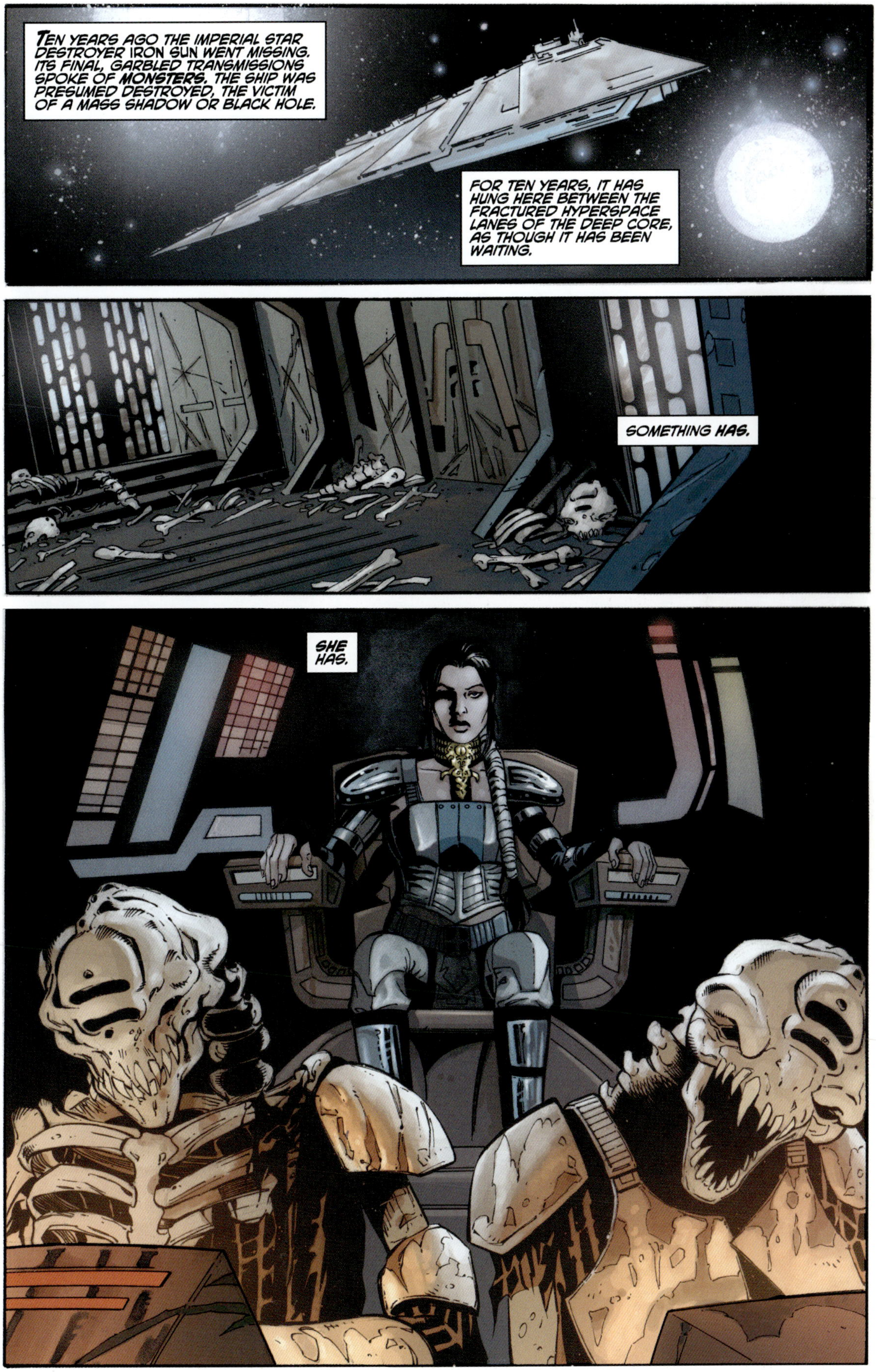
TEN YEARS AGO THE IMPERIAL STAR DESTROYER IRON SUN WENT MISSING. ITS FINAL, GARBLED TRANSMISSIONS SPOKE OF MONSTERS. THE SHIP WAS PRESUMED DESTROYED, THE VICTIM OF A MASS SHADOW OR BLACK HOLE.
FOR TEN YEARS, IT HAS HUNG HERE BETWEEN THE FRACTURED HYPERSPACE LANES OF THE DEEP CORE, AS THOUGH IT HAS BEEN WAITING.
SOMETHING HAS.
SHE HAS.

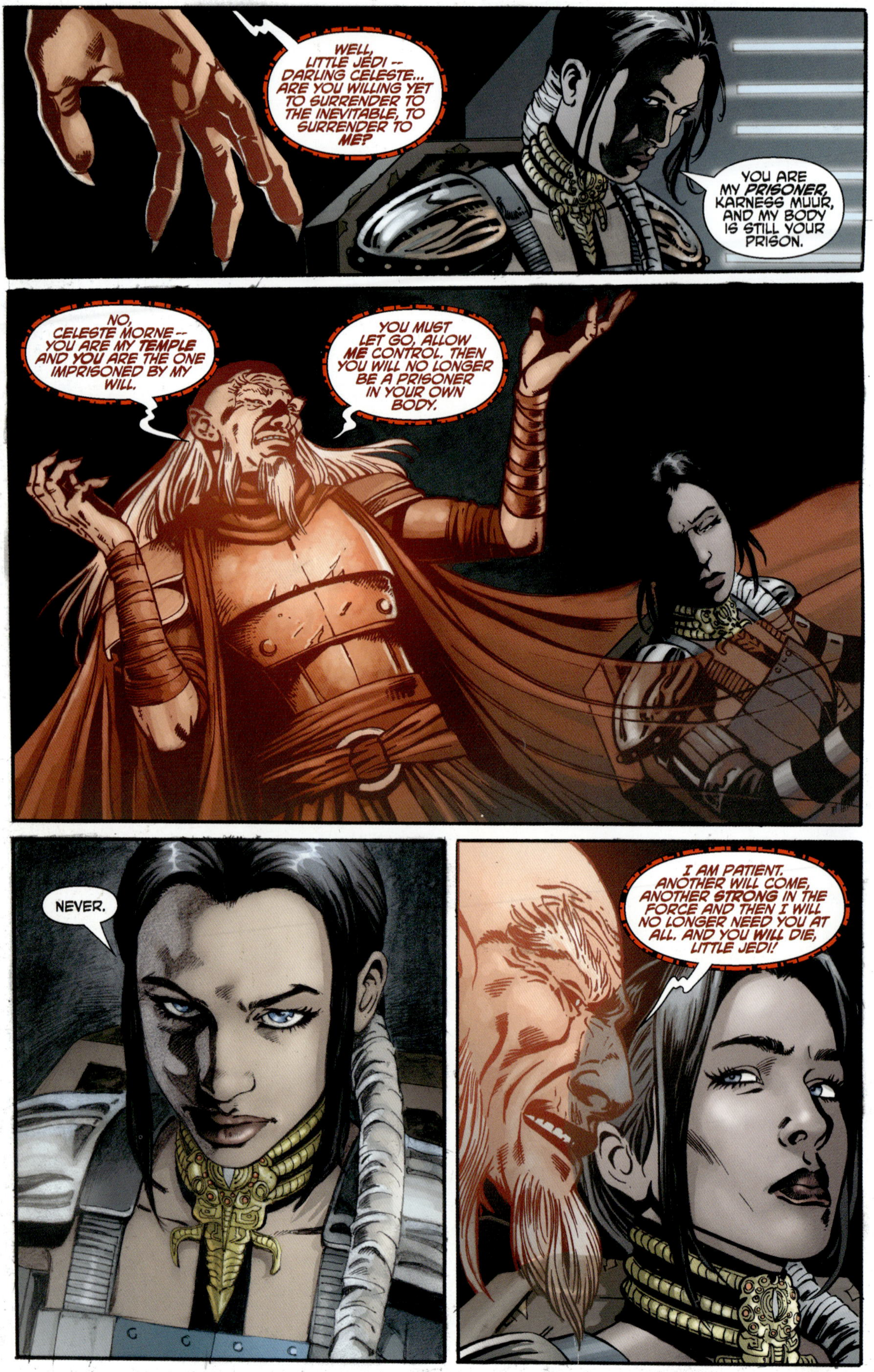
WELL, LITTLE JEDI -- DARLING CELESTE... ARE YOU WILLING YET TO SURRENDER TO THE INEVITABLE, TO SURRENDER TO ME?
YOU ARE MY PRISONER, KARNESS MUUR, AND MY BODY IS STILL YOUR PRISON.
NO, CELESTE MORNE -- YOU ARE MY TEMPLE AND YOU ARE THE ONE IMPRISONED BY MY WILL.
YOU MUST LET GO, ALLOW ME CONTROL. THEN YOU WILL NO LONGER BE A PRISONER IN YOUR OWN BODY.
NEVER.
I AM PATIENT. ANOTHER WILL COME, ANOTHER STRONG IN THE FORCE AND THEN I WILL NO LONGER NEED YOU AT ALL. AND YOU WILL DIE, LITTLE JEDI!

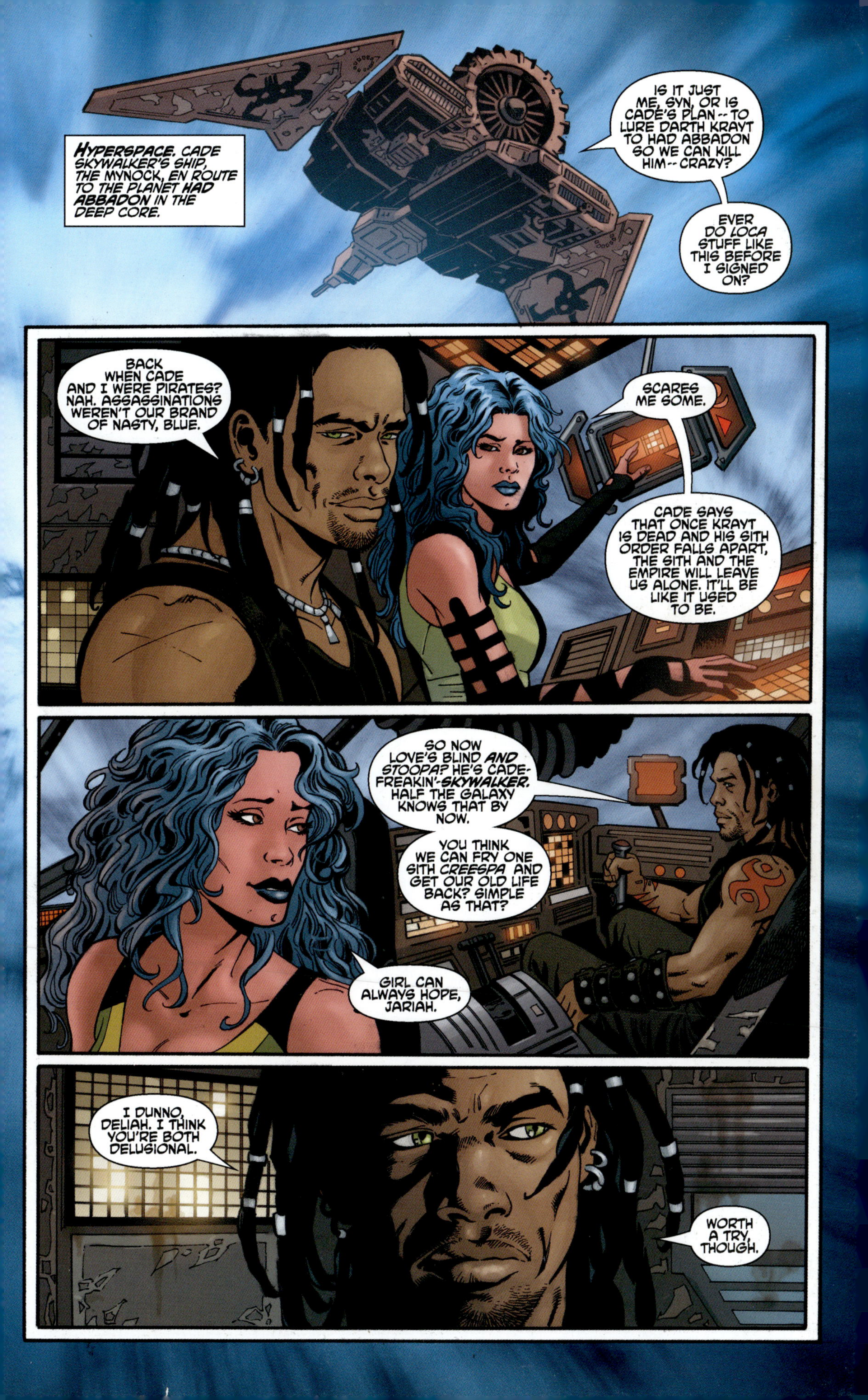
HYPERSPACE. CADE SKYWALKER'S SHIP, THE MYNOCK, EN ROUTE TO THE PLANET HAD ABBADON IN THE DEEP CORE.
IS IT JUST ME, SYN, OR IS CADE'S PLAN-- TO LURE DARTH KRAYT TO HAD ABBADON SO WE CAN KILL HIM-- CRAZY?
EVER DO LOCA STUFF LIKE THIS BEFORE I SIGNED ON?
BACK WHEN CADE AND I WERE PIRATES? NAH. ASSASSINATIONS WEREN'T OUR BRAND OF NASTY, BLUE.
SCARES ME SOME.
CADE SAYS THAT ONCE KRAYT IS DEAD AND HIS SITH ORDER FALLS APART, THE SITH AND THE EMPIRE WILL LEAVE US ALONE. IT'LL BE LIKE IT USED TO BE.
SO NOW LOVE'S BLIND AND STOOPA? HE'S CADE-FREAKIN'-SKYWALKER. HALF THE GALAXY KNOWS THAT BY NOW.
YOU THINK WE CAN FRY ONE SITH CREESPA AND GET OUR OLD LIFE BACK? SIMPLE AS THAT?
GIRL CAN ALWAYS HOPE, JARIAH.
I DUNNO, DELIAH. I THINK YOU'RE BOTH DELUSIONAL.
WORTH A TRY, THOUGH.

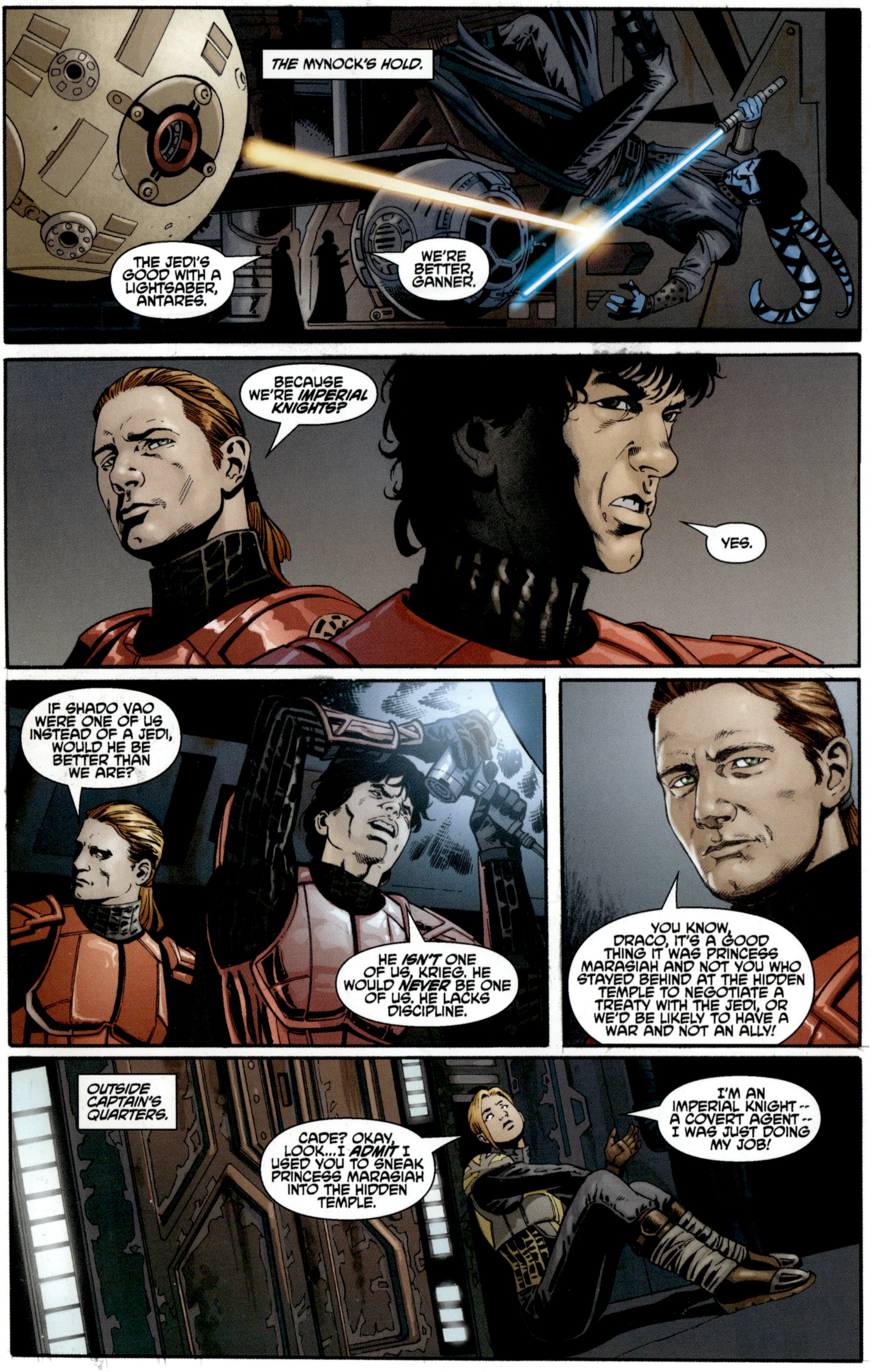
THE MYNOCK'S HOLD.
THE JEDI'S GOOD WITH A LIGHTSABER, ANTARES.
WE'RE BETTER, GANNER.
BECAUSE WE'RE IMPERIAL KNIGHTS?
YES.
IF SHADO VAO WERE ONE OF US INSTEAD OF A JEDI, WOULD HE BE BETTER THAN WE ARE?
HE ISN'T ONE OF US, KRIEG. HE WOULD NEVER BE ONE OF US. HE LACKS DISCIPLINE.
YOU KNOW, DRACO, IT'S A GOOD THING IT WAS PRINCESS MARASIAH AND NOT YOU WHO STAYED BEHIND AT THE HIDDEN TEMPLE TO NEGOTIATE A TREATY WITH THE JEDI, OR WE'D BE LIKELY TO HAVE A WAR AND NOT AN ALLY!
OUTSIDE CAPTAIN'S QUARTERS.
CADE? OKAY, LOOK...I ADMIT I USED YOU TO SNEAK PRINCESS MARASIAH INTO THE HIDDEN TEMPLE.
I'M AN IMPERIAL KNIGHT -- A COVERT AGENT -- I WAS JUST DOING MY JOB!

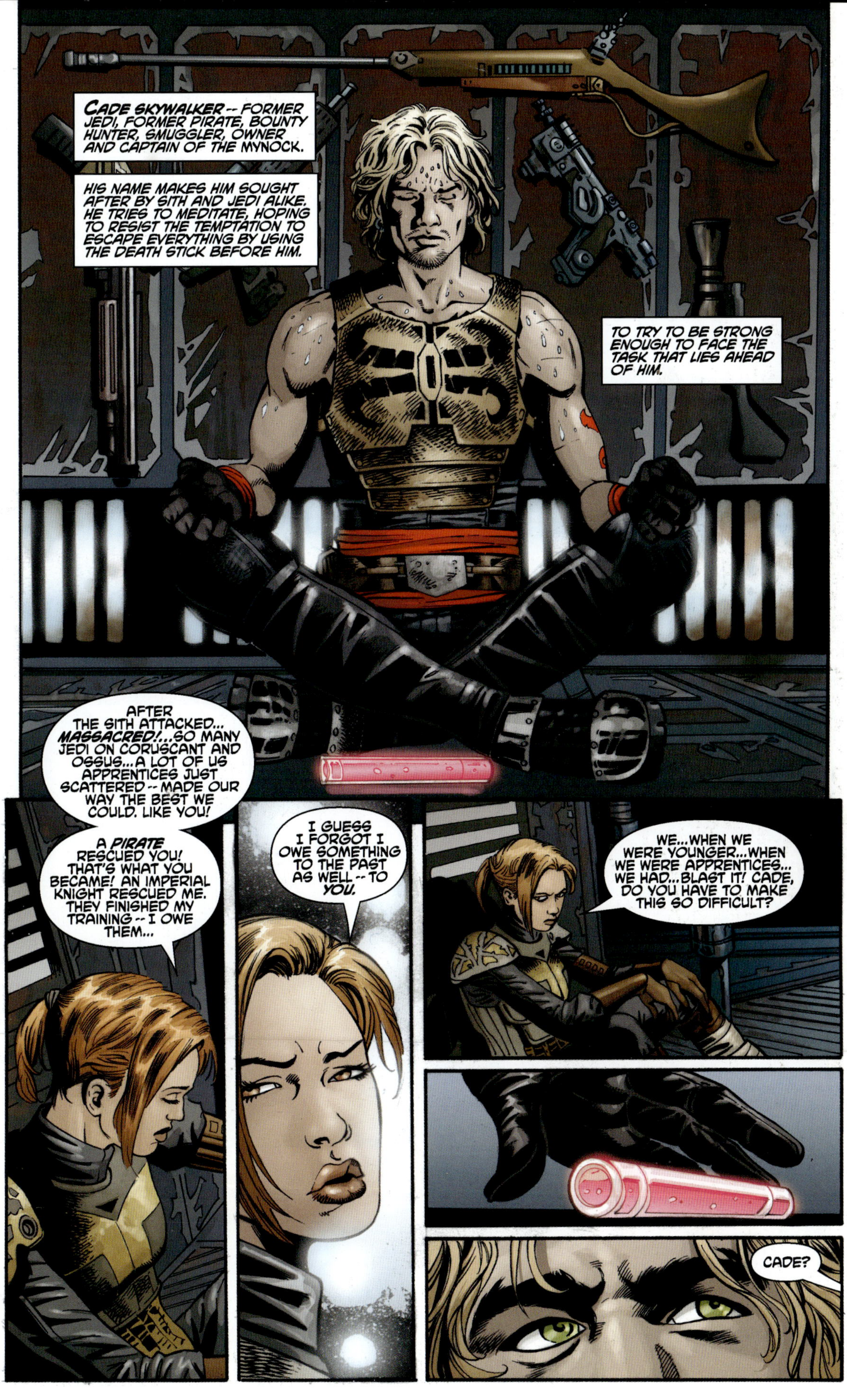
CADE SKYWALKER -- FORMER JEDI, FORMER PIRATE, BOUNTY HUNTER, SMUGGLER, OWNER AND CAPTAIN OF THE MYNOCK.
HIS NAME MAKES HIM SOUGHT AFTER BY SITH AND JEDI ALIKE. HE TRIES TO MEDITATE, HOPING TO RESIST THE TEMPTATION TO ESCAPE EVERYTHING BY USING THE DEATH STICK BEFORE HIM.
TO TRY TO BE STRONG ENOUGH TO FACE THE TASK THAT LIES AHEAD OF HIM.
AFTER THE SITH ATTACKED... MASSACRED!...SO MANY JEDI ON CORUSCANT AND OSSUS...A LOT OF US APPRENTICES JUST SCATTERED -- MADE OUR WAY THE BEST WE COULD. LIKE YOU!
A PIRATE RESCUED YOU! THAT'S WHAT YOU BECAME! AN IMPERIAL KNIGHT RESCUED ME. THEY FINISHED MY TRAINING -- I OWE THEM...
I GUESS I FORGOT I OWE SOMETHING TO THE PAST AS WELL -- TO YOU.
WE...WHEN WE WERE YOUNGER...WHEN WE WERE APPRENTICES... WE HAD...BLAST IT! CADE, DO YOU HAVE TO MAKE THIS SO DIFFICULT?
CADE?

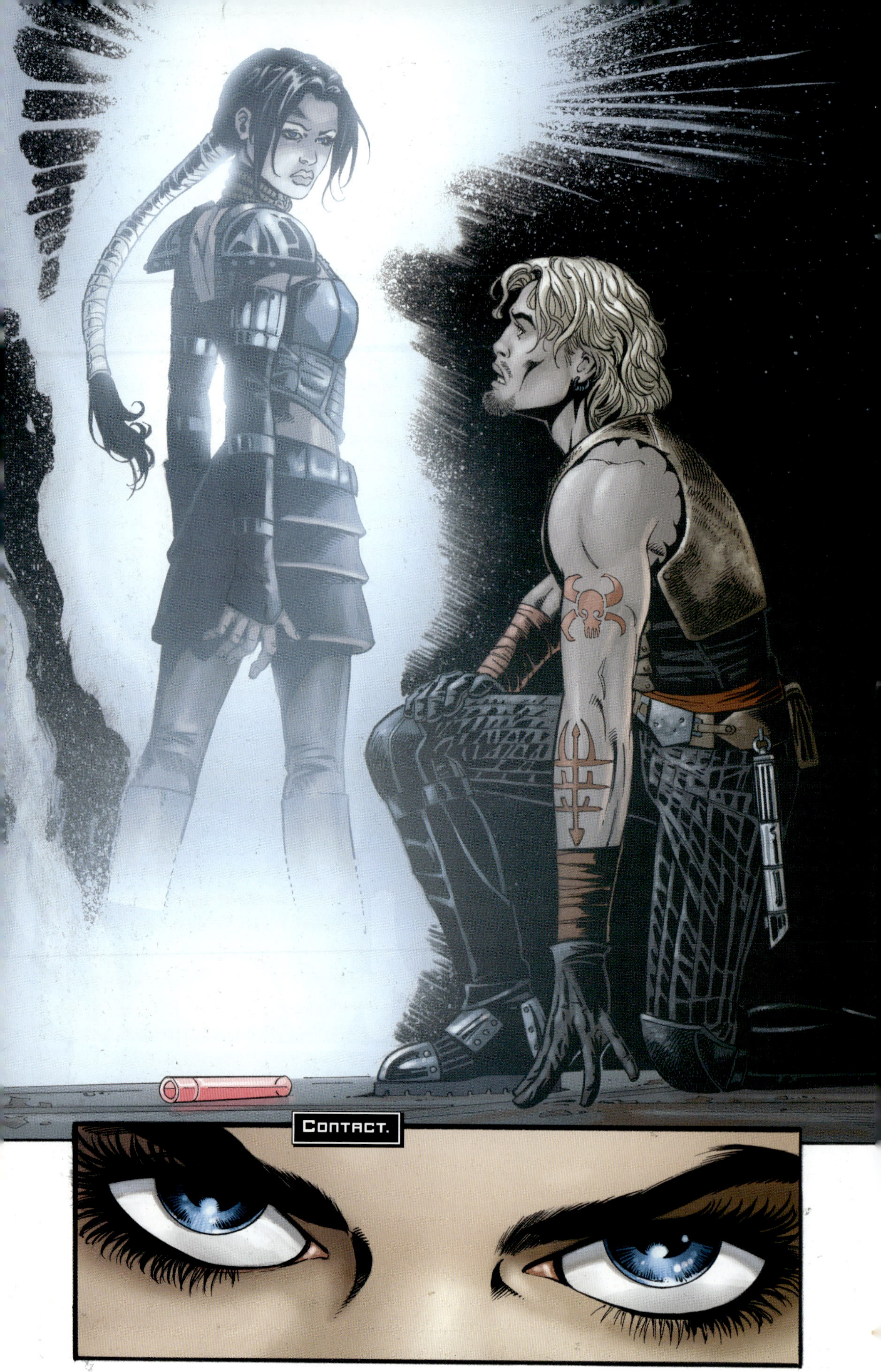
CONTACT.

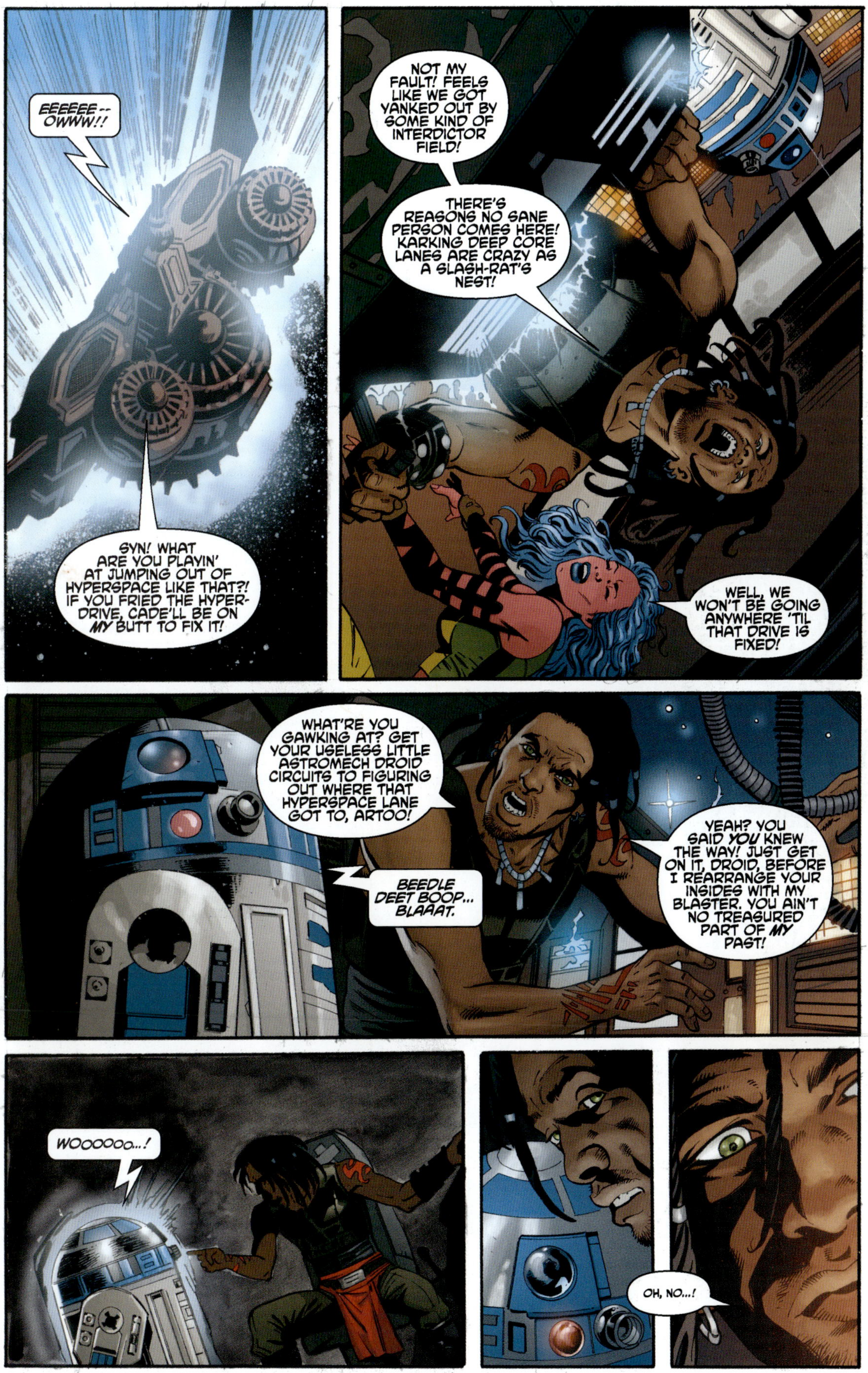
EEEEEE--OWWW!!
SYN! WHAT ARE YOU PLAYIN' AT JUMPING OUT OF HYPERSPACE LIKE THAT?! IF YOU FRIED THE HYPER-DRIVE, CADE'LL BE ON MY BUTT TO FIX IT!
NOT MY FAULT! FEELS LIKE WE GOT YANKED OUT BY SOME KIND OF INTERDICTOR FIELD!
THERE'S REASONS NO SANE PERSON COMES HERE! KARKING DEEP CORE LANES ARE CRAZY AS A SLASH-RAT'S NEST!
WELL, WE WON'T BE GOING ANYWHERE 'TIL THAT DRIVE IS FIXED!
WHAT'RE YOU GAWKING AT? GET YOUR USELESS LITTLE ASTROMECH DROID CIRCUITS TO FIGURING OUT WHERE THAT HYPERSPACE LANE GOT TO, ARTOO!
BEEDLE DEET BOOP... BLAAAT.
YEAH? YOU SAID YOU KNEW THE WAY! JUST GET ON IT, DROID, BEFORE I REARRANGE YOUR INSIDES WITH MY BLASTER. YOU AIN'T NO TREASURED PART OF MY PAST!
WOOOOOO...!
OH, NO...!

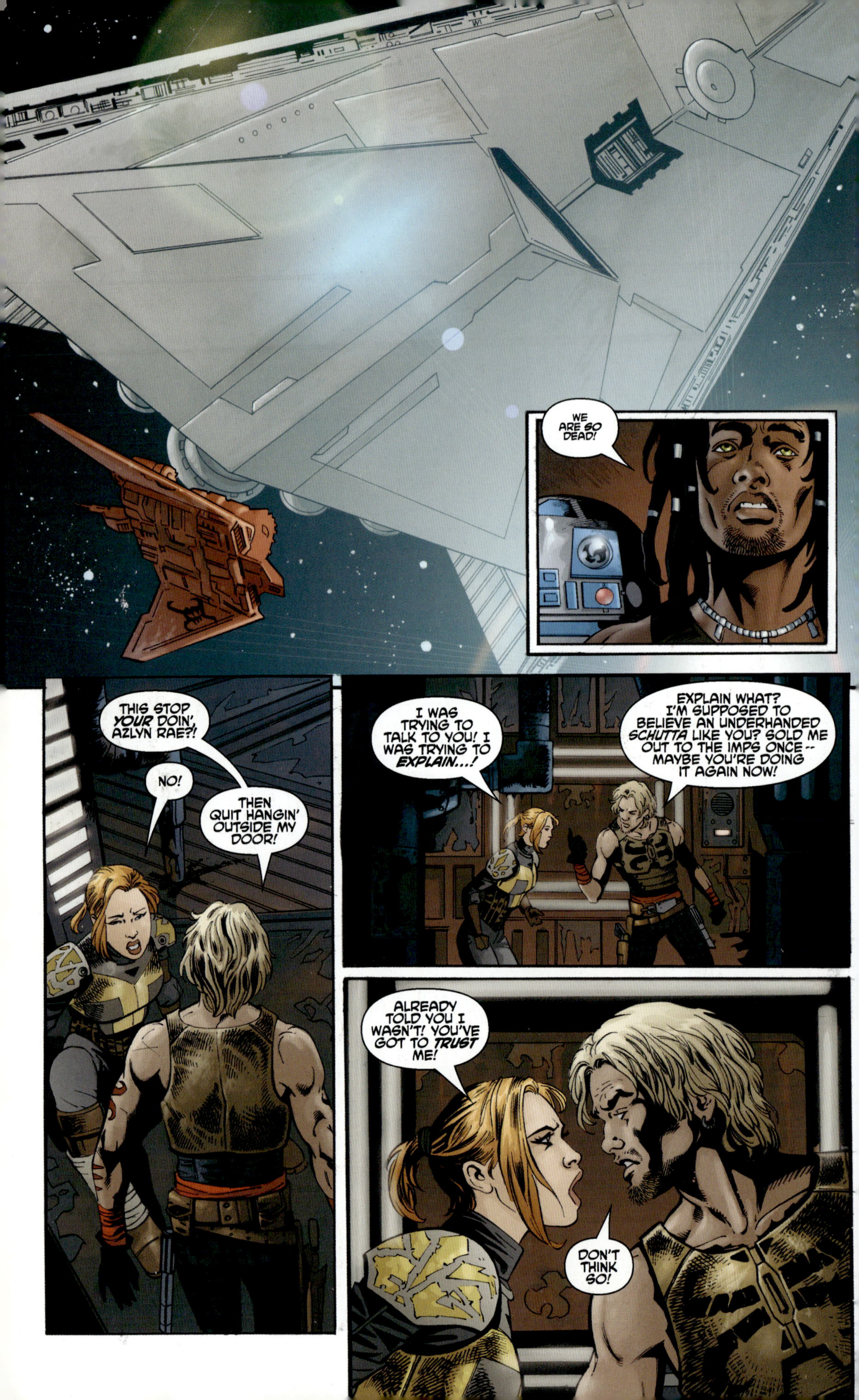

WE ARE SO DEAD!
THIS STOP *YOUR* DOIN', AZLYN RAE?!
NO!
THEN QUIT HANGIN' OUTSIDE MY DOOR!
I WAS TRYING TO TALK TO YOU! I WAS TRYING TO *EXPLAIN...!*
EXPLAIN WHAT? I'M SUPPOSED TO BELIEVE AN UNDERHANDED *SCHUTTA* LIKE YOU? SOLD ME OUT TO THE IMPS ONCE-- MAYBE YOU'RE DOING IT AGAIN NOW!
ALREADY TOLD YOU I WASN'T! YOU'VE GOT TO *TRUST* ME!
DON'T THINK SO!

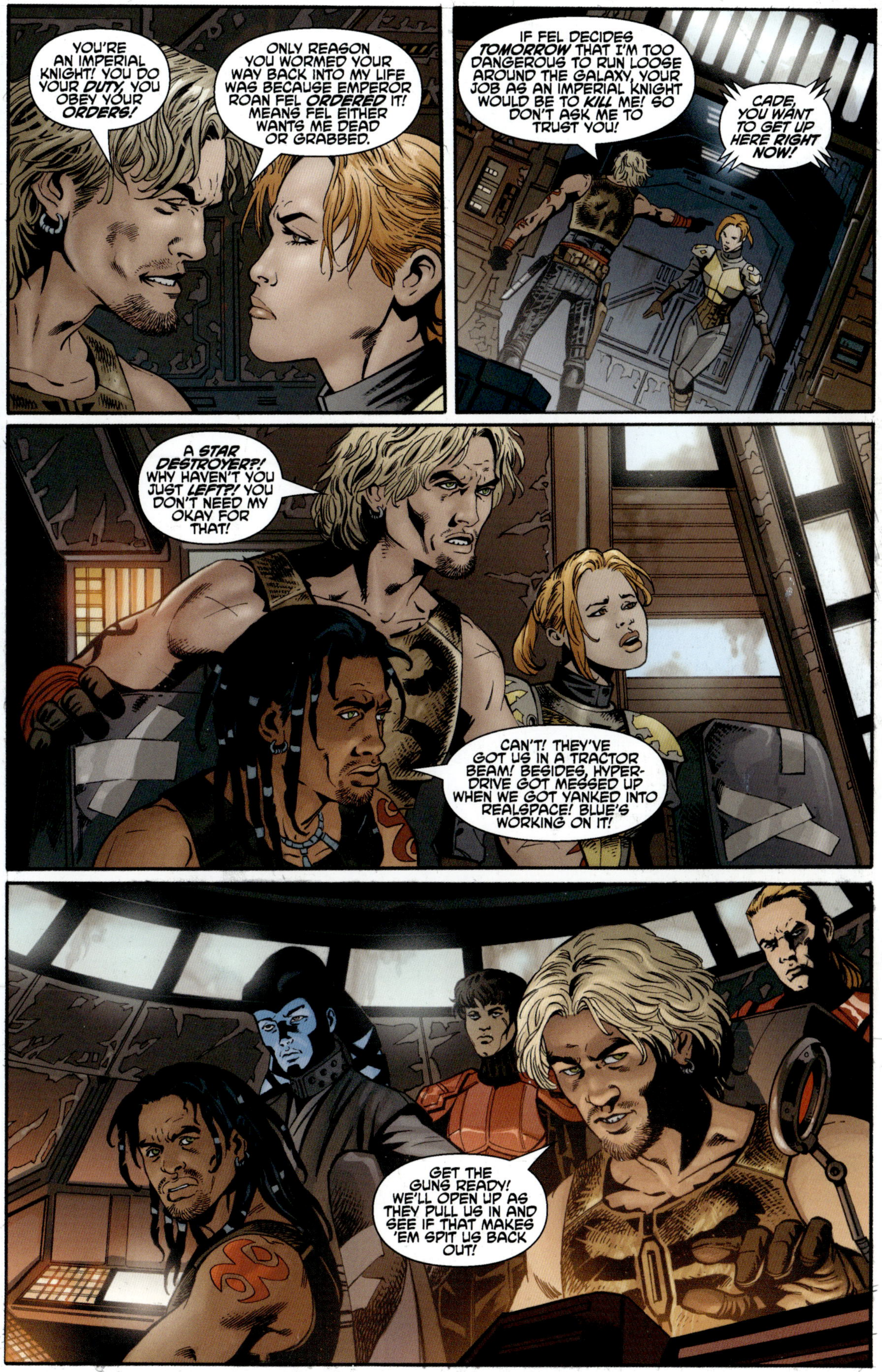
YOU'RE AN IMPERIAL KNIGHT! YOU DO YOUR DUTY, YOU OBEY YOUR ORDERS!
ONLY REASON YOU WORMED YOUR WAY BACK INTO MY LIFE WAS BECAUSE EMPEROR ROAN FEL ORDERED IT! MEANS FEL EITHER WANTS ME DEAD OR GRABBED.
IF FEL DECIDES TOMORROW THAT I'M TOO DANGEROUS TO RUN LOOSE AROUND THE GALAXY, YOUR JOB AS AN IMPERIAL KNIGHT WOULD BE TO KILL ME! SO DON'T ASK ME TO TRUST YOU!
CADE, YOU WANT TO GET UP HERE RIGHT NOW!
A STAR DESTROYER?! WHY HAVEN'T YOU JUST LEFT?! YOU DON'T NEED MY OKAY FOR THAT!
CAN'T! THEY'VE GOT US IN A TRACTOR BEAM! BESIDES, HYPER-DRIVE GOT MESSED UP WHEN WE GOT YANKED INTO REALSPACE! BLUE'S WORKING ON IT!
GET THE GUNS READY! WE'LL OPEN UP AS THEY PULL US IN AND SEE IF THAT MAKES 'EM SPIT US BACK OUT!

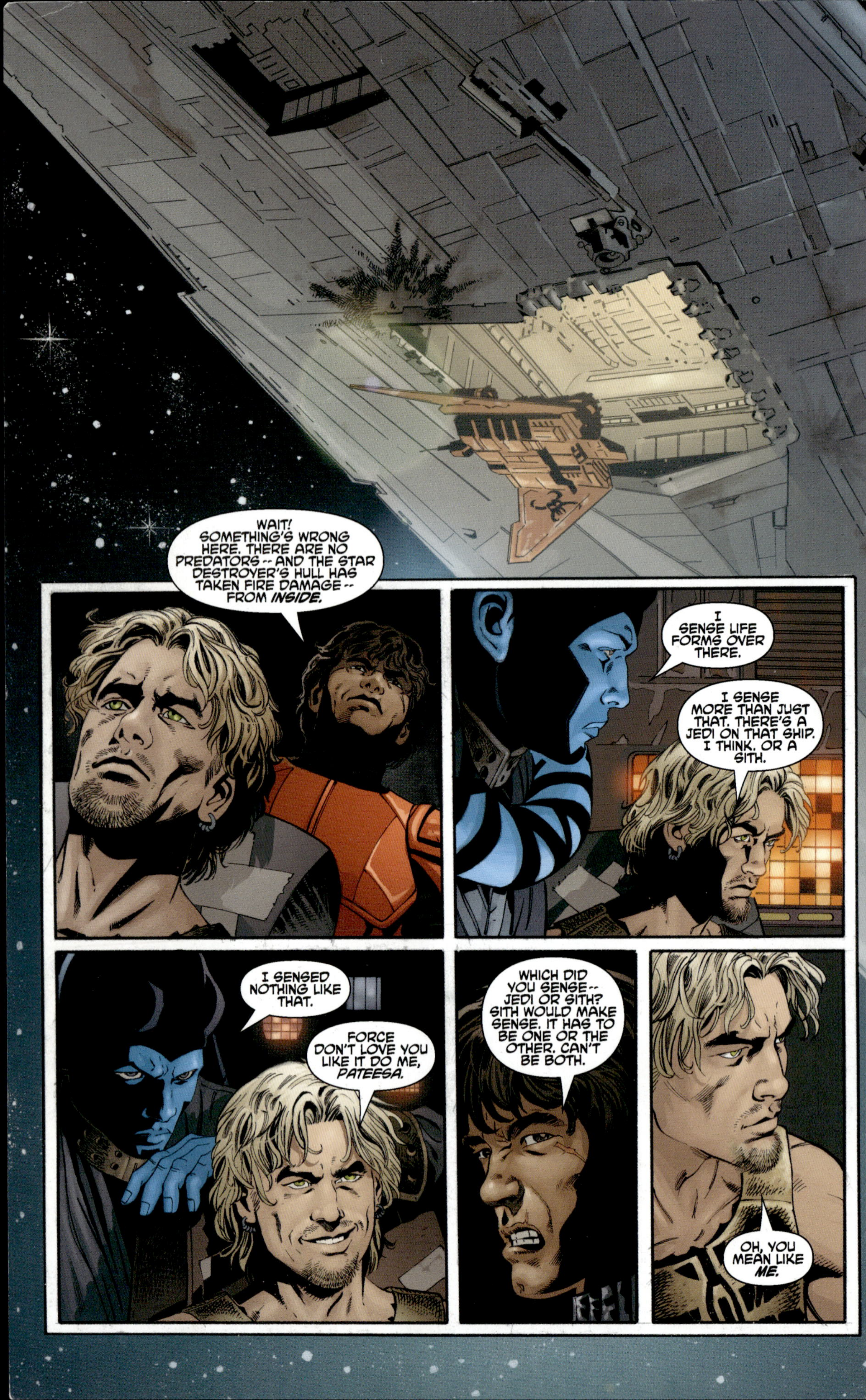
WAIT! SOMETHING'S WRONG HERE. THERE ARE NO PREDATORS-- AND THE STAR DESTROYER'S HULL HAS TAKEN FIRE DAMAGE-- FROM *INSIDE.*
I SENSE LIFE FORMS OVER THERE.
I SENSE MORE THAN JUST THAT. THERE'S A JEDI ON THAT SHIP. I THINK. OR A SITH.
I SENSED NOTHING LIKE THAT.
FORCE DON'T LOVE YOU LIKE IT DO ME, *PATEESA.*
WHICH DID YOU SENSE-- JEDI OR SITH? SITH WOULD MAKE SENSE. IT HAS TO BE ONE OR THE OTHER. CAN'T BE BOTH.
OH, YOU MEAN LIKE *ME.*

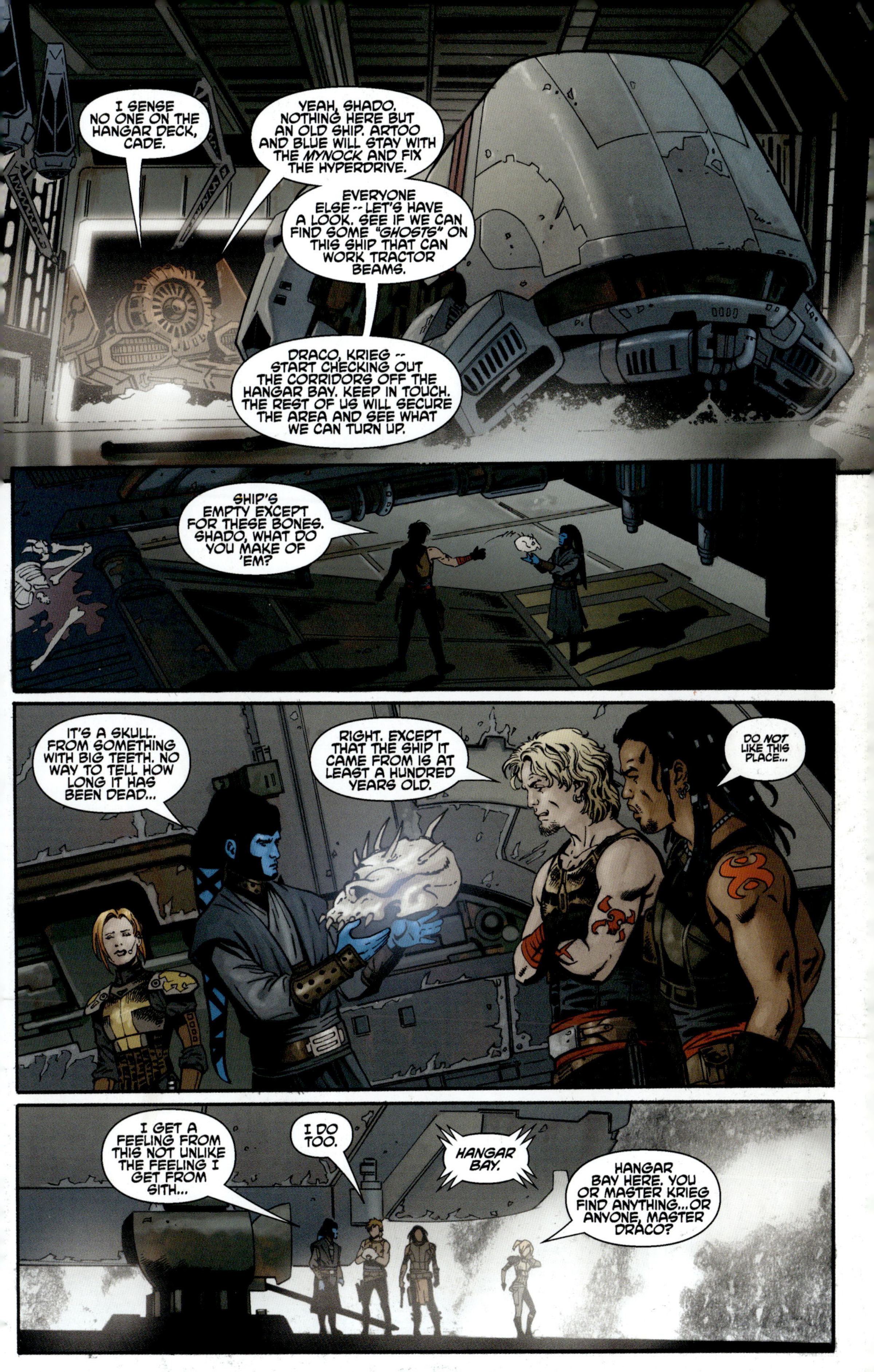
I SENSE NO ONE ON THE HANGAR DECK, CADE.
YEAH, SHADO. NOTHING HERE BUT AN OLD SHIP. ARTOO AND BLUE WILL STAY WITH THE *MYNOCK* AND FIX THE HYPERDRIVE.
EVERYONE ELSE -- LET'S HAVE A LOOK. SEE IF WE CAN FIND SOME "*GHOSTS*" ON THIS SHIP THAT CAN WORK TRACTOR BEAMS.
DRACO, KRIEG -- START CHECKING OUT THE CORRIDORS OFF THE HANGAR BAY. KEEP IN TOUCH. THE REST OF US WILL SECURE THE AREA AND SEE WHAT WE CAN TURN UP.
SHIP'S EMPTY EXCEPT FOR THESE BONES. SHADO, WHAT DO YOU MAKE OF 'EM?
IT'S A SKULL. FROM SOMETHING WITH BIG TEETH. NO WAY TO TELL HOW LONG IT HAS BEEN DEAD...
RIGHT. EXCEPT THAT THE SHIP IT CAME FROM IS AT LEAST A HUNDRED YEARS OLD.
DO *NOT* LIKE THIS PLACE...
I GET A FEELING FROM THIS NOT UNLIKE THE FEELING I GET FROM SITH...
I DO TOO.
HANGAR BAY.
HANGAR BAY HERE. YOU OR MASTER KRIEG FIND ANYTHING...OR ANYONE, MASTER DRACO?

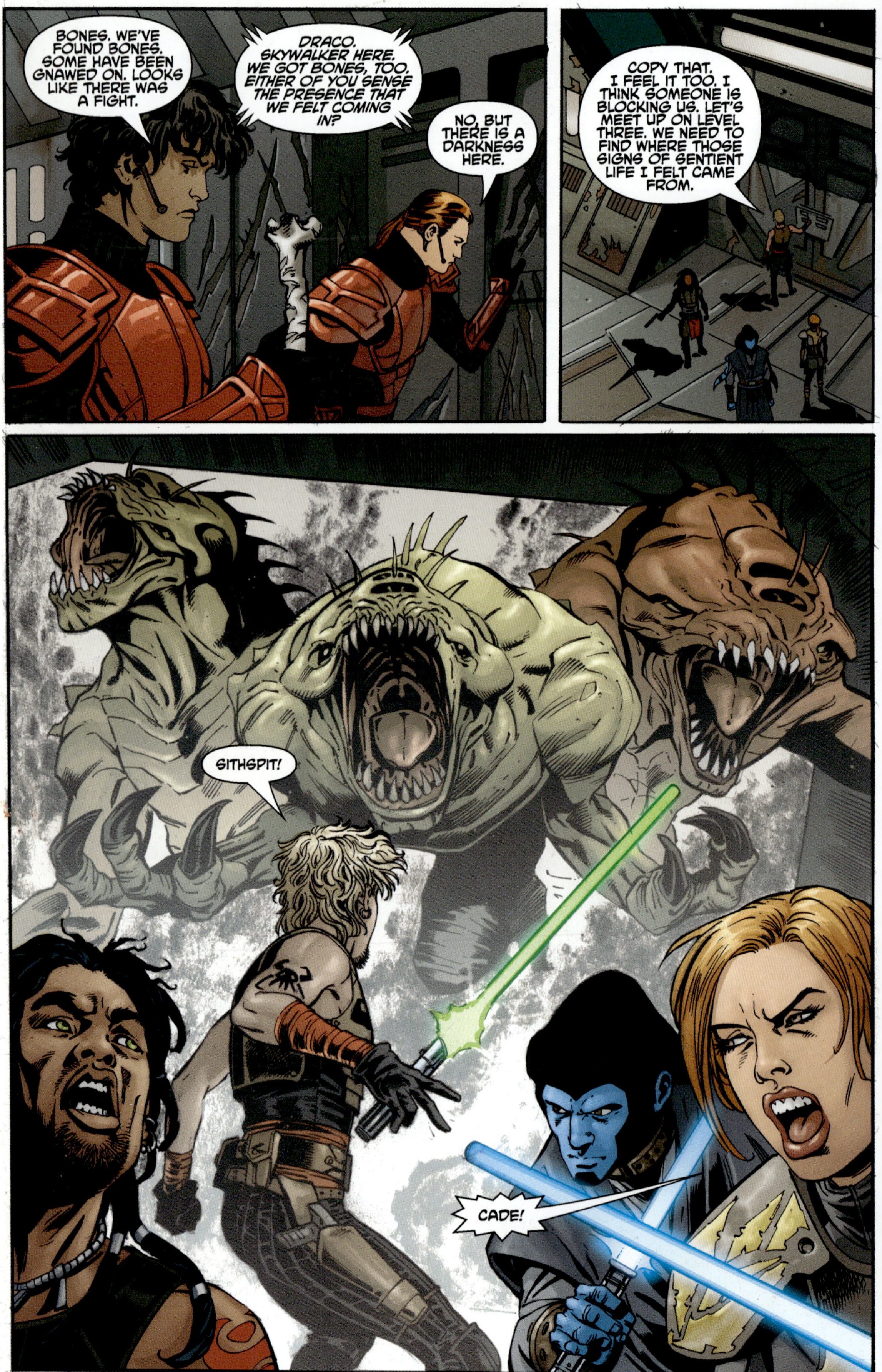
BONES. WE'VE FOUND BONES. SOME HAVE BEEN GNAWED ON. LOOKS LIKE THERE WAS A FIGHT.
DRACO. SKYWALKER HERE. WE GOT BONES, TOO. EITHER OF YOU SENSE THE PRESENCE THAT WE FELT COMING IN?
NO, BUT THERE IS A DARKNESS HERE.
COPY THAT. I FEEL IT TOO. I THINK SOMEONE IS BLOCKING US. LET'S MEET UP ON LEVEL THREE. WE NEED TO FIND WHERE THOSE SIGNS OF SENTIENT LIFE I FELT CAME FROM.
SITHSPIT!
CADE!

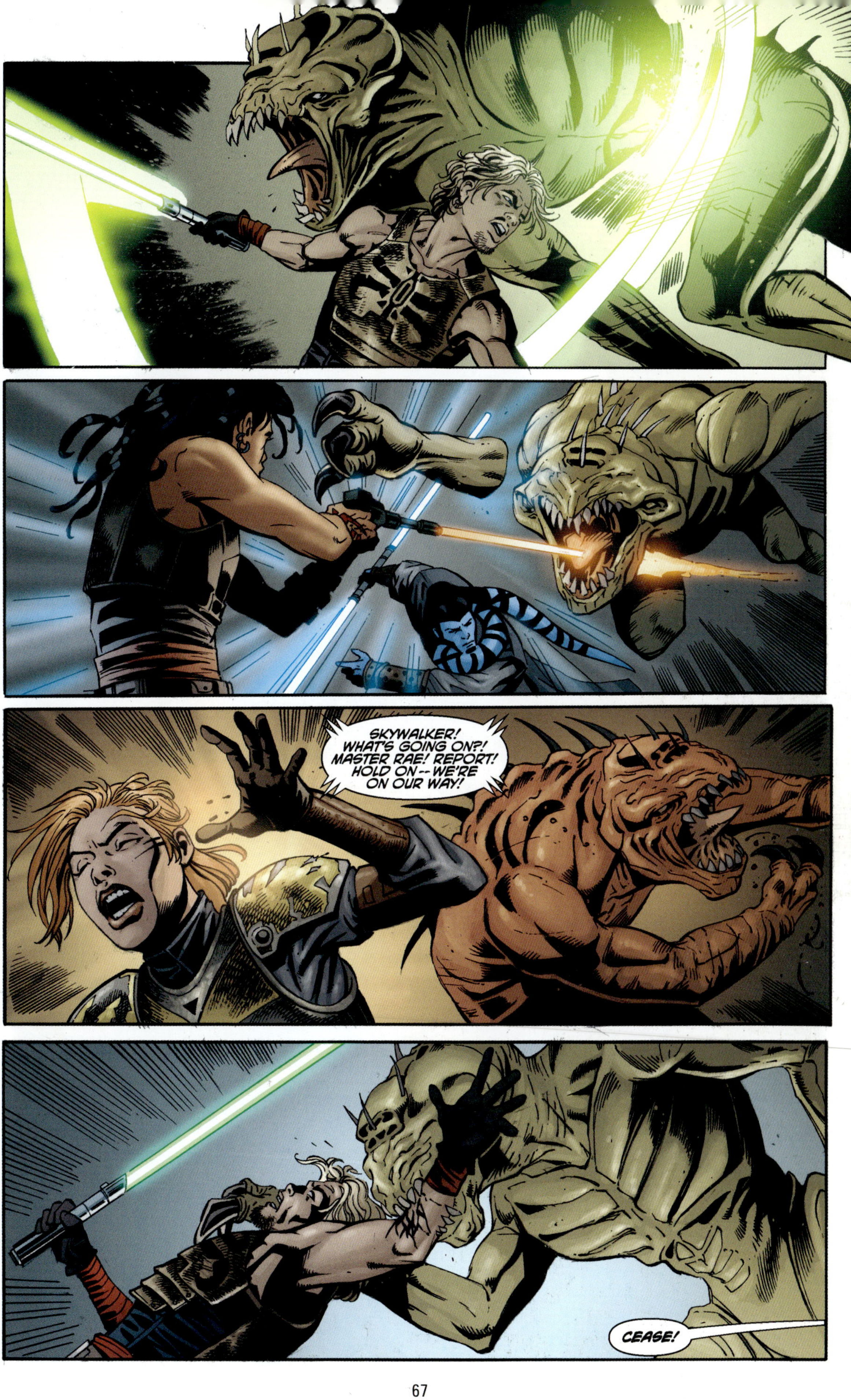
SKYWALKER! WHAT'S GOING ON?! MASTER RAE! REPORT! HOLD ON -- WE'RE ON OUR WAY!
CEASE!

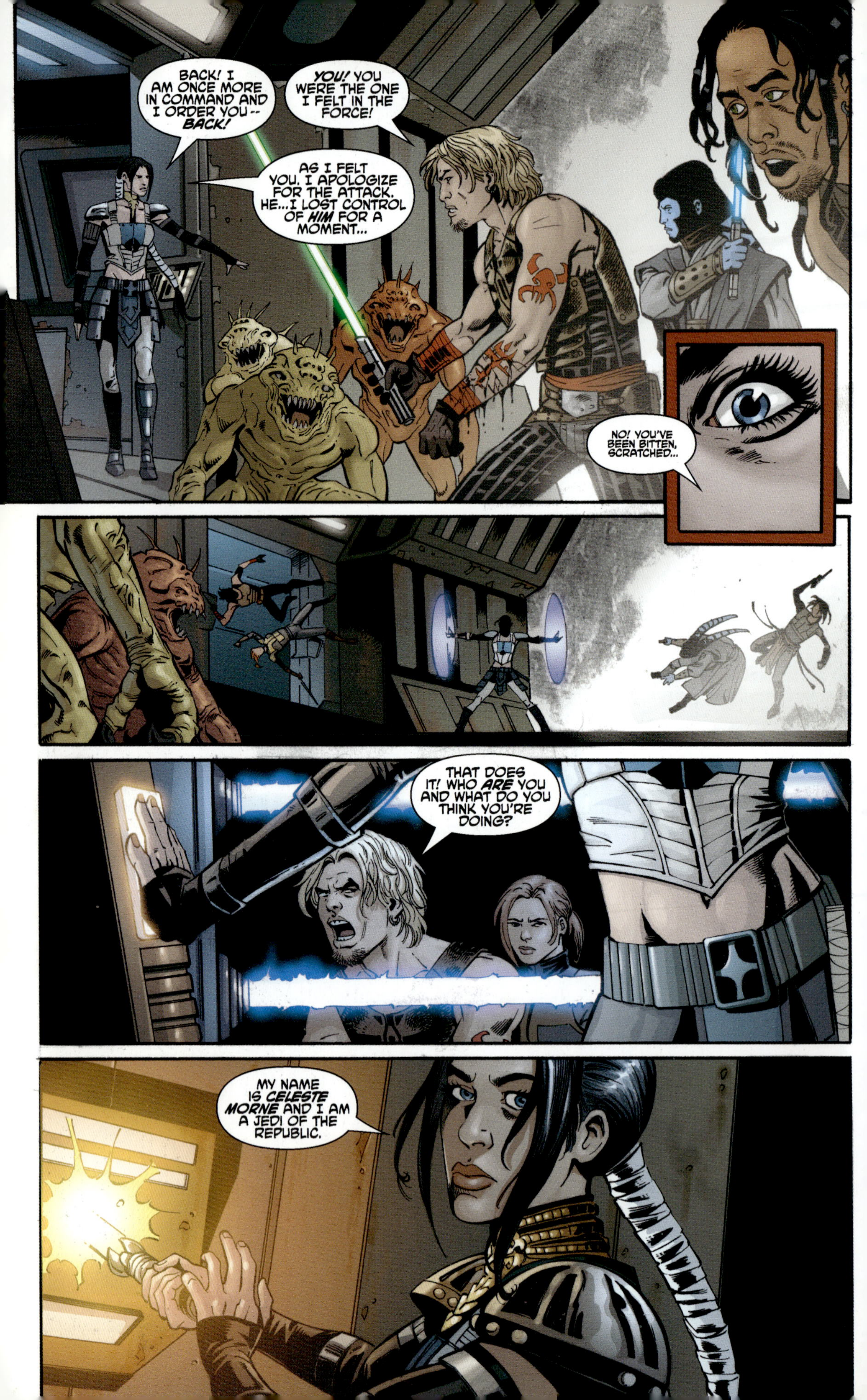
BACK! I AM ONCE MORE IN COMMAND AND I ORDER YOU-- BACK!
YOU! YOU WERE THE ONE I FELT IN THE FORCE!
AS I FELT YOU. I APOLOGIZE FOR THE ATTACK. HE...I LOST CONTROL OF HIM FOR A MOMENT...
NO! YOU'VE BEEN BITTEN, SCRATCHED...
THAT DOES IT! WHO ARE YOU AND WHAT DO YOU THINK YOU'RE DOING?
MY NAME IS CELESTE MORNE AND I AM A JEDI OF THE REPUBLIC.

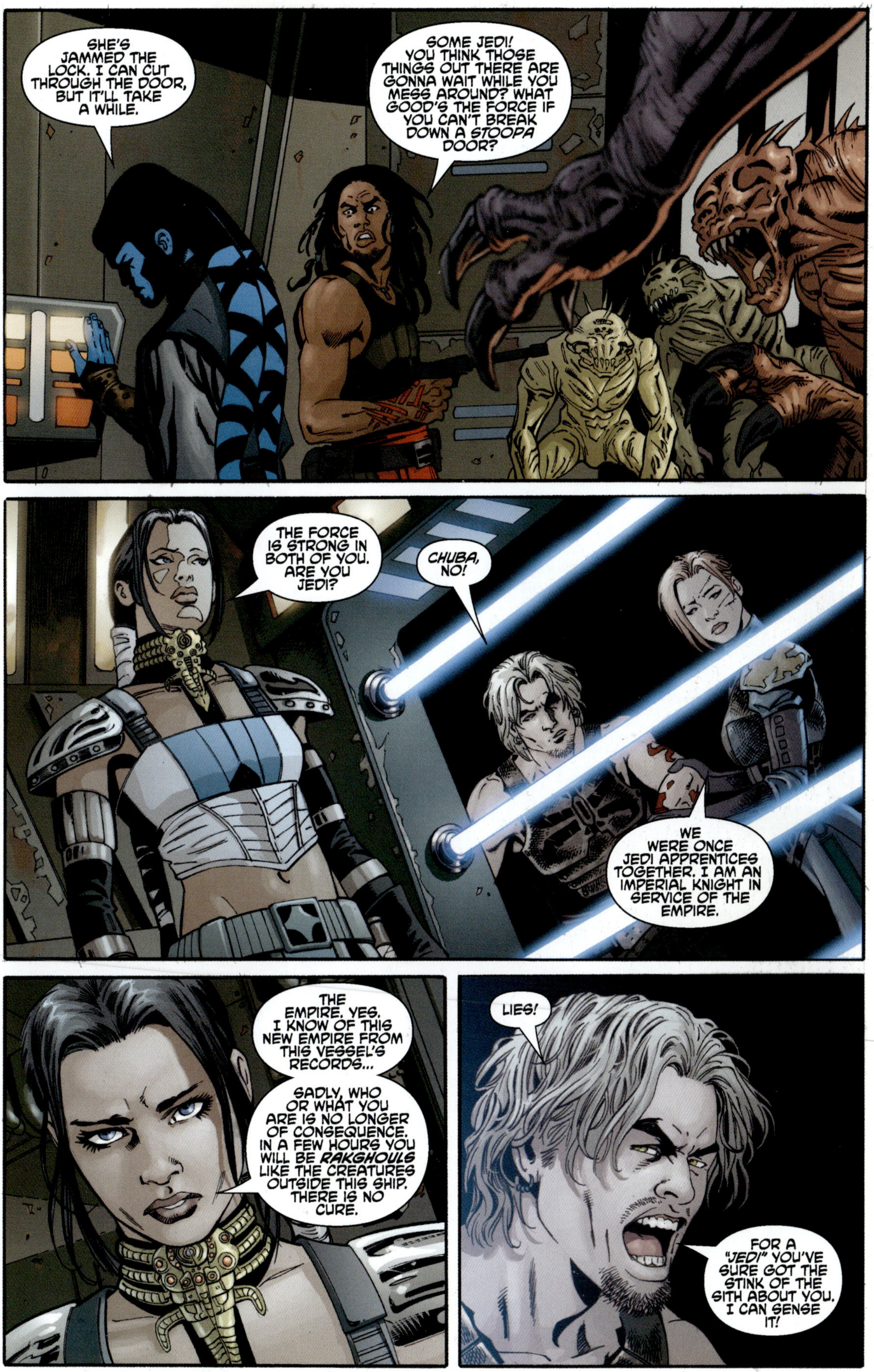
SHE'S JAMMED THE LOCK. I CAN CUT THROUGH THE DOOR, BUT IT'LL TAKE A WHILE.
SOME JEDI! YOU THINK THOSE THINGS OUT THERE ARE GONNA WAIT WHILE YOU MESS AROUND? WHAT GOOD'S THE FORCE IF YOU CAN'T BREAK DOWN A *STOOPA* DOOR?
THE FORCE IS STRONG IN BOTH OF YOU. ARE YOU JEDI?
CHUBA, NO!
WE WERE ONCE JEDI APPRENTICES TOGETHER. I AM AN IMPERIAL KNIGHT IN SERVICE OF THE EMPIRE.
THE EMPIRE. YES. I KNOW OF THIS NEW EMPIRE FROM THIS VESSEL'S RECORDS...
SADLY, WHO OR WHAT YOU ARE IS NO LONGER OF CONSEQUENCE. IN A FEW HOURS YOU WILL BE *RAKGHOULS* LIKE THE CREATURES OUTSIDE THIS SHIP. THERE IS NO CURE.
LIES!
FOR A *"JEDI"* YOU'VE SURE GOT THE STINK OF THE SITH ABOUT YOU. I CAN SENSE IT!

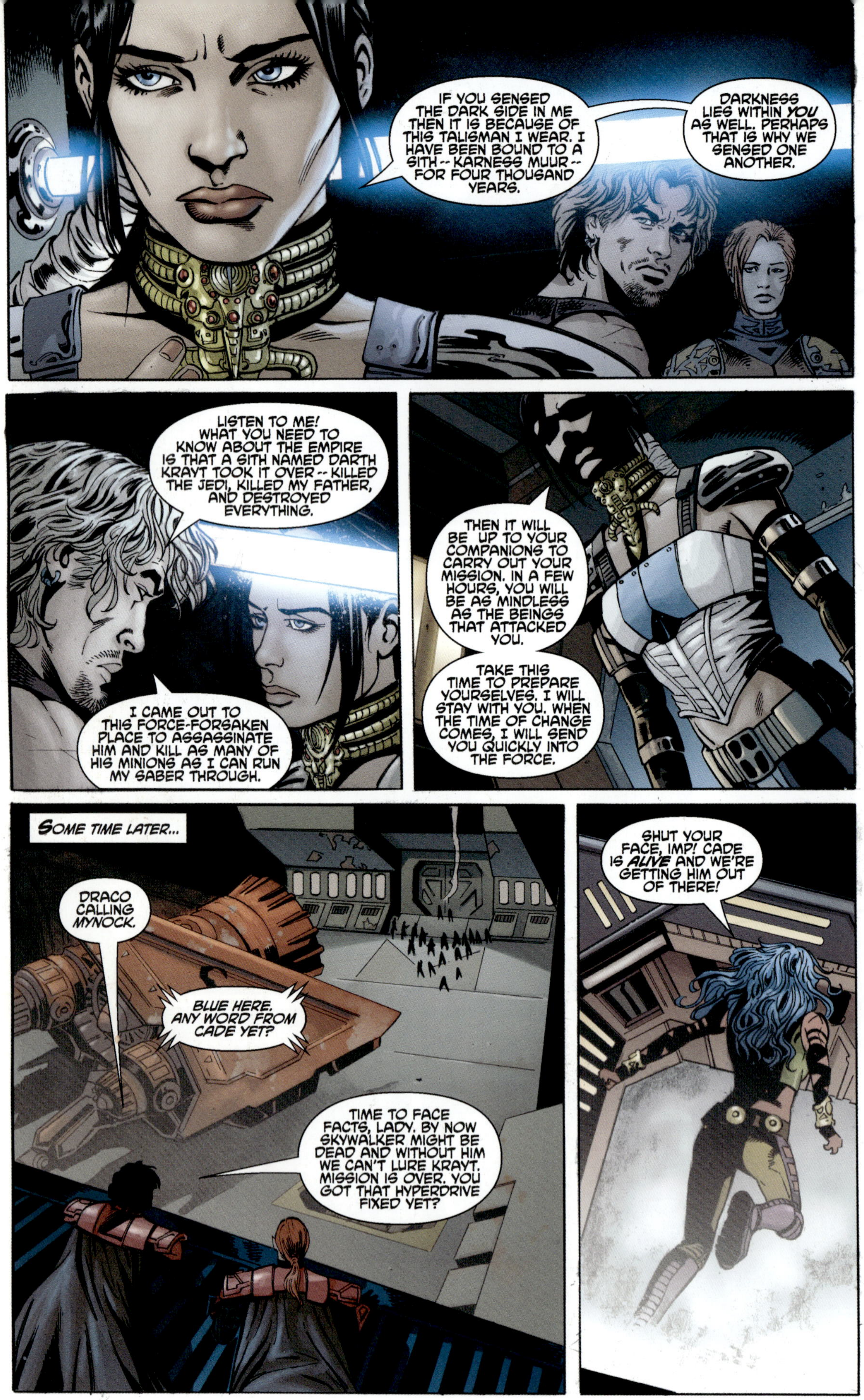

IF YOU SENSED THE DARK SIDE IN ME THEN IT IS BECAUSE OF THIS TALISMAN I WEAR. I HAVE BEEN BOUND TO A SITH -- KARNESS MUUR -- FOR FOUR THOUSAND YEARS.
DARKNESS LIES WITHIN *YOU* AS WELL. PERHAPS THAT IS WHY WE SENSED ONE ANOTHER.
LISTEN TO ME! WHAT YOU NEED TO KNOW ABOUT THE EMPIRE IS THAT A SITH NAMED DARTH KRAYT TOOK IT OVER -- KILLED THE JEDI, KILLED MY FATHER, AND DESTROYED EVERYTHING.
I CAME OUT TO THIS FORCE-FORSAKEN PLACE TO ASSASSINATE HIM AND KILL AS MANY OF HIS MINIONS AS I CAN RUN MY SABER THROUGH.
THEN IT WILL BE UP TO YOUR COMPANIONS TO CARRY OUT YOUR MISSION. IN A FEW HOURS, YOU WILL BE AS MINDLESS AS THE BEINGS THAT ATTACKED YOU.
TAKE THIS TIME TO PREPARE YOURSELVES. I WILL STAY WITH YOU. WHEN THE TIME OF CHANGE COMES, I WILL SEND YOU QUICKLY INTO THE FORCE.
SOME TIME LATER...
DRACO CALLING MYNOCK.
BLUE HERE. ANY WORD FROM CADE YET?
TIME TO FACE FACTS, LADY. BY NOW SKYWALKER MIGHT BE DEAD AND WITHOUT HIM WE CAN'T LURE KRAYT. MISSION IS OVER. YOU GOT THAT HYPERDRIVE FIXED YET?
SHUT YOUR FACE, IMP! CADE IS *ALIVE* AND WE'RE GETTING HIM OUT OF THERE!

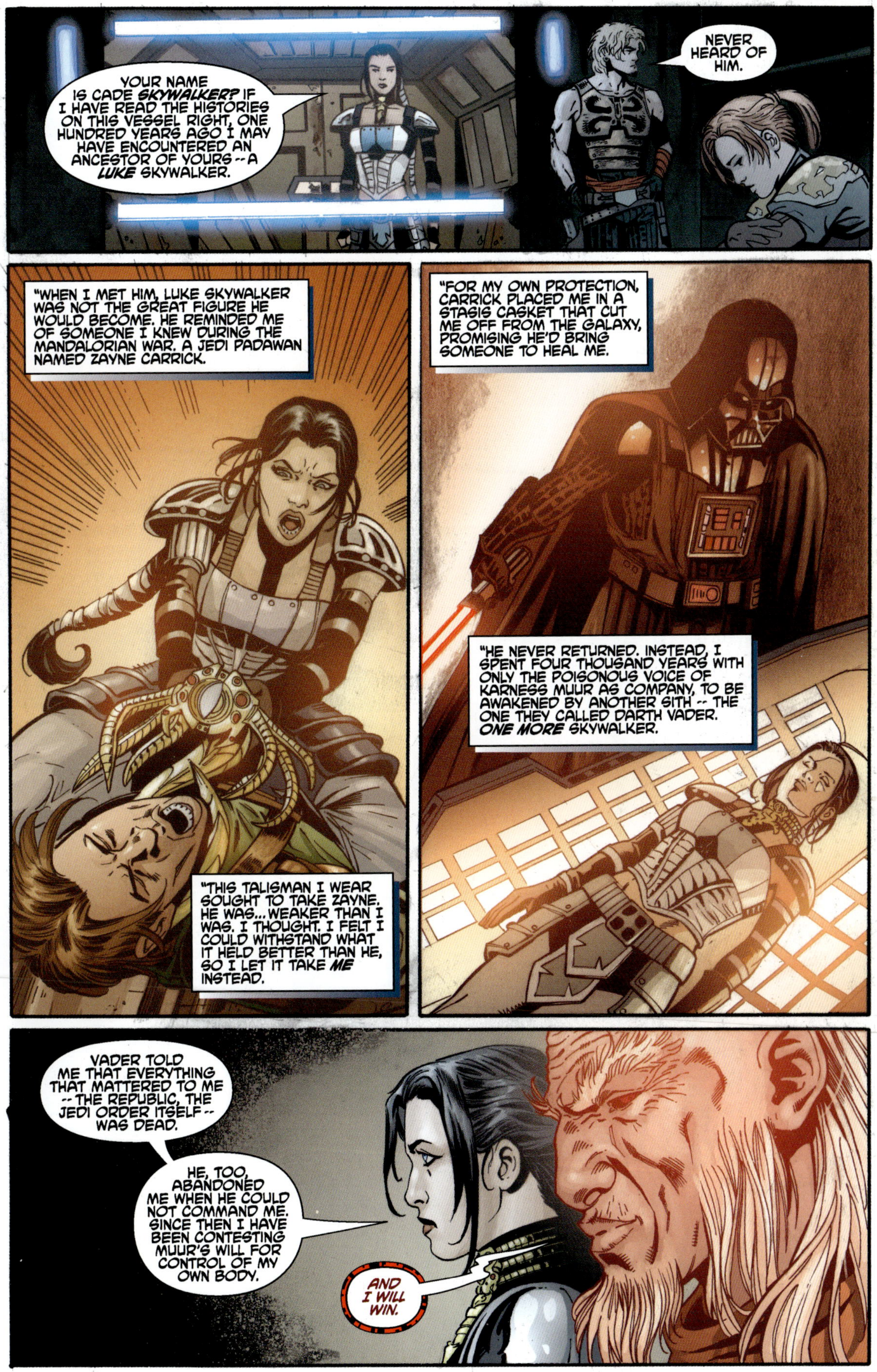
YOUR NAME IS CADE SKYWALKER? IF I HAVE READ THE HISTORIES ON THIS VESSEL RIGHT, ONE HUNDRED YEARS AGO I MAY HAVE ENCOUNTERED AN ANCESTOR OF YOURS -- A LUKE SKYWALKER.
NEVER HEARD OF HIM.
"WHEN I MET HIM, LUKE SKYWALKER WAS NOT THE GREAT FIGURE HE WOULD BECOME. HE REMINDED ME OF SOMEONE I KNEW DURING THE MANDALORIAN WAR. A JEDI PADAWAN NAMED ZAYNE CARRICK.
"THIS TALISMAN I WEAR SOUGHT TO TAKE ZAYNE. HE WAS... WEAKER THAN I WAS, I THOUGHT. I FELT I COULD WITHSTAND WHAT IT HELD BETTER THAN HE, SO I LET IT TAKE ME INSTEAD.
"FOR MY OWN PROTECTION, CARRICK PLACED ME IN A STASIS CASKET THAT CUT ME OFF FROM THE GALAXY, PROMISING HE'D BRING SOMEONE TO HEAL ME.
"HE NEVER RETURNED. INSTEAD, I SPENT FOUR THOUSAND YEARS WITH ONLY THE POISONOUS VOICE OF KARNESS MUUR AS COMPANY, TO BE AWAKENED BY ANOTHER SITH -- THE ONE THEY CALLED DARTH VADER. ONE MORE SKYWALKER.
VADER TOLD ME THAT EVERYTHING THAT MATTERED TO ME -- THE REPUBLIC, THE JEDI ORDER ITSELF -- WAS DEAD.
HE, TOO, ABANDONED ME WHEN HE COULD NOT COMMAND ME. SINCE THEN I HAVE BEEN CONTESTING MUUR'S WILL FOR CONTROL OF MY OWN BODY.
AND I WILL WIN.

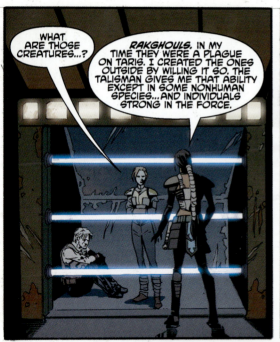

WHAT ARE THOSE CREATURES...?

RAKGHOULS. IN MY TIME THEY WERE A PLAGUE ON TARIS. I CREATED THE ONES OUTSIDE BY WILLING IT SO. THE TALISMAN GIVES ME THAT ABILITY EXCEPT IN SOME NONHUMAN SPECIES...AND INDIVIDUALS STRONG IN THE FORCE.

THE RAKGHOULS BEGAN AS CREATIONS OF KARNESS MUUR'S SITH MAGIC, BUT SCRATCHES OR BITES SPREAD THE PLAGUE -- EVEN TO FORCE USERS LIKE YOU.

AFTER I COMMANDEERED THE VESSEL IN WHICH WE NOW STAND, I FELT A SUDDEN YEARNING TO EXPLORE.

BUT THEN I REALIZED THAT WAS WHAT *MUUR* WANTED. HIS INTENTION IS TO CREATE ARMIES OF RAKGHOULS WITH WHICH TO DOMINATE THE GALAXY. I FLED TO THE DEEP CORE TO LOSE MYSELF...

...AND TO PROTECT THE GALAXY.

TEN YEARS AGO, MY SHIP WAS FOUND AND TAKEN ABOARD BY THE *IRON SUN.* I ASSUMED IT WAS THE SAME EMPIRE VADER SERVED. SO I...CREATED A NEW ARMY FROM ITS CREW.

FOOD RAN OUT; THE RAKGHOULS HAVE BEEN CANNIBALIZING ONE ANOTHER. I DIDN'T STOP THEM -- THEY NEEDED TO EAT.

AND IT WAS ENTERTAINING.

IF THE TALISMAN IS THAT NASTY, WHY NOT JUST BURY IT SOMEWHERE?

AND HAVE IT FOUND AGAIN BY SOMEONE ELSE? SOMEONE OF WEAKER WILL WHO WOULD CREATE AN ARMY OF RAKS AND SET THEM LOOSE ON THE GALAXY?

NO. I AM MUUR'S CAGE AND HE IS MY PRISONER AND THAT IS HOW IT MUST BE.

C-CADE...? I FEEL.... WRONG...!

IT BEGINS. I WILL GIVE YOU DEATH. IT IS THE ONLY MERCY I CAN OFFER.

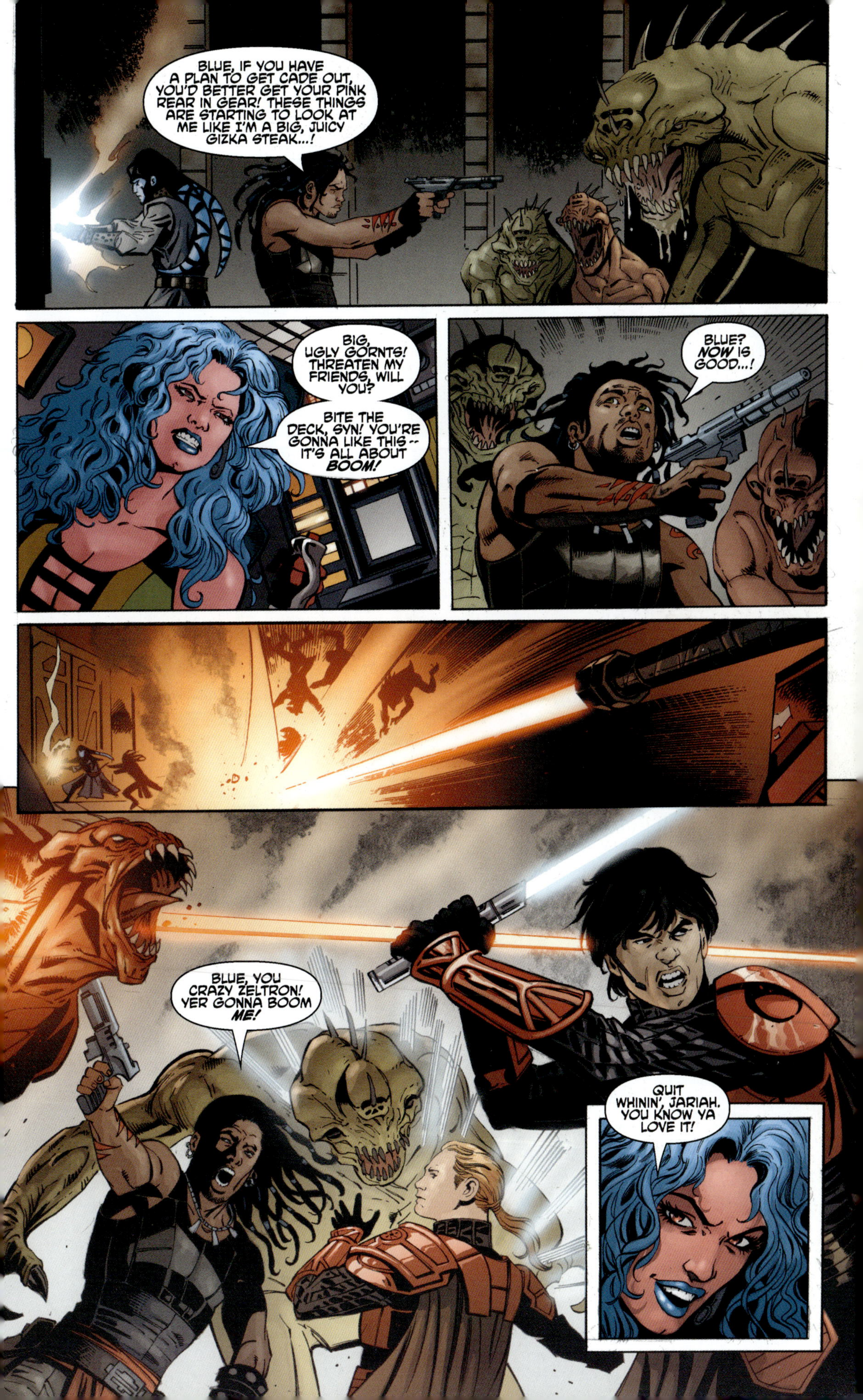
BLUE, IF YOU HAVE A PLAN TO GET CADE OUT, YOU'D BETTER GET YOUR PINK REAR IN GEAR! THESE THINGS ARE STARTING TO LOOK AT ME LIKE I'M A BIG, JUICY GIZKA STEAK...!
BIG, UGLY GORNTS! THREATEN MY FRIENDS, WILL YOU?
BITE THE DECK, SYN! YOU'RE GONNA LIKE THIS -- IT'S ALL ABOUT *BOOM!*
BLUE? *NOW* IS GOOD...!
BLUE, YOU CRAZY ZELTRON! YER GONNA BOOM *ME!*
QUIT WHININ', JARIAH. YOU KNOW YA LOVE IT!

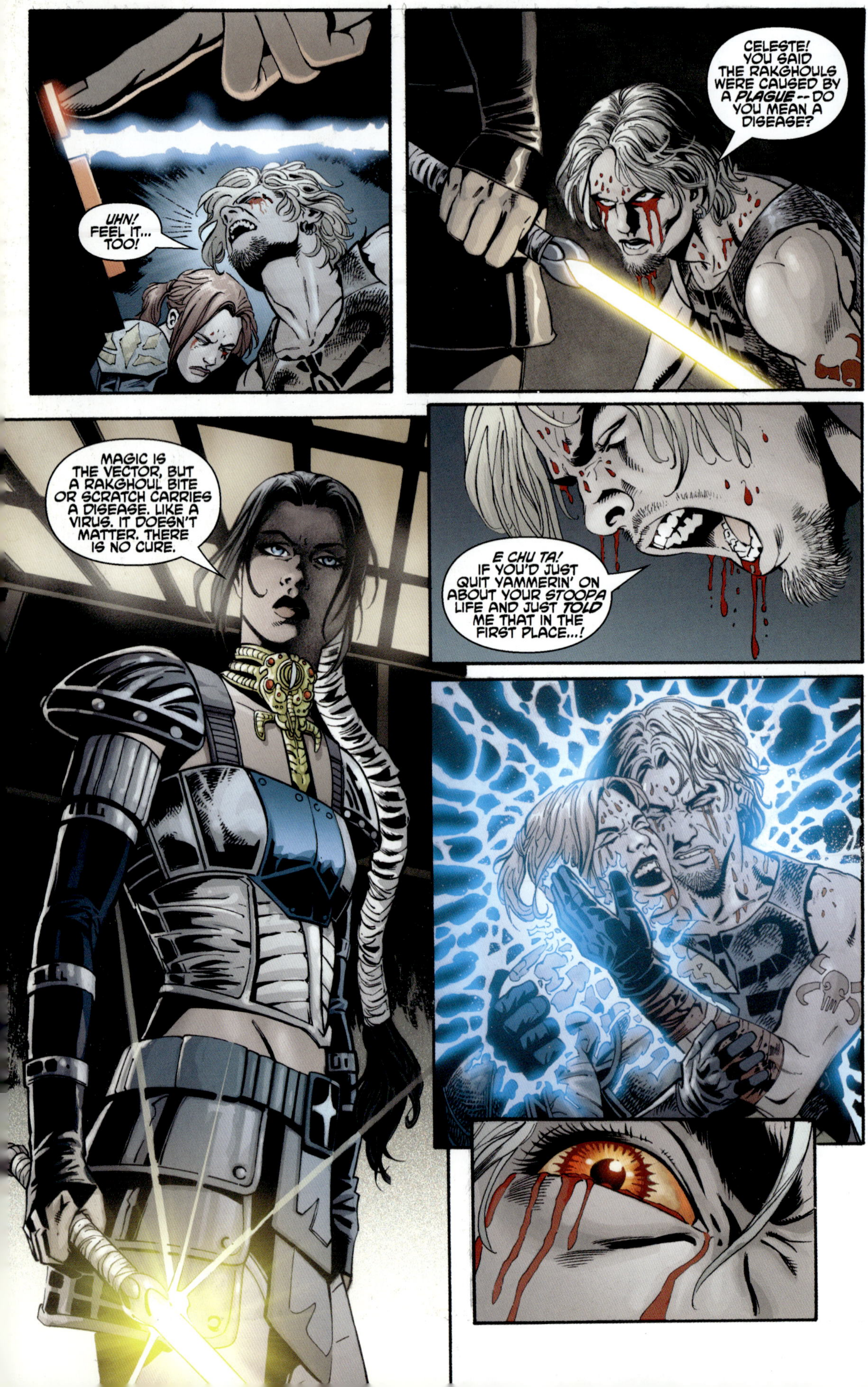
UHN! FEEL IT... TOO!
CELESTE! YOU SAID THE RAKGHOULS WERE CAUSED BY A *PLAGUE* -- DO YOU MEAN A DISEASE?
MAGIC IS THE VECTOR, BUT A RAKGHOUL BITE OR SCRATCH CARRIES A DISEASE. LIKE A VIRUS. IT DOESN'T MATTER. THERE IS NO CURE.
E CHU TA! IF YOU'D JUST QUIT YAMMERIN' ON ABOUT YOUR *STOOPA* LIFE AND JUST *TOLD* ME THAT IN THE FIRST PLACE...!

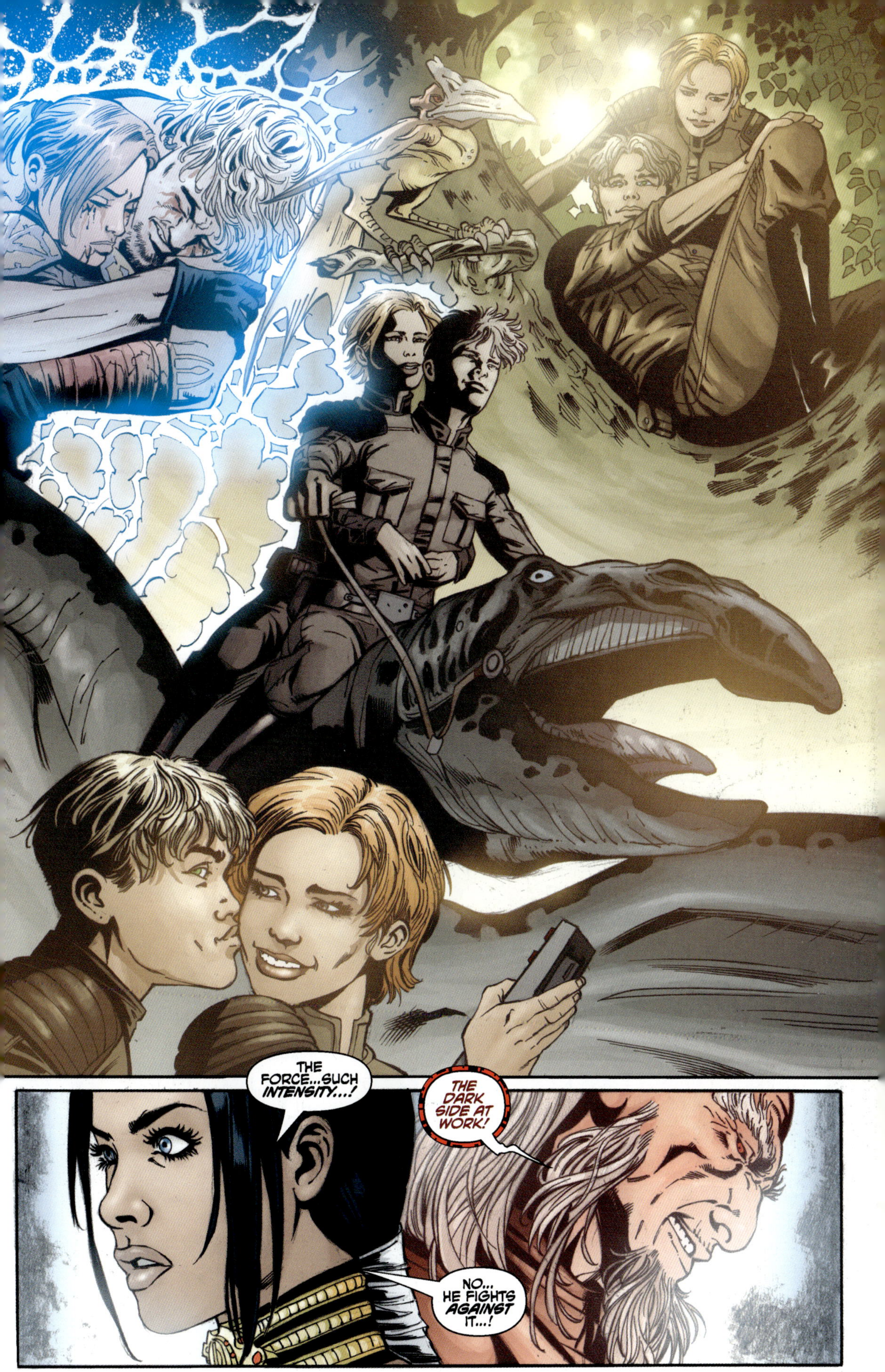
THE FORCE...SUCH INTENSITY...!
THE DARK SIDE AT WORK!
NO... HE FIGHTS AGAINST IT...!

GIVING UP, *JEDI*? PERHAPS IF I WERE TO USE AN *IMPERIAL* LIGHTSABER...

IF YOU CLOSED YOUR MOUTH AND OPENED YOUR MIND, *IMPERIAL*, PERHAPS YOU COULD SENSE IT. SOMETHING HAS HAPPENED IN THERE...

CADE!

WHAT? JUST MAKIN' SOME FRIENDS, BLUE...!

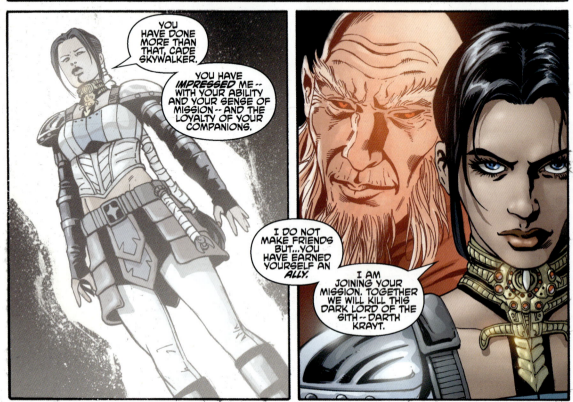

YOU HAVE DONE MORE THAN THAT, CADE SKYWALKER.

YOU HAVE *IMPRESSED* ME -- WITH YOUR ABILITY AND YOUR SENSE OF MISSION -- AND THE LOYALTY OF YOUR COMPANIONS.

I DO NOT MAKE FRIENDS BUT...YOU HAVE EARNED YOURSELF AN *ALLY*.

I AM JOINING YOUR MISSION. TOGETHER WE WILL KILL THIS DARK LORD OF THE SITH -- DARTH KRAYT.

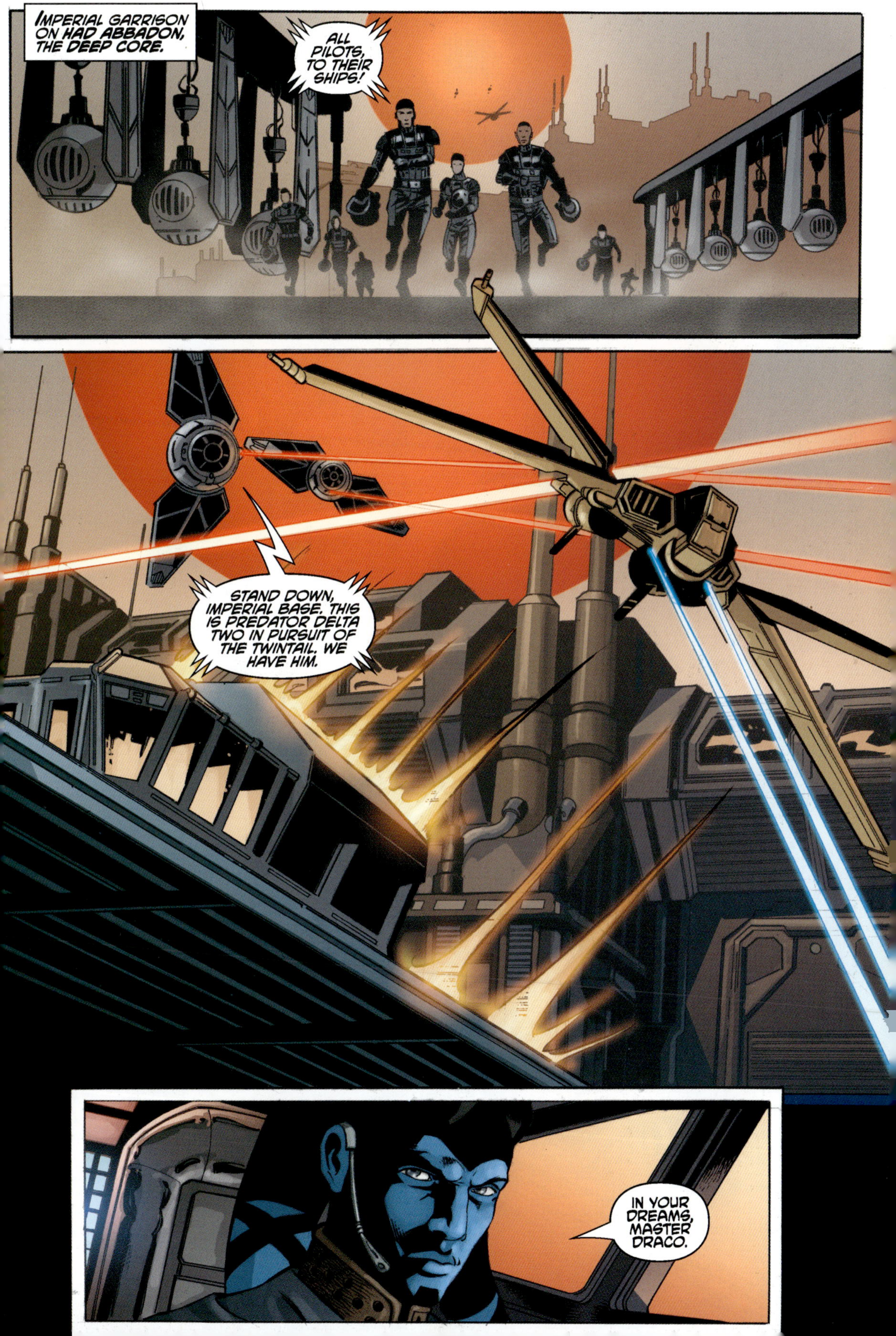
IMPERIAL GARRISON ON HAD ABBADON, THE DEEP CORE.
ALL PILOTS, TO THEIR SHIPS!
STAND DOWN, IMPERIAL BASE. THIS IS PREDATOR DELTA TWO IN PURSUIT OF THE TWINTAIL. WE HAVE HIM.
IN YOUR DREAMS, MASTER DRACO.

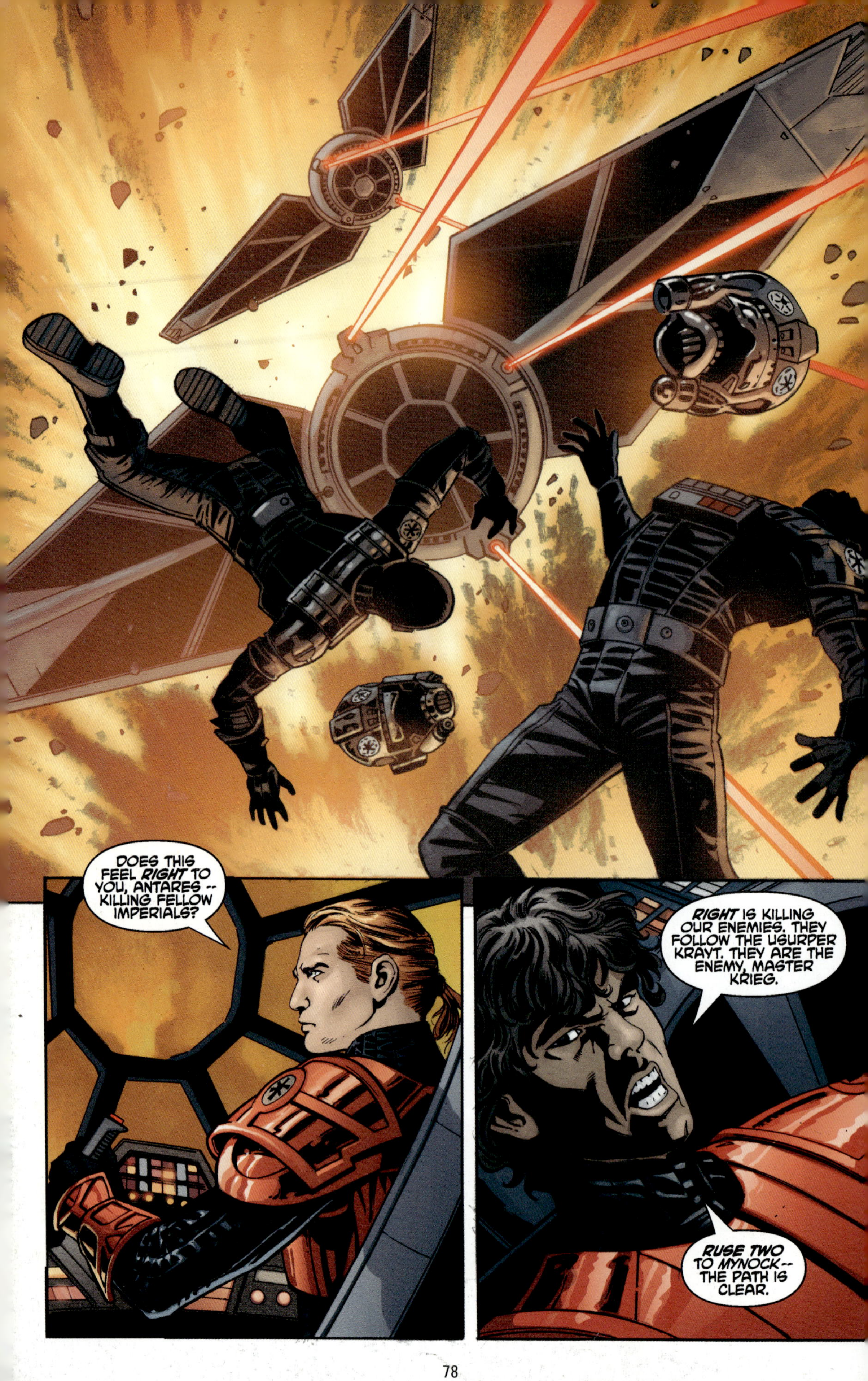
DOES THIS FEEL RIGHT TO YOU, ANTARES -- KILLING FELLOW IMPERIALS?
RIGHT IS KILLING OUR ENEMIES. THEY FOLLOW THE USURPER KRAYT. THEY ARE THE ENEMY, MASTER KRIEG.
RUSE TWO TO MYNOCK-- THE PATH IS CLEAR.

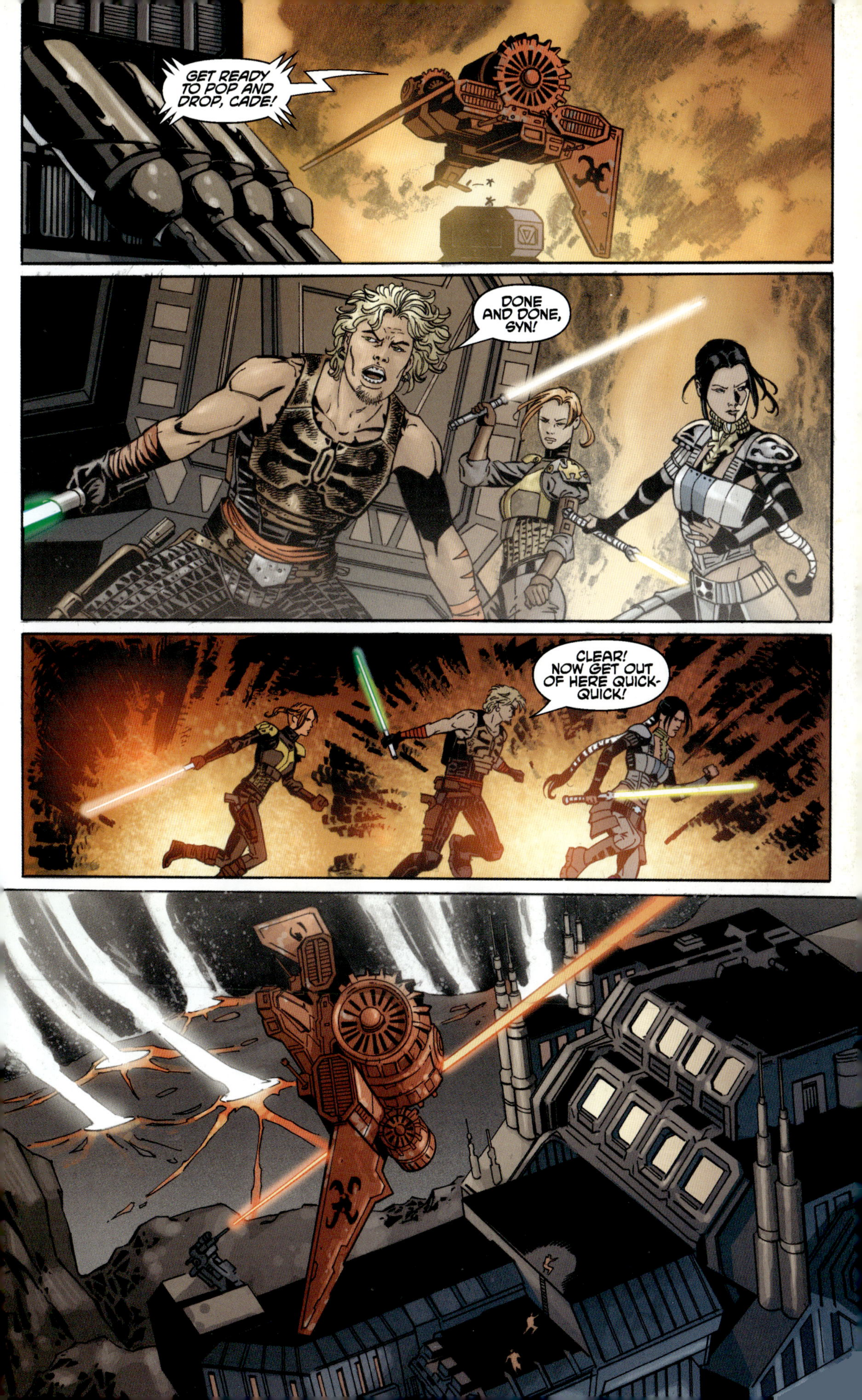
GET READY TO POP AND DROP, CADE!
DONE AND DONE, SYN!
CLEAR! NOW GET OUT OF HERE QUICK-QUICK!

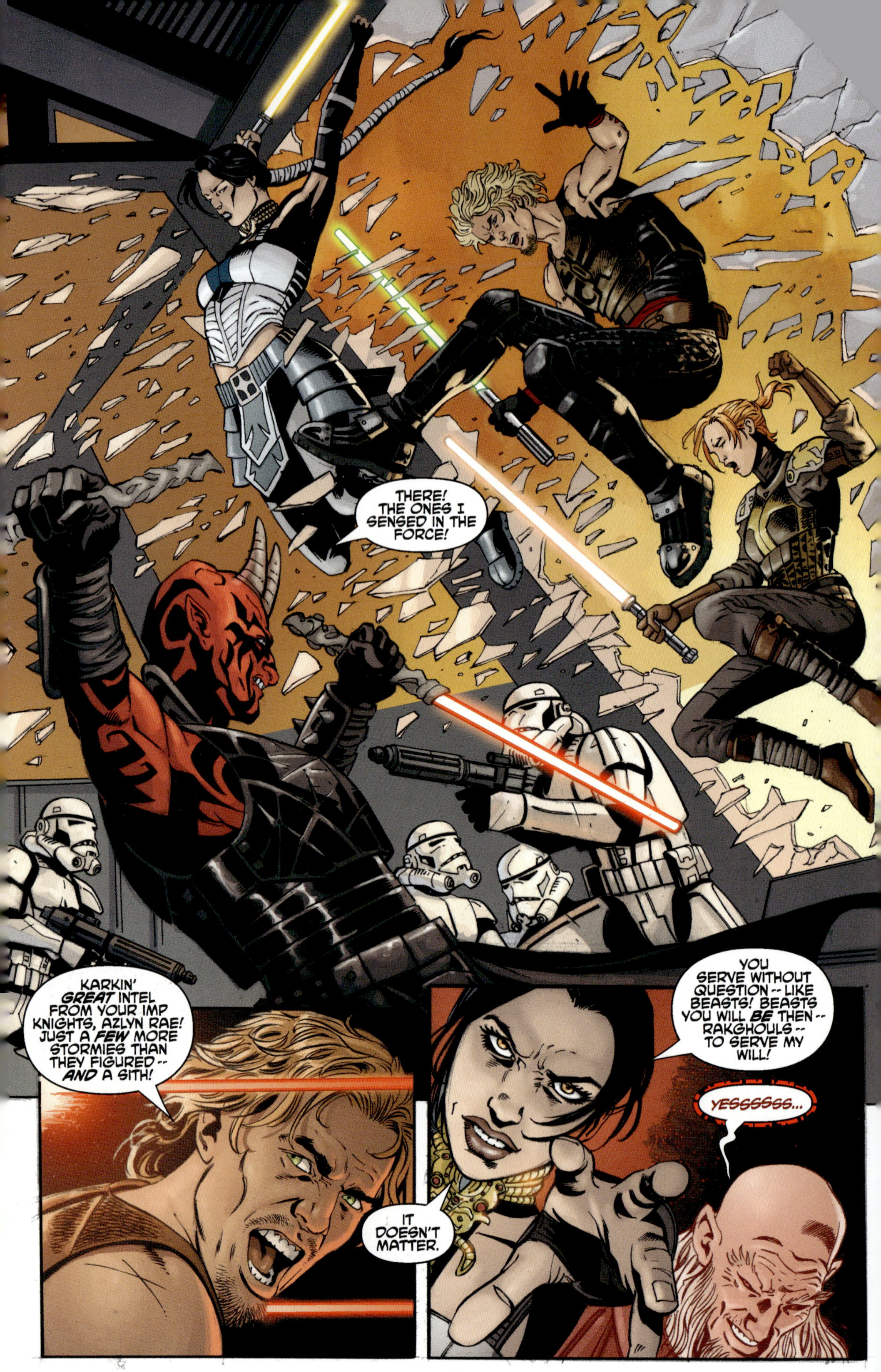

THERE! THE ONES I SENSED IN THE FORCE!
KARKIN' GREAT INTEL FROM YOUR IMP KNIGHTS, AZLYN RAE! JUST A FEW MORE STORMIES THAN THEY FIGURED -- AND A SITH!
IT DOESN'T MATTER.
YOU SERVE WITHOUT QUESTION -- LIKE BEASTS! BEASTS YOU WILL BE THEN -- RAKGHOULS -- TO SERVE MY WILL!
YESSSSSS...

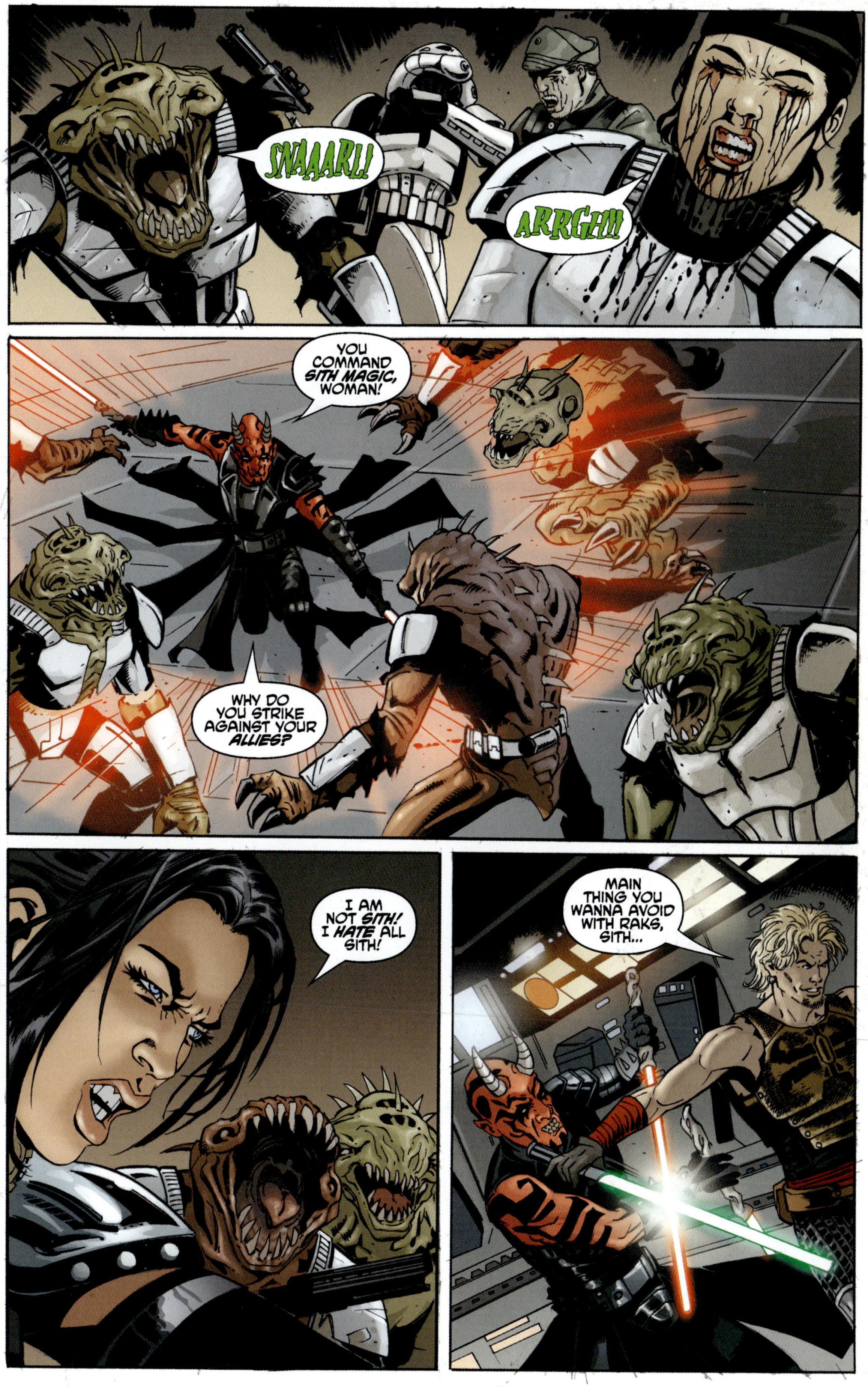
SNAAARL!
ARRGH!!
YOU COMMAND SITH MAGIC, WOMAN!
WHY DO YOU STRIKE AGAINST YOUR ALLIES?
I AM NOT SITH! I HATE ALL SITH!
MAIN THING YOU WANNA AVOID WITH RAKS, SITH...

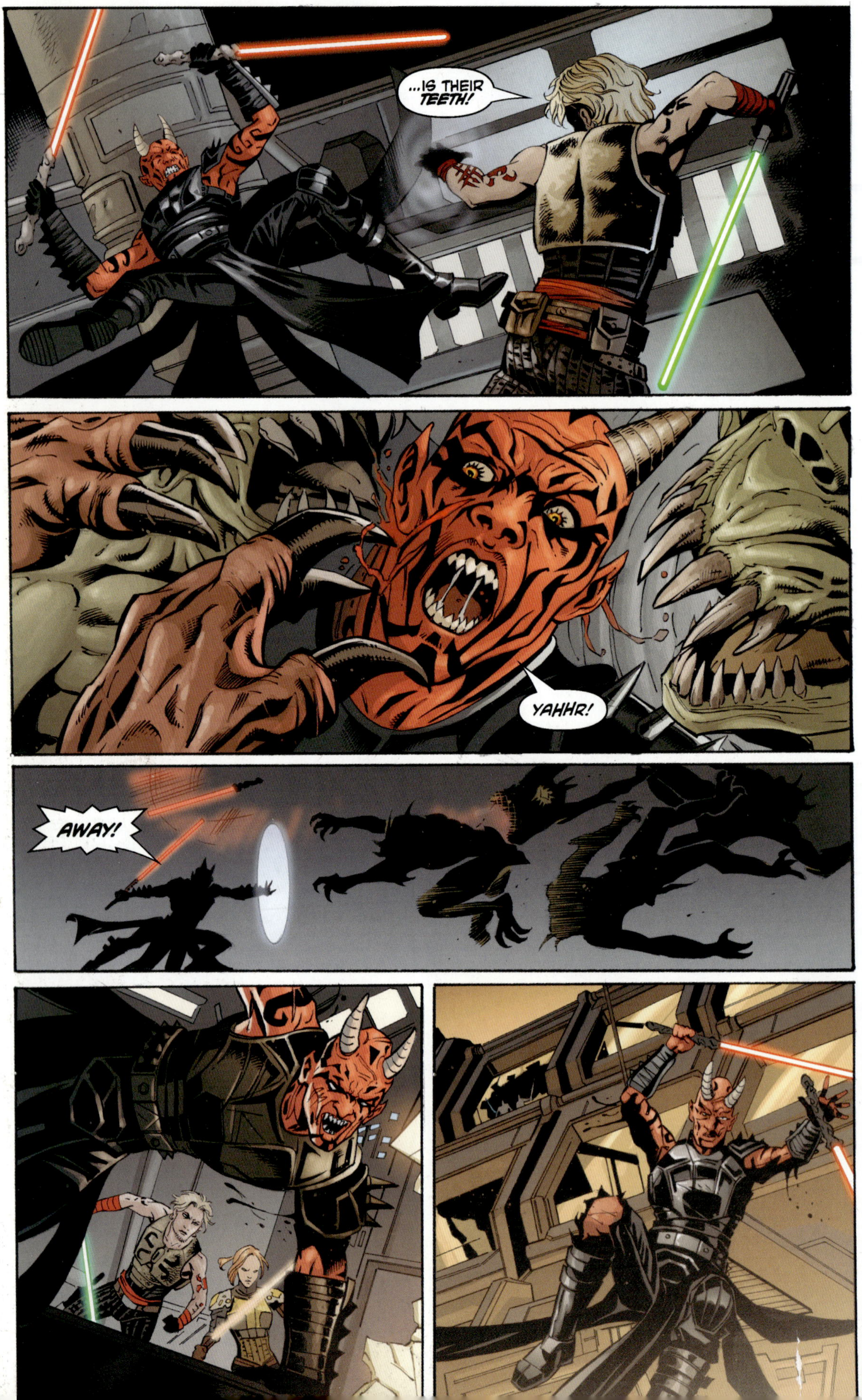
...IS THEIR TEETH!
YAHHR!
AWAY!

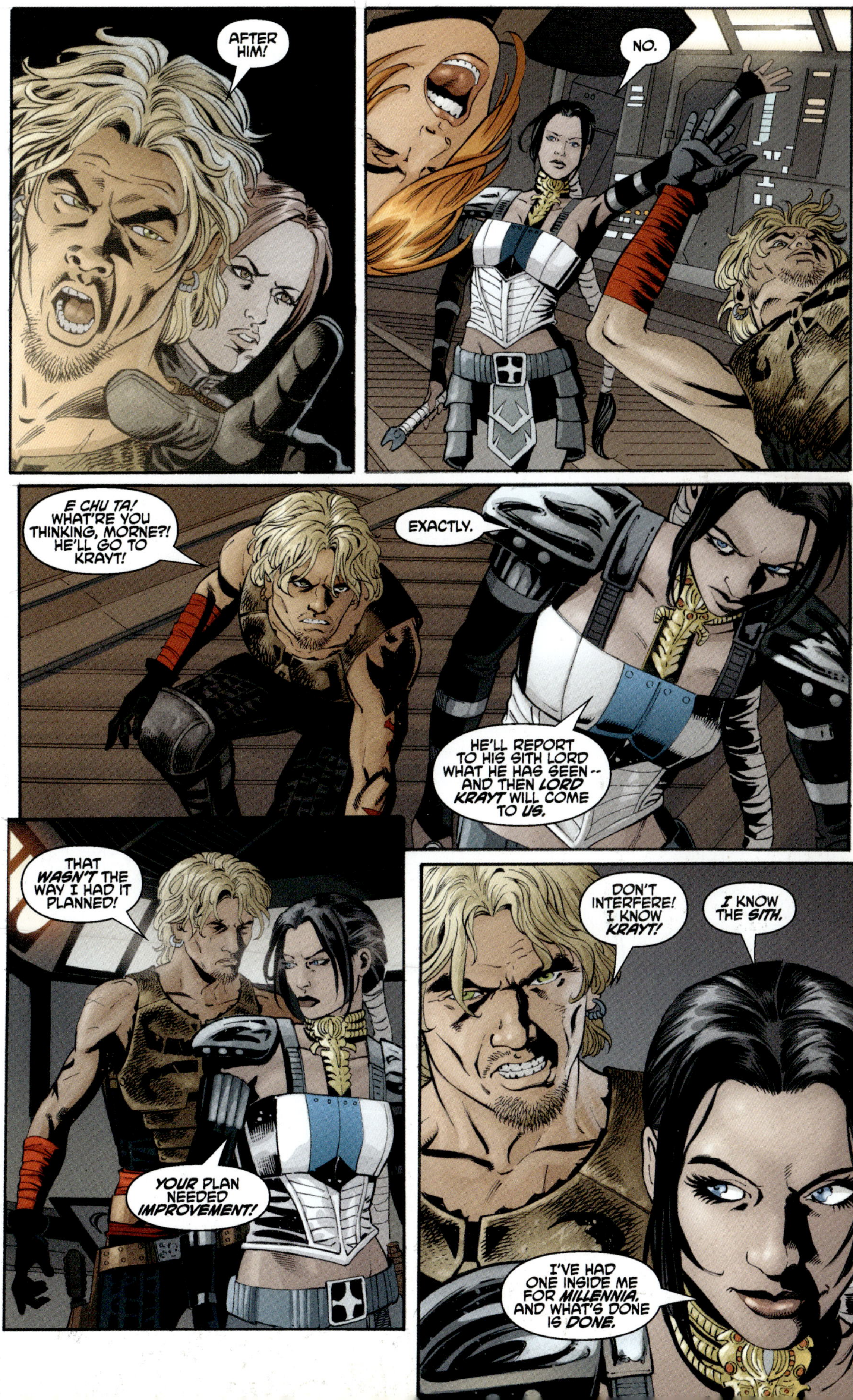
AFTER HIM!
NO.
E CHU TA! WHAT'RE YOU THINKING, MORNE?! HE'LL GO TO KRAYT!
EXACTLY.
HE'LL REPORT TO HIS SITH LORD WHAT HE HAS SEEN-- AND THEN LORD KRAYT WILL COME TO US.
THAT WASN'T THE WAY I HAD IT PLANNED!
YOUR PLAN NEEDED IMPROVEMENT!
DON'T INTERFERE! I KNOW KRAYT!
I KNOW THE SITH.
I'VE HAD ONE INSIDE ME FOR MILLENNIA. AND WHAT'S DONE IS DONE.

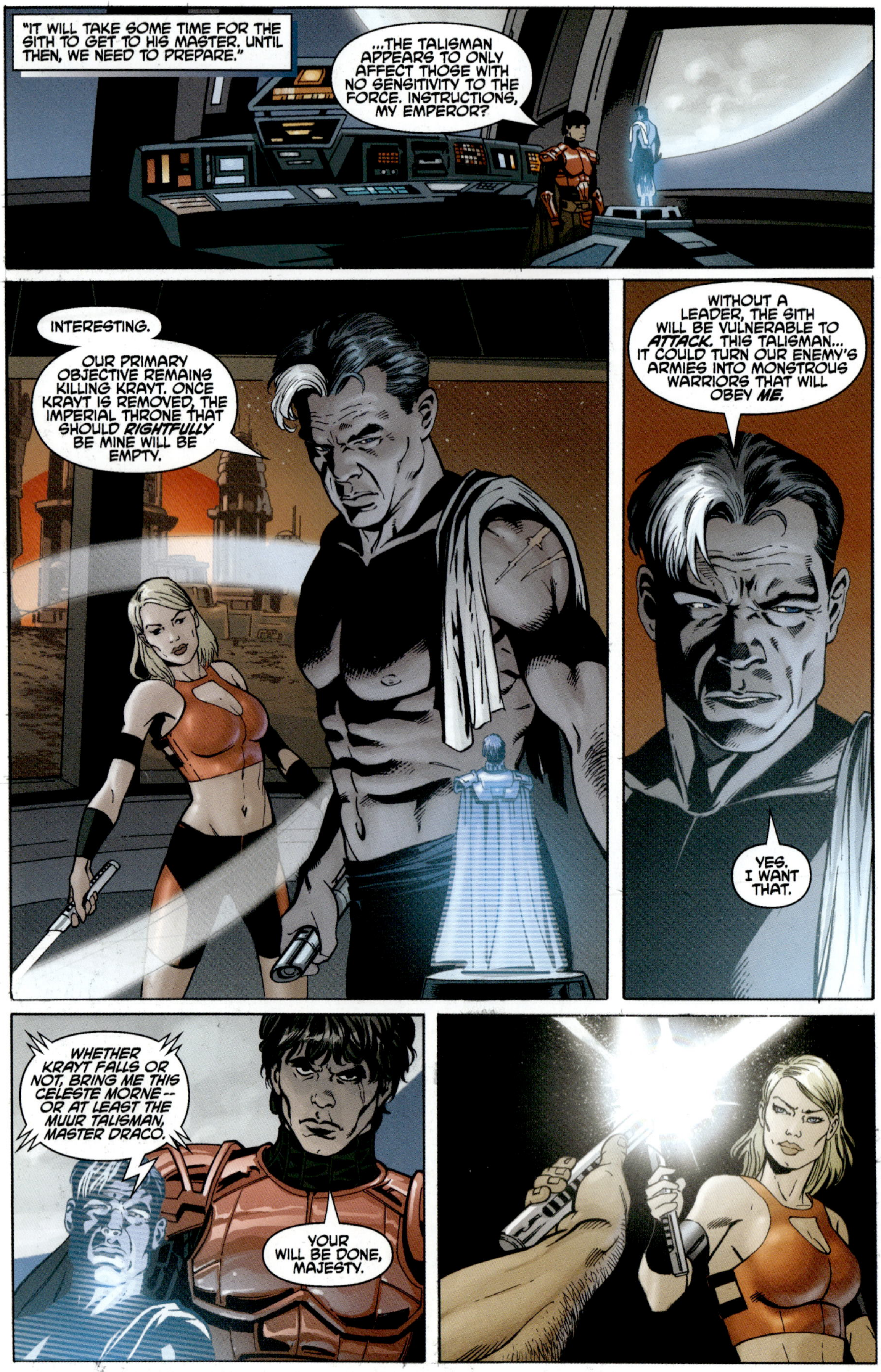
"IT WILL TAKE SOME TIME FOR THE SITH TO GET TO HIS MASTER. UNTIL THEN, WE NEED TO PREPARE."
...THE TALISMAN APPEARS TO ONLY AFFECT THOSE WITH NO SENSITIVITY TO THE FORCE. INSTRUCTIONS, MY EMPEROR?
INTERESTING.
OUR PRIMARY OBJECTIVE REMAINS KILLING KRAYT. ONCE KRAYT IS REMOVED, THE IMPERIAL THRONE THAT SHOULD RIGHTFULLY BE MINE WILL BE EMPTY.
WITHOUT A LEADER, THE SITH WILL BE VULNERABLE TO ATTACK. THIS TALISMAN... IT COULD TURN OUR ENEMY'S ARMIES INTO MONSTROUS WARRIORS THAT WILL OBEY ME.
YES. I WANT THAT.
WHETHER KRAYT FALLS OR NOT, BRING ME THIS CELESTE MORNE-- OR AT LEAST THE MUUR TALISMAN, MASTER DRACO.
YOUR WILL BE DONE, MAJESTY.

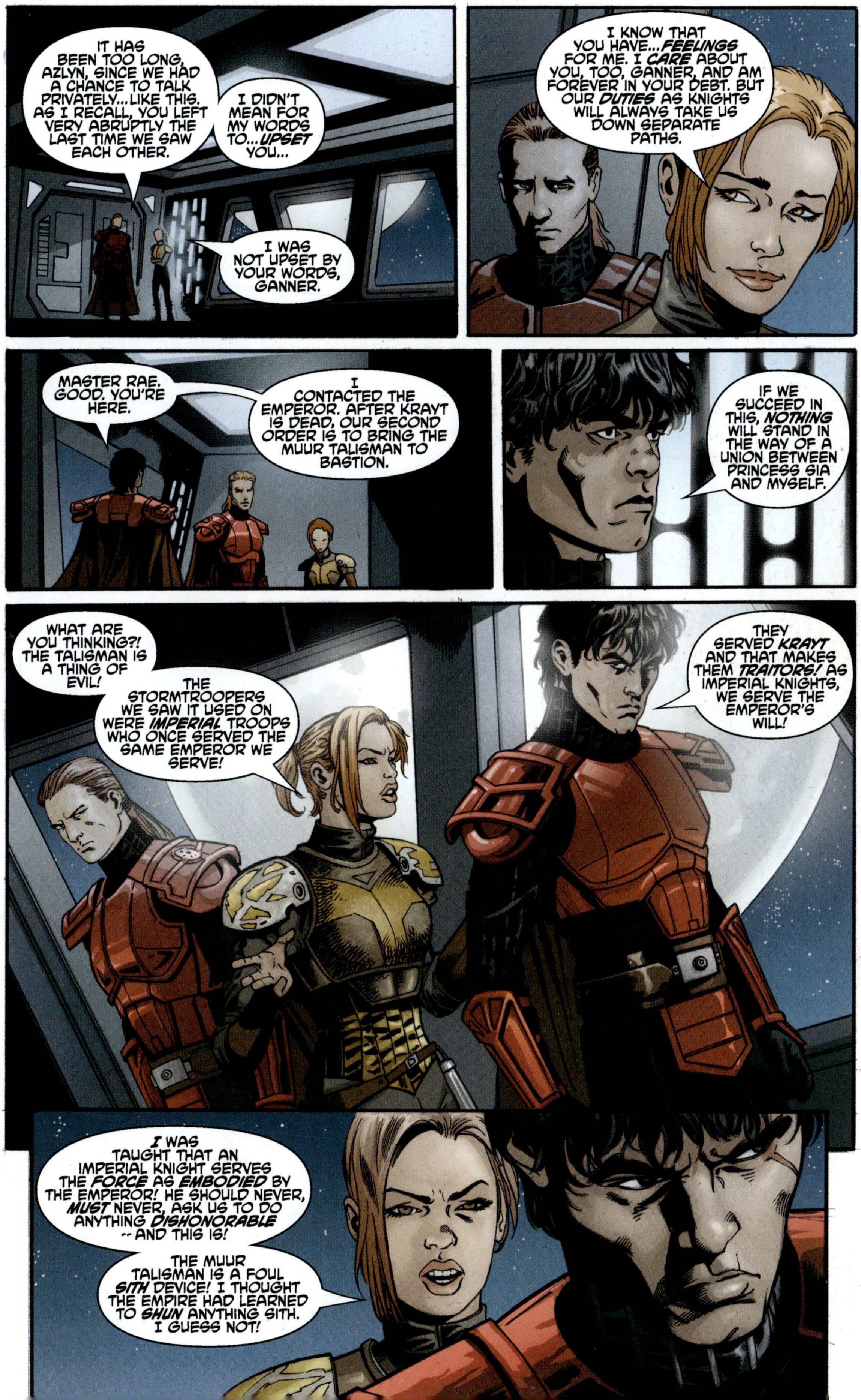
IT HAS BEEN TOO LONG, AZLYN, SINCE WE HAD A CHANCE TO TALK PRIVATELY...LIKE THIS. AS I RECALL, YOU LEFT VERY ABRUPTLY THE LAST TIME WE SAW EACH OTHER.
I DIDN'T MEAN FOR MY WORDS TO...*UPSET* YOU...
I WAS NOT UPSET BY YOUR WORDS, GANNER.
I KNOW THAT YOU HAVE...*FEELINGS* FOR ME. I *CARE* ABOUT YOU, TOO, GANNER, AND AM FOREVER IN YOUR DEBT. BUT OUR *DUTIES* AS KNIGHTS WILL ALWAYS TAKE US DOWN SEPARATE PATHS.
MASTER RAE. GOOD. YOU'RE HERE.
I CONTACTED THE EMPEROR. AFTER KRAYT IS DEAD, OUR SECOND ORDER IS TO BRING THE MUUR TALISMAN TO BASTION.
IF WE SUCCEED IN THIS, *NOTHING* WILL STAND IN THE WAY OF A UNION BETWEEN PRINCESS SIA AND MYSELF.
WHAT ARE YOU THINKING?! THE TALISMAN IS A THING OF EVIL!
THE STORMTROOPERS WE SAW IT USED ON WERE *IMPERIAL* TROOPS WHO ONCE SERVED THE SAME EMPEROR WE SERVE!
THEY SERVED *KRAYT* AND THAT MAKES THEM *TRAITORS!* AS IMPERIAL KNIGHTS, WE SERVE THE EMPEROR'S WILL!
I WAS TAUGHT THAT AN IMPERIAL KNIGHT SERVES THE *FORCE* AS *EMBODIED* BY THE EMPEROR! HE SHOULD NEVER, *MUST* NEVER, ASK US TO DO ANYTHING *DISHONORABLE* -- AND THIS IS!
THE MUUR TALISMAN IS A FOUL *SITH* DEVICE! I THOUGHT THE EMPIRE HAD LEARNED TO *SHUN* ANYTHING SITH. I GUESS NOT!

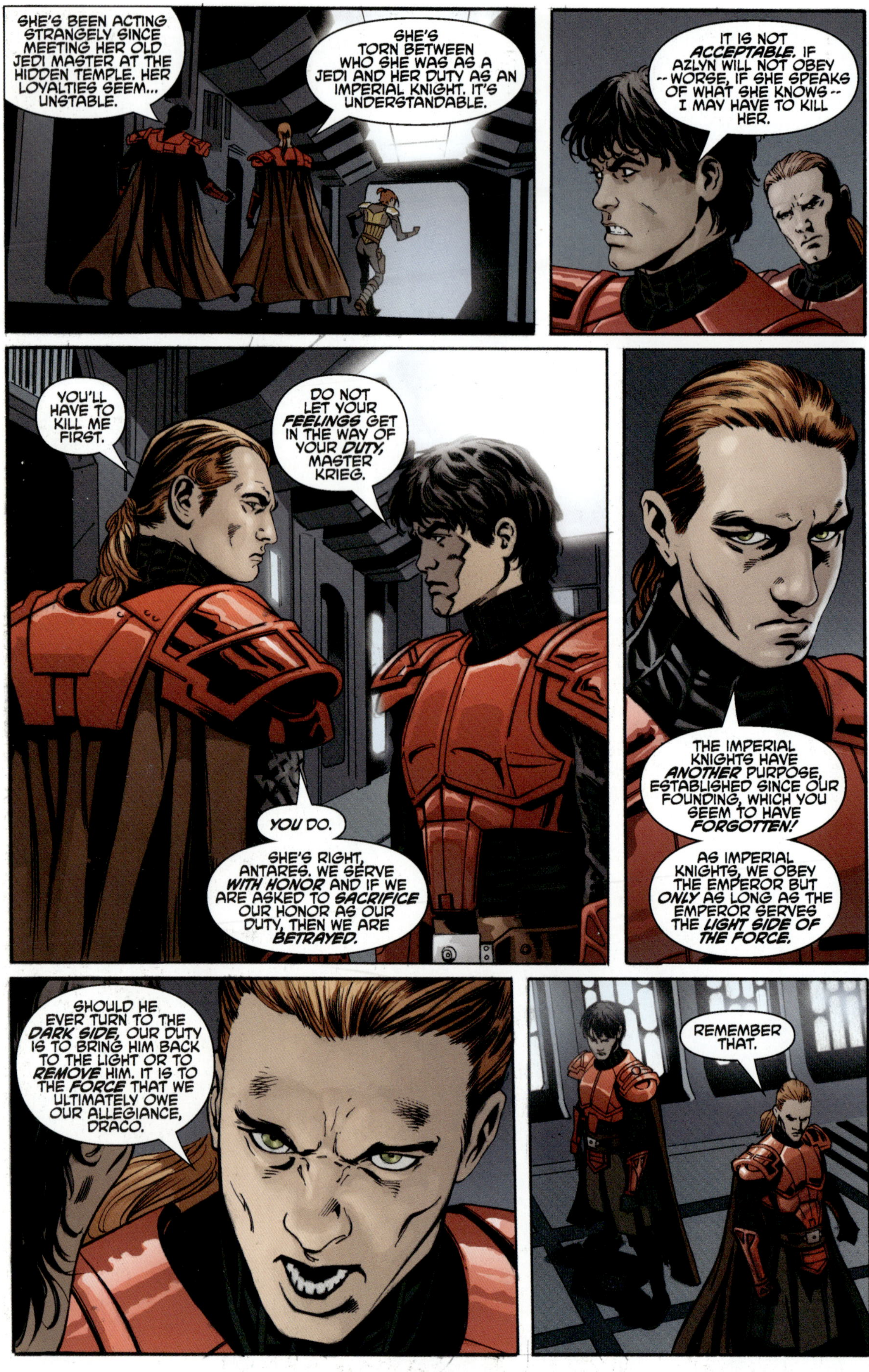
SHE'S BEEN ACTING STRANGELY SINCE MEETING HER OLD JEDI MASTER AT THE HIDDEN TEMPLE. HER LOYALTIES SEEM... UNSTABLE.
SHE'S TORN BETWEEN WHO SHE WAS AS A JEDI AND HER DUTY AS AN IMPERIAL KNIGHT. IT'S UNDERSTANDABLE.
IT IS NOT ACCEPTABLE. IF AZLYN WILL NOT OBEY -- WORSE, IF SHE SPEAKS OF WHAT SHE KNOWS -- I MAY HAVE TO KILL HER.
YOU'LL HAVE TO KILL ME FIRST.
DO NOT LET YOUR FEELINGS GET IN THE WAY OF YOUR DUTY, MASTER KRIEG.
YOU DO.
SHE'S RIGHT, ANTARES. WE SERVE WITH HONOR AND IF WE ARE ASKED TO SACRIFICE OUR HONOR AS OUR DUTY, THEN WE ARE BETRAYED.
THE IMPERIAL KNIGHTS HAVE ANOTHER PURPOSE, ESTABLISHED SINCE OUR FOUNDING, WHICH YOU SEEM TO HAVE FORGOTTEN!
AS IMPERIAL KNIGHTS, WE OBEY THE EMPEROR BUT ONLY AS LONG AS THE EMPEROR SERVES THE LIGHT SIDE OF THE FORCE.
SHOULD HE EVER TURN TO THE DARK SIDE, OUR DUTY IS TO BRING HIM BACK TO THE LIGHT OR TO REMOVE HIM. IT IS TO THE FORCE THAT WE ULTIMATELY OWE OUR ALLEGIANCE, DRACO.
REMEMBER THAT.

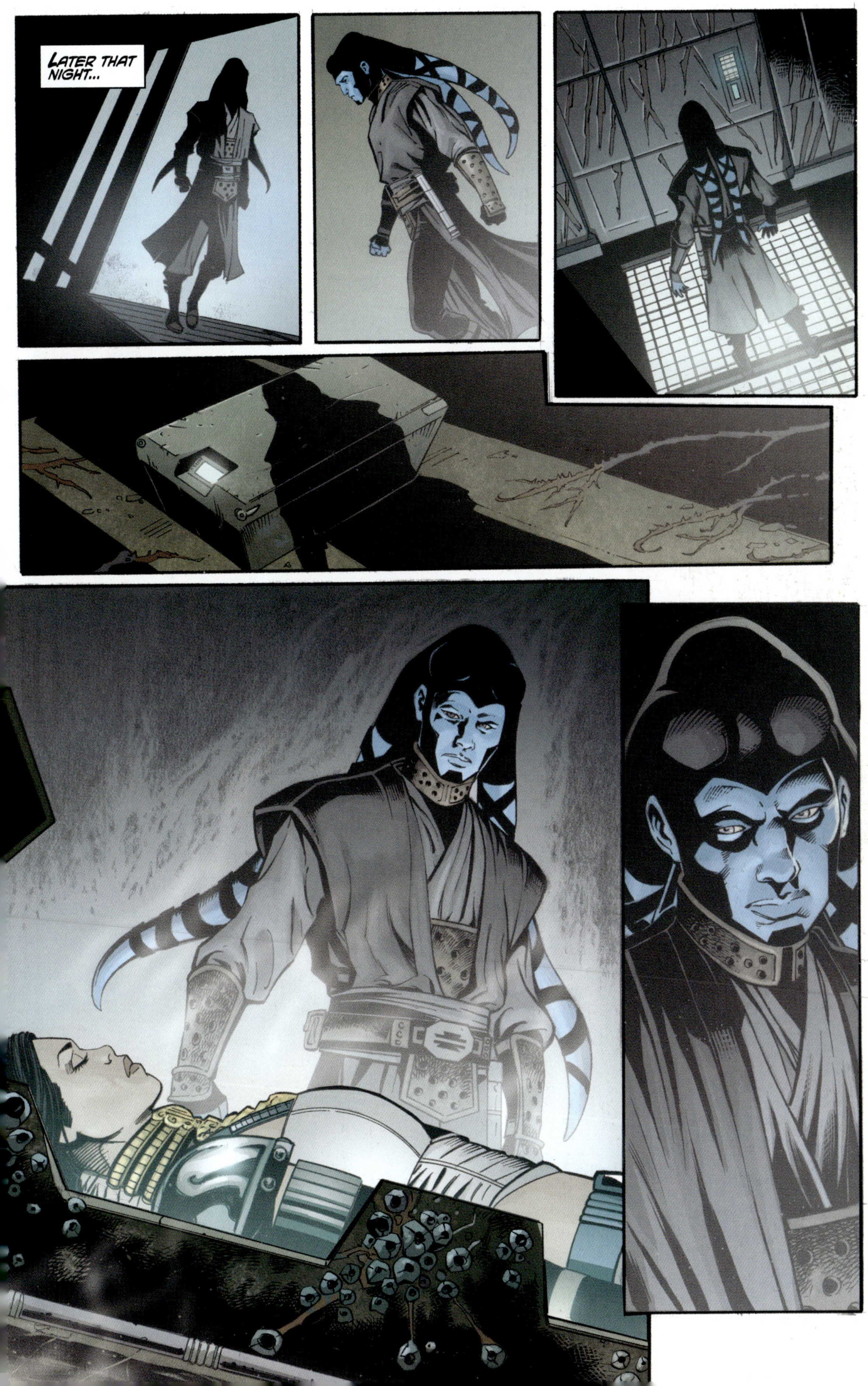
LATER THAT NIGHT...

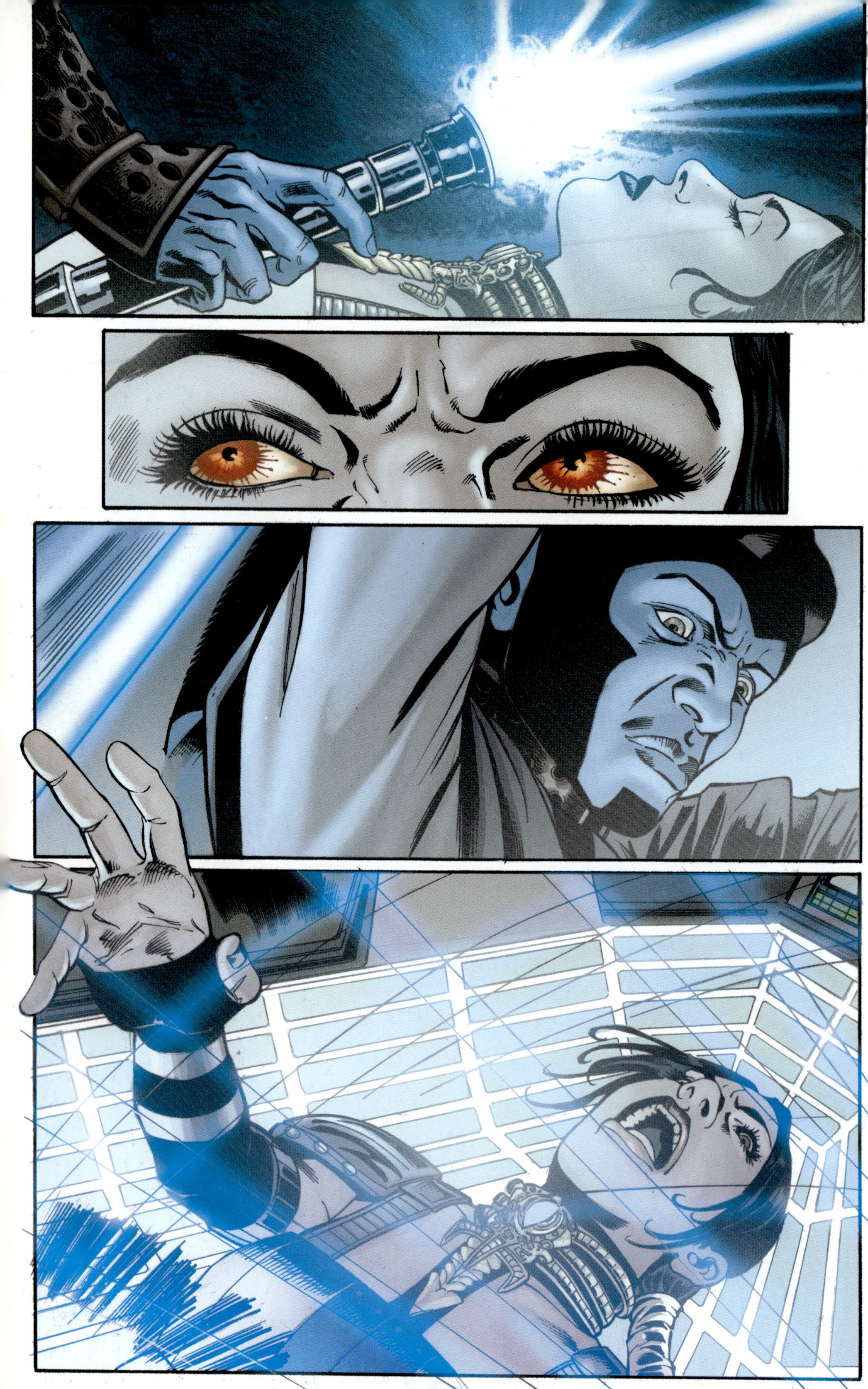

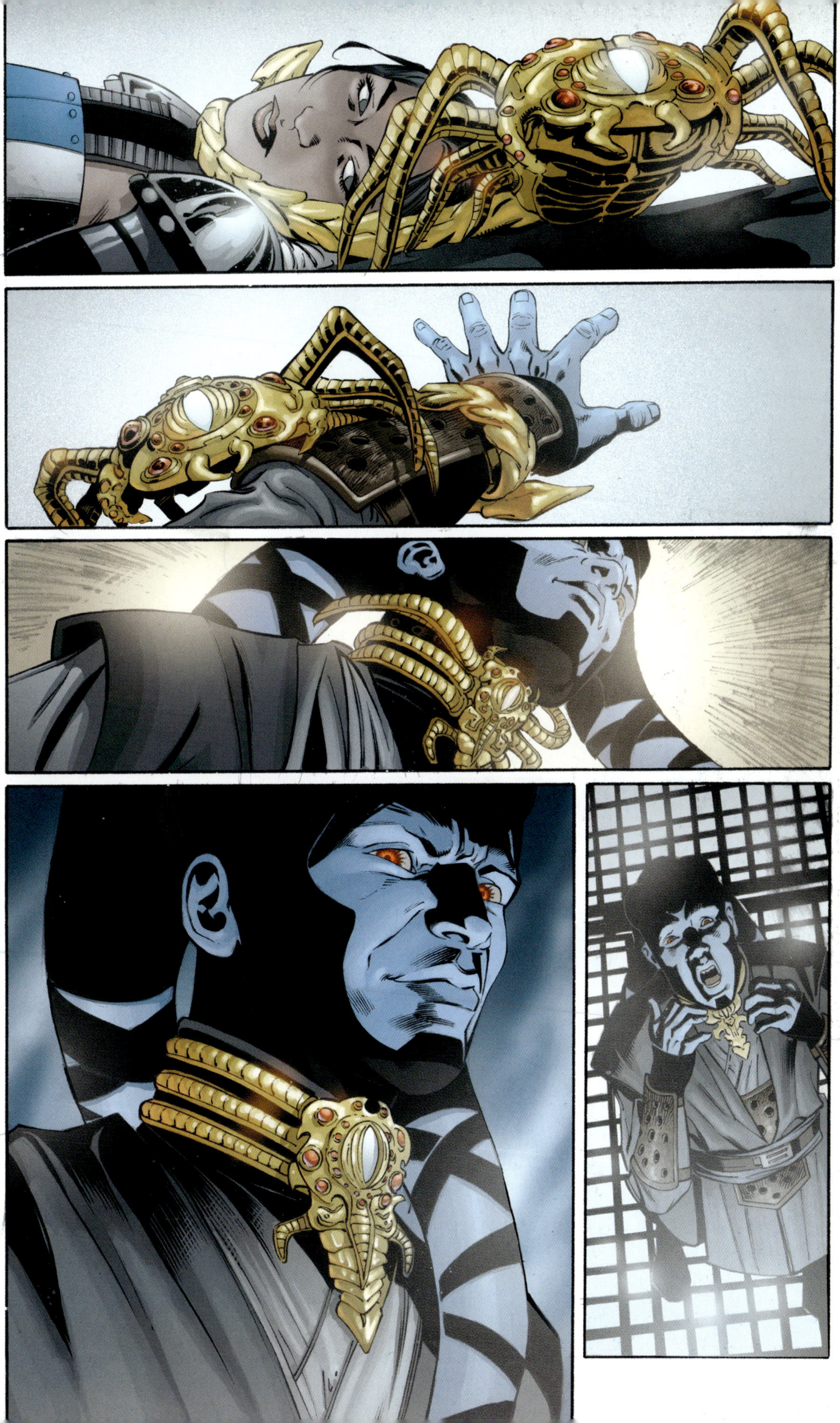

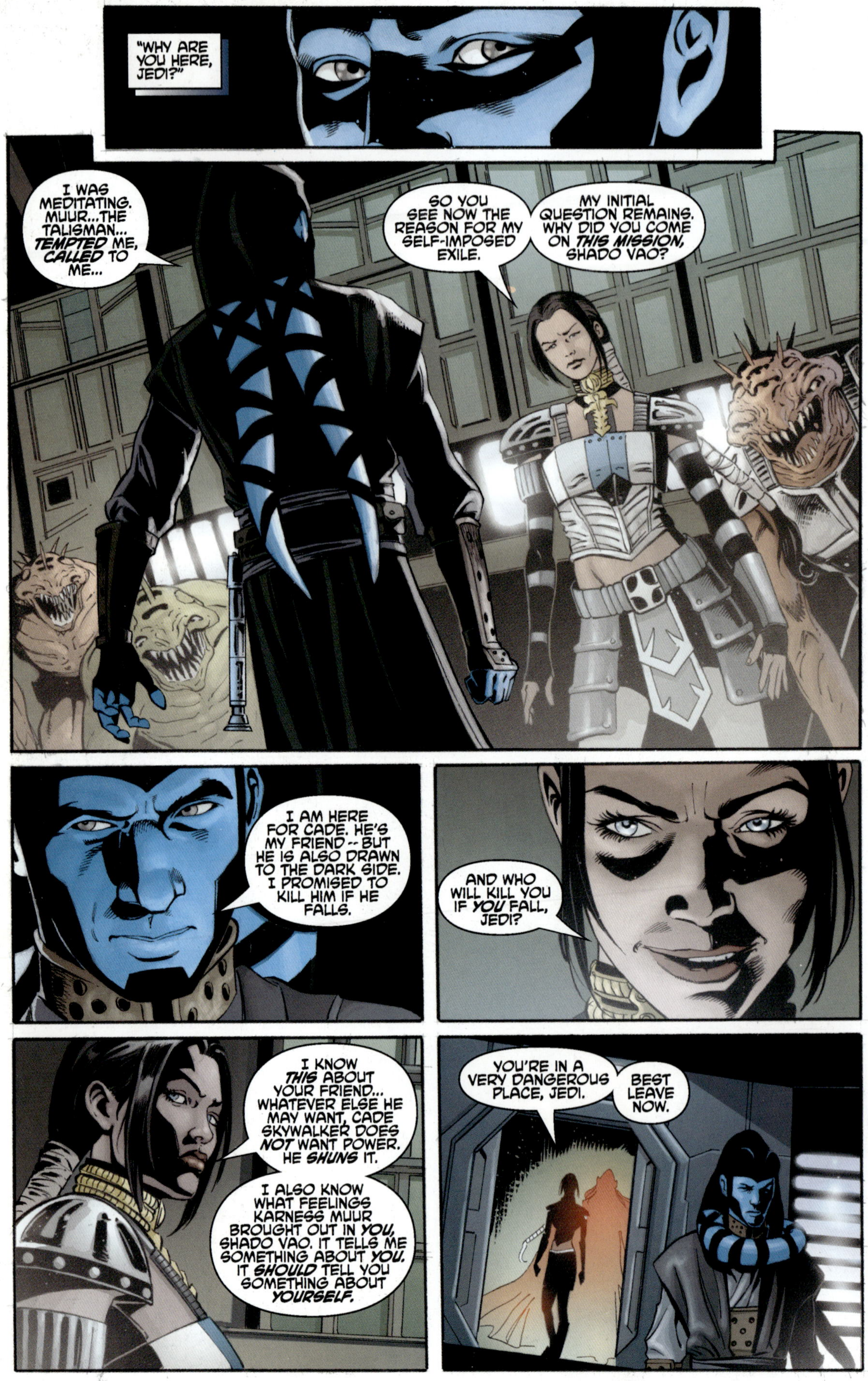
"WHY ARE YOU HERE, JEDI?"
I WAS MEDITATING. MUUR...THE TALISMAN... *TEMPTED* ME, *CALLED* TO ME...
SO YOU SEE NOW THE REASON FOR MY SELF-IMPOSED EXILE.
MY INITIAL QUESTION REMAINS. WHY DID YOU COME ON *THIS MISSION,* SHADO VAO?
I AM HERE FOR CADE. HE'S MY FRIEND -- BUT HE IS ALSO DRAWN TO THE DARK SIDE. I PROMISED TO KILL HIM IF HE FALLS.
AND WHO WILL KILL YOU IF *YOU* FALL, JEDI?
I KNOW *THIS* ABOUT YOUR FRIEND... WHATEVER ELSE HE MAY WANT, CADE SKYWALKER DOES *NOT* WANT POWER. HE *SHUNS* IT.
I ALSO KNOW WHAT FEELINGS KARNESS MUUR BROUGHT OUT IN *YOU,* SHADO VAO. IT TELLS ME SOMETHING ABOUT *YOU.* IT *SHOULD* TELL YOU SOMETHING ABOUT *YOURSELF.*
YOU'RE IN A VERY DANGEROUS PLACE, JEDI.
BEST LEAVE NOW.

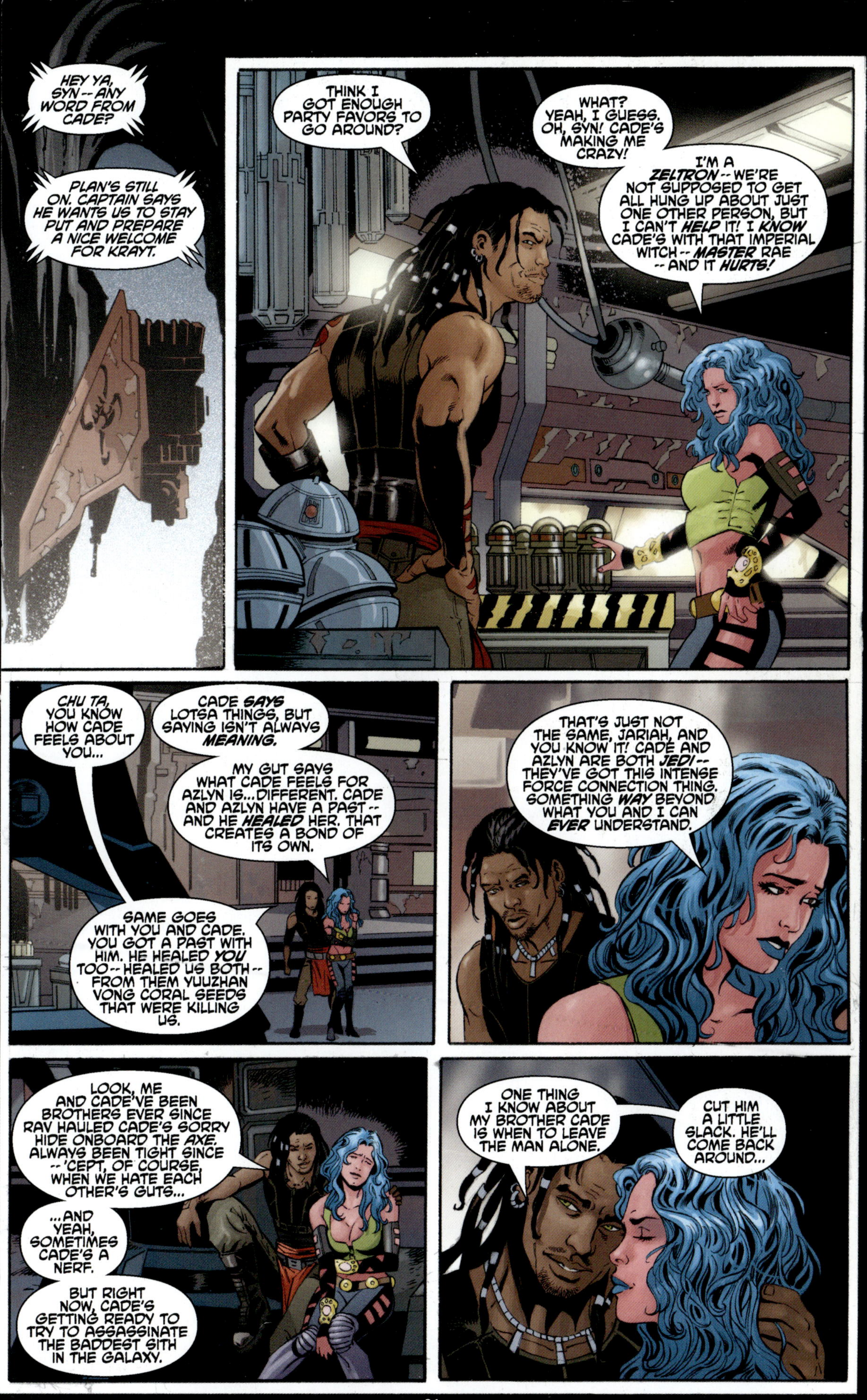
HEY YA, SYN -- ANY WORD FROM CADE?
PLAN'S STILL ON. CAPTAIN SAYS HE WANTS US TO STAY PUT AND PREPARE A NICE WELCOME FOR KRAYT.
THINK I GOT ENOUGH PARTY FAVORS TO GO AROUND?
WHAT? YEAH, I GUESS. OH, SYN! CADE'S MAKING ME CRAZY!
I'M A ZELTRON -- WE'RE NOT SUPPOSED TO GET ALL HUNG UP ABOUT JUST ONE OTHER PERSON, BUT I CAN'T HELP IT! I KNOW CADE'S WITH THAT IMPERIAL WITCH -- MASTER RAE -- AND IT HURTS!
CHU TA, YOU KNOW HOW CADE FEELS ABOUT YOU...
CADE SAYS LOTSA THINGS, BUT SAYING ISN'T ALWAYS MEANING.
MY GUT SAYS WHAT CADE FEELS FOR AZLYN IS...DIFFERENT. CADE AND AZLYN HAVE A PAST -- AND HE HEALED HER. THAT CREATES A BOND OF ITS OWN.
SAME GOES WITH YOU AND CADE. YOU GOT A PAST WITH HIM. HE HEALED YOU TOO -- HEALED US BOTH -- FROM THEM YUUZHAN VONG CORAL SEEDS THAT WERE KILLING US.
THAT'S JUST NOT THE SAME, JARIAH, AND YOU KNOW IT! CADE AND AZLYN ARE BOTH JEDI -- THEY'VE GOT THIS INTENSE FORCE CONNECTION THING. SOMETHING WAY BEYOND WHAT YOU AND I CAN EVER UNDERSTAND.
LOOK, ME AND CADE'VE BEEN BROTHERS EVER SINCE RAV HAULED CADE'S SORRY HIDE ONBOARD THE AXE. ALWAYS BEEN TIGHT SINCE -- 'CEPT, OF COURSE, WHEN WE HATE EACH OTHER'S GUTS...
...AND YEAH, SOMETIMES CADE'S A NERF.
BUT RIGHT NOW, CADE'S GETTING READY TO TRY TO ASSASSINATE THE BADDEST SITH IN THE GALAXY.
ONE THING I KNOW ABOUT MY BROTHER CADE IS WHEN TO LEAVE THE MAN ALONE.
CUT HIM A LITTLE SLACK. HE'LL COME BACK AROUND...

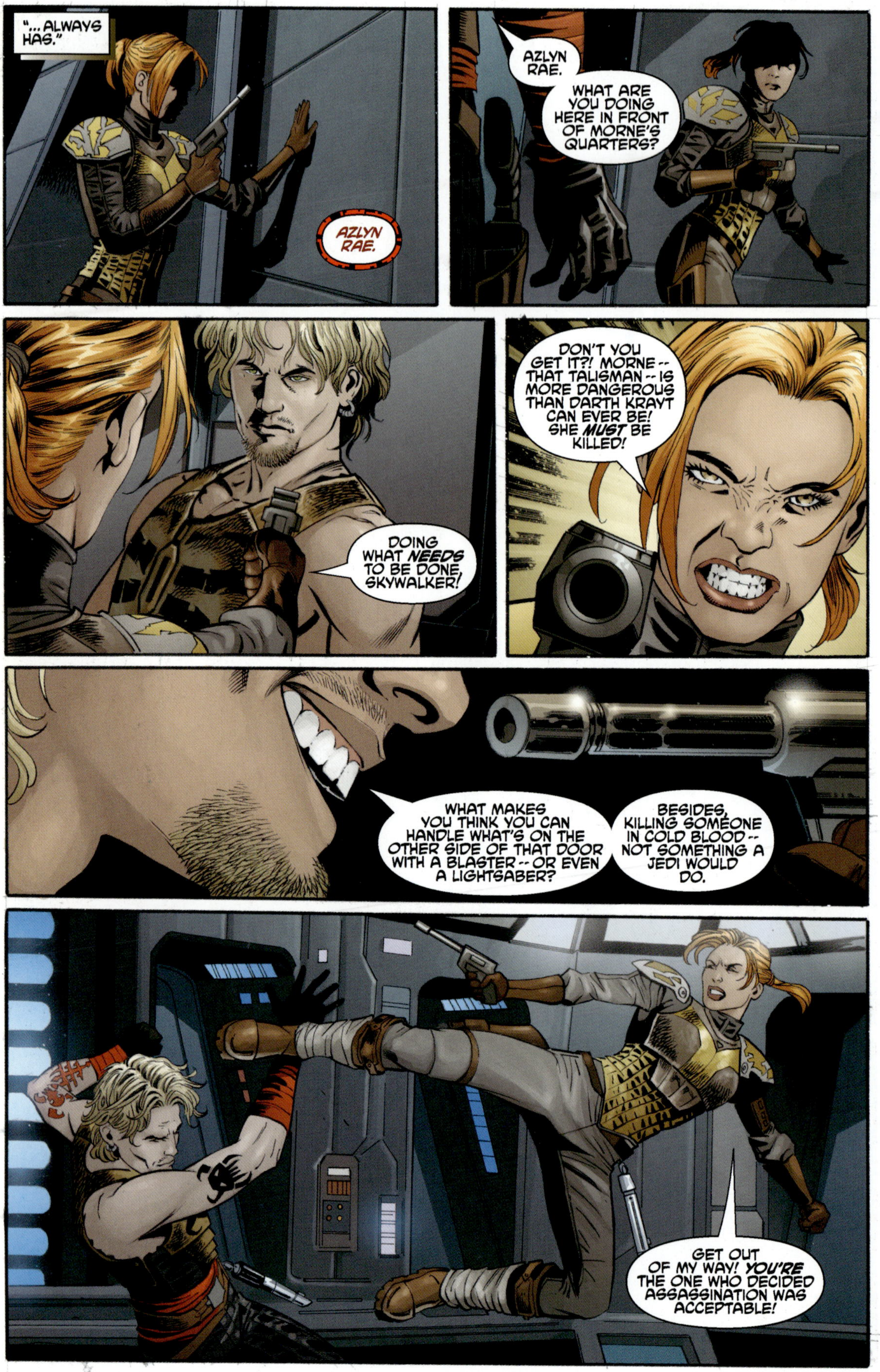
"...ALWAYS HAS."
AZLYN RAE.
AZLYN RAE.
WHAT ARE YOU DOING HERE IN FRONT OF MORNE'S QUARTERS?
DOING WHAT NEEDS TO BE DONE, SKYWALKER!
DON'T YOU GET IT?! MORNE -- THAT TALISMAN -- IS MORE DANGEROUS THAN DARTH KRAYT CAN EVER BE! SHE MUST BE KILLED!
WHAT MAKES YOU THINK YOU CAN HANDLE WHAT'S ON THE OTHER SIDE OF THAT DOOR WITH A BLASTER -- OR EVEN A LIGHTSABER?
BESIDES, KILLING SOMEONE IN COLD BLOOD -- NOT SOMETHING A JEDI WOULD DO.
GET OUT OF MY WAY! YOU'RE THE ONE WHO DECIDED ASSASSINATION WAS ACCEPTABLE!

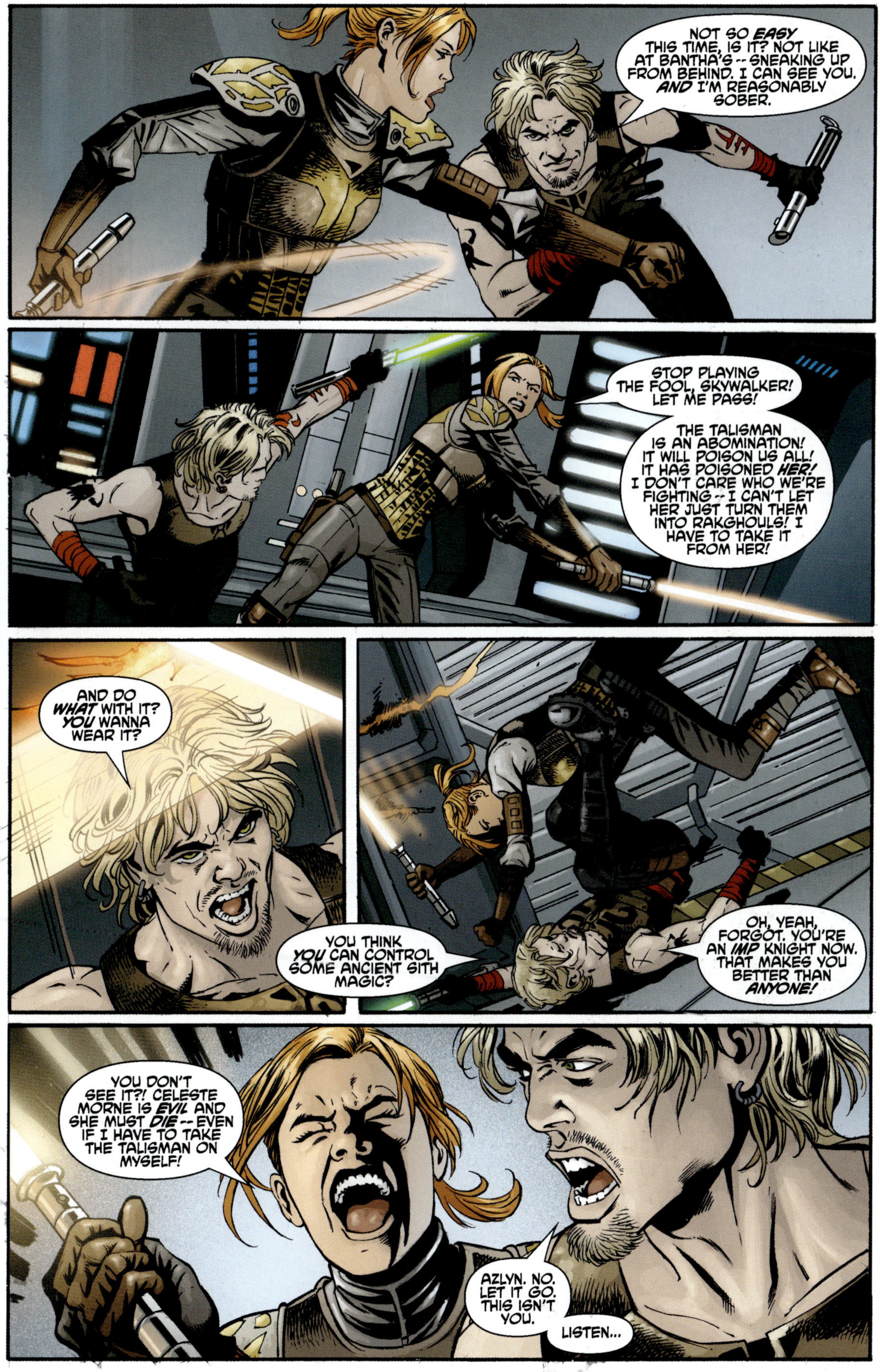
NOT SO EASY THIS TIME, IS IT? NOT LIKE AT BANTHA'S -- SNEAKING UP FROM BEHIND. I CAN SEE YOU. AND I'M REASONABLY SOBER.
STOP PLAYING THE FOOL, SKYWALKER! LET ME PASS!
THE TALISMAN IS AN ABOMINATION! IT WILL POISON US ALL! IT HAS POISONED HER! I DON'T CARE WHO WE'RE FIGHTING -- I CAN'T LET HER JUST TURN THEM INTO RAKGHOULS! I HAVE TO TAKE IT FROM HER!
AND DO WHAT WITH IT? YOU WANNA WEAR IT?
YOU THINK YOU CAN CONTROL SOME ANCIENT SITH MAGIC?
OH, YEAH, FORGOT. YOU'RE AN IMP KNIGHT NOW. THAT MAKES YOU BETTER THAN ANYONE!
YOU DON'T SEE IT?! CELESTE MORNE IS EVIL AND SHE MUST DIE -- EVEN IF I HAVE TO TAKE THE TALISMAN ON MYSELF!
AZLYN. NO. LET IT GO. THIS ISN'T YOU.
LISTEN...

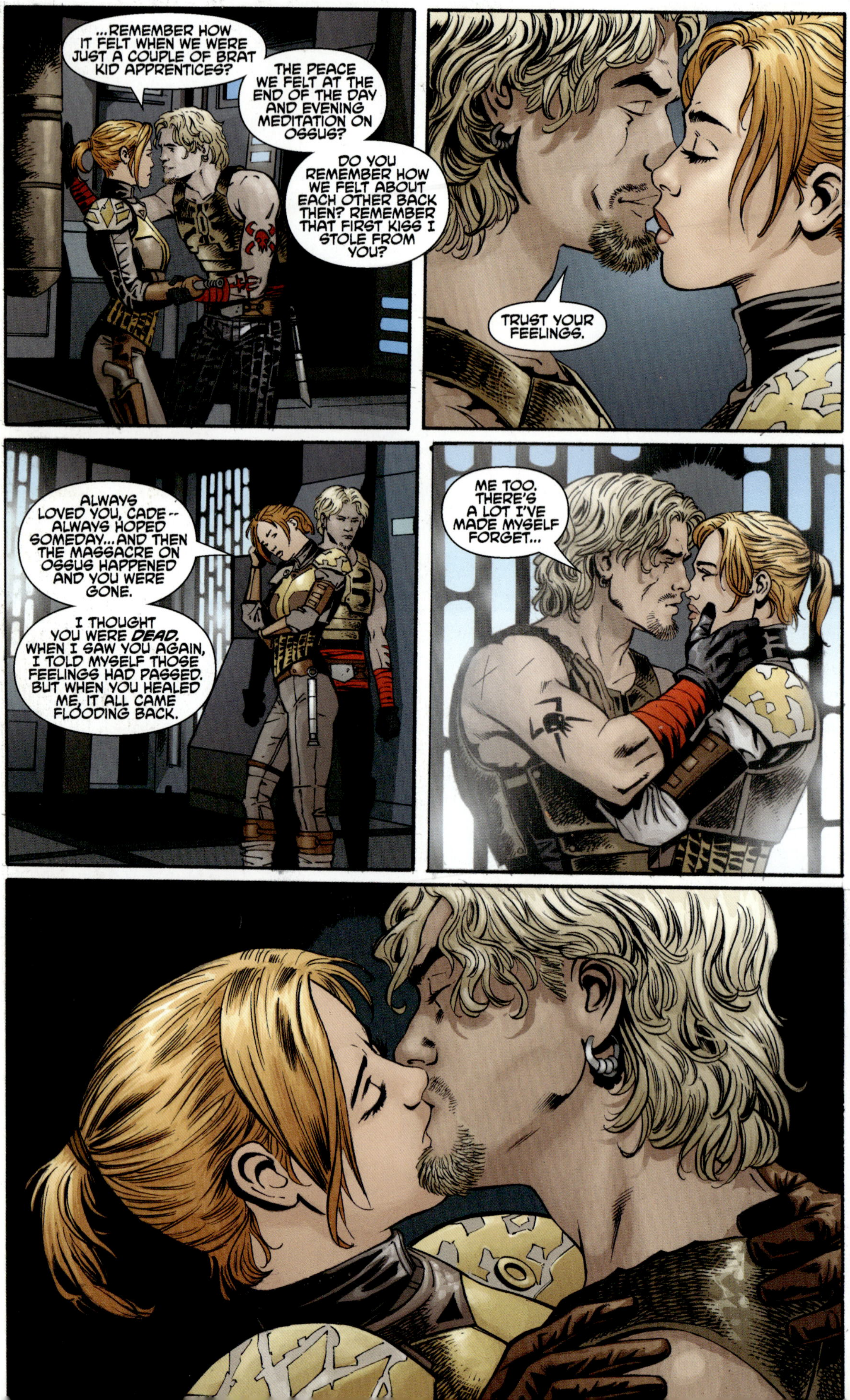
...REMEMBER HOW IT FELT WHEN WE WERE JUST A COUPLE OF BRAT KID APPRENTICES?
THE PEACE WE FELT AT THE END OF THE DAY AND EVENING MEDITATION ON OSSUS?
DO YOU REMEMBER HOW WE FELT ABOUT EACH OTHER BACK THEN? REMEMBER THAT FIRST KISS I STOLE FROM YOU?
TRUST YOUR FEELINGS.
ALWAYS LOVED YOU, CADE-- ALWAYS HOPED SOMEDAY...AND THEN THE MASSACRE ON OSSUS HAPPENED AND YOU WERE GONE.
I THOUGHT YOU WERE *DEAD*. WHEN I SAW YOU AGAIN, I TOLD MYSELF THOSE FEELINGS HAD PASSED. BUT WHEN YOU HEALED ME, IT ALL CAME FLOODING BACK.
ME TOO. THERE'S A LOT I'VE MADE MYSELF FORGET...

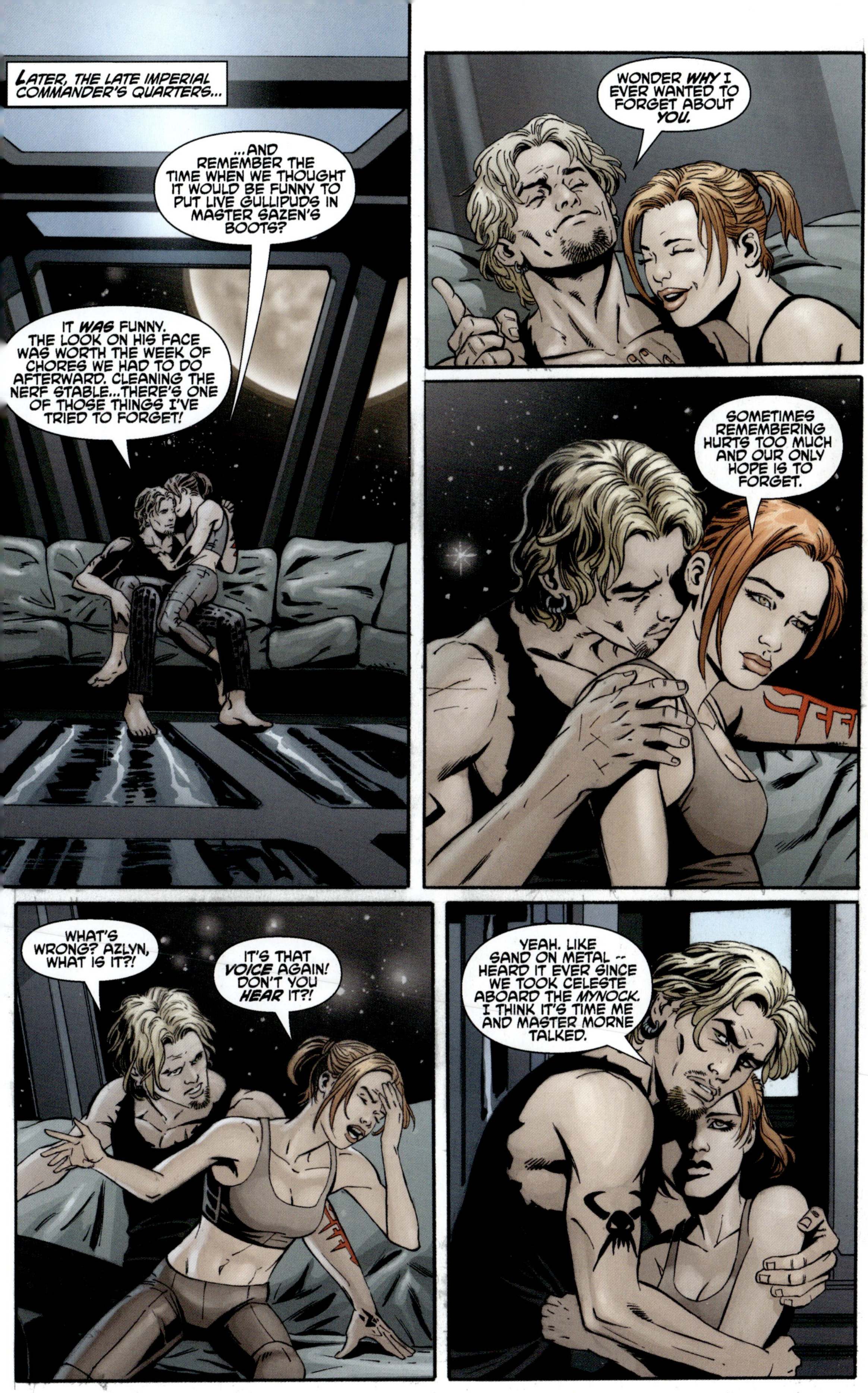
LATER, THE LATE IMPERIAL COMMANDER'S QUARTERS...
...AND REMEMBER THE TIME WHEN WE THOUGHT IT WOULD BE FUNNY TO PUT LIVE GULLIPUDS IN MASTER SAZEN'S BOOTS?
IT WAS FUNNY. THE LOOK ON HIS FACE WAS WORTH THE WEEK OF CHORES WE HAD TO DO AFTERWARD. CLEANING THE NERF STABLE...THERE'S ONE OF THOSE THINGS I'VE TRIED TO FORGET!
WONDER WHY I EVER WANTED TO FORGET ABOUT YOU.
SOMETIMES REMEMBERING HURTS TOO MUCH AND OUR ONLY HOPE IS TO FORGET.
WHAT'S WRONG? AZLYN, WHAT IS IT?!
IT'S THAT VOICE AGAIN! DON'T YOU HEAR IT?!
YEAH. LIKE SAND ON METAL -- HEARD IT EVER SINCE WE TOOK CELESTE ABOARD THE MYNOCK. I THINK IT'S TIME ME AND MASTER MORNE TALKED.

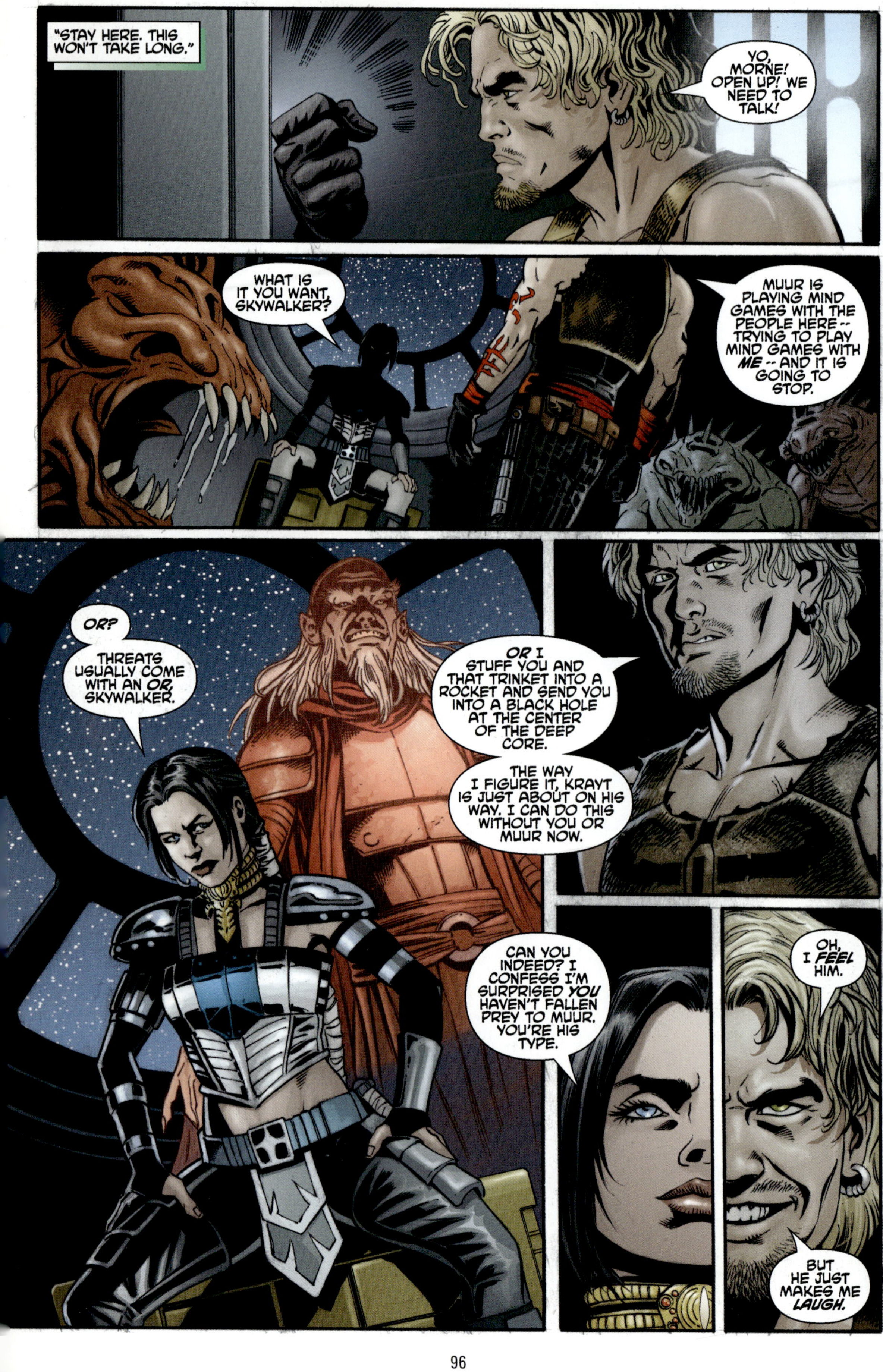
"STAY HERE. THIS WON'T TAKE LONG."
YO, MORNE! OPEN UP! WE NEED TO TALK!
WHAT IS IT YOU WANT, SKYWALKER?
MUUR IS PLAYING MIND GAMES WITH THE PEOPLE HERE -- TRYING TO PLAY MIND GAMES WITH *ME* -- AND IT IS GOING TO STOP.
OR?
THREATS USUALLY COME WITH AN *OR,* SKYWALKER.
OR I STUFF YOU AND THAT TRINKET INTO A ROCKET AND SEND YOU INTO A BLACK HOLE AT THE CENTER OF THE DEEP CORE.
THE WAY I FIGURE IT, KRAYT IS JUST ABOUT ON HIS WAY. I CAN DO THIS WITHOUT YOU OR MUUR NOW.
CAN YOU INDEED? I CONFESS I'M SURPRISED *YOU* HAVEN'T FALLEN PREY TO MUUR. YOU'RE HIS TYPE.
OH, I *FEEL* HIM.
BUT HE JUST MAKES ME *LAUGH.*

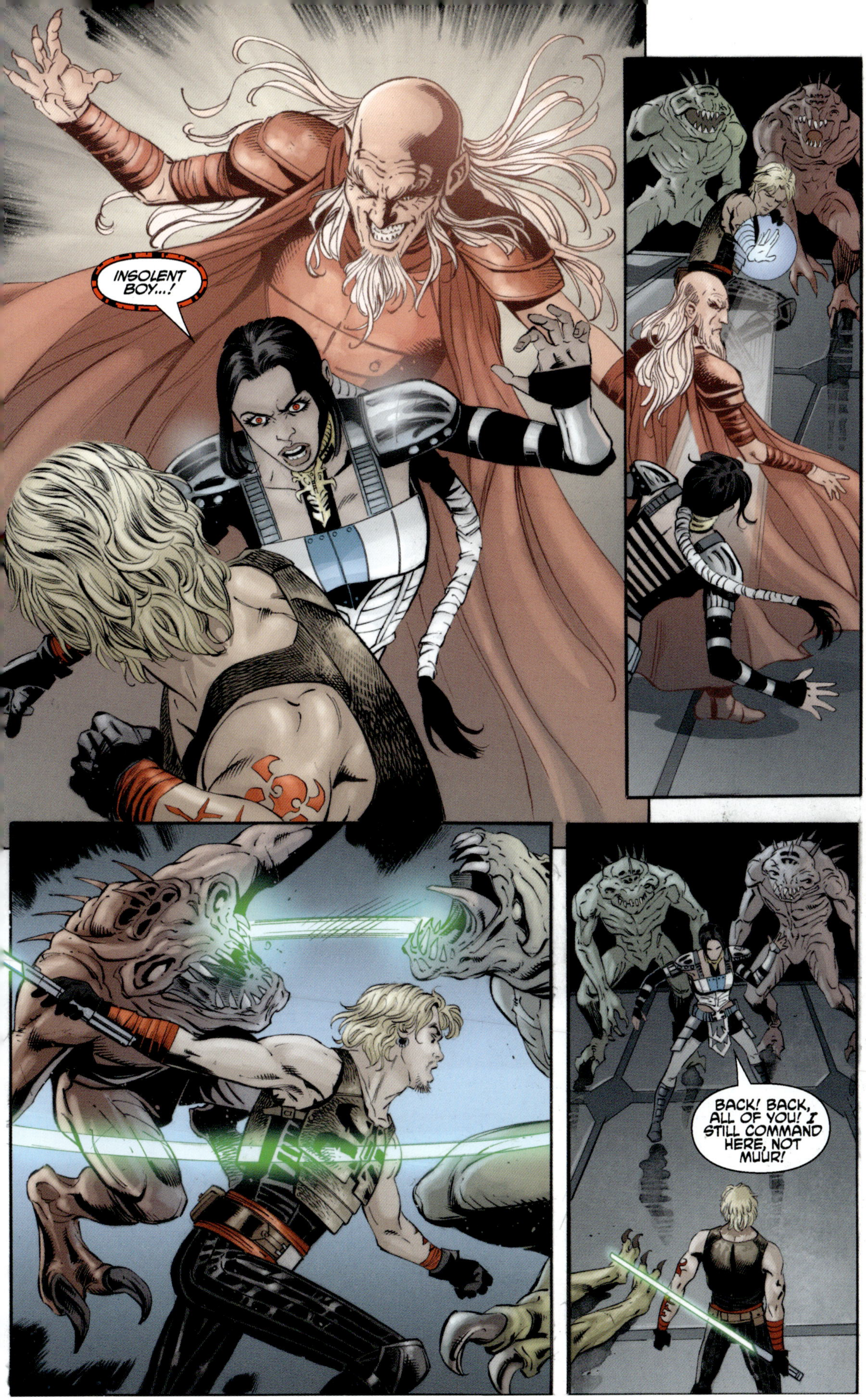
INSOLENT BOY...!
BACK! BACK, ALL OF YOU! I STILL COMMAND HERE, NOT MUUR!

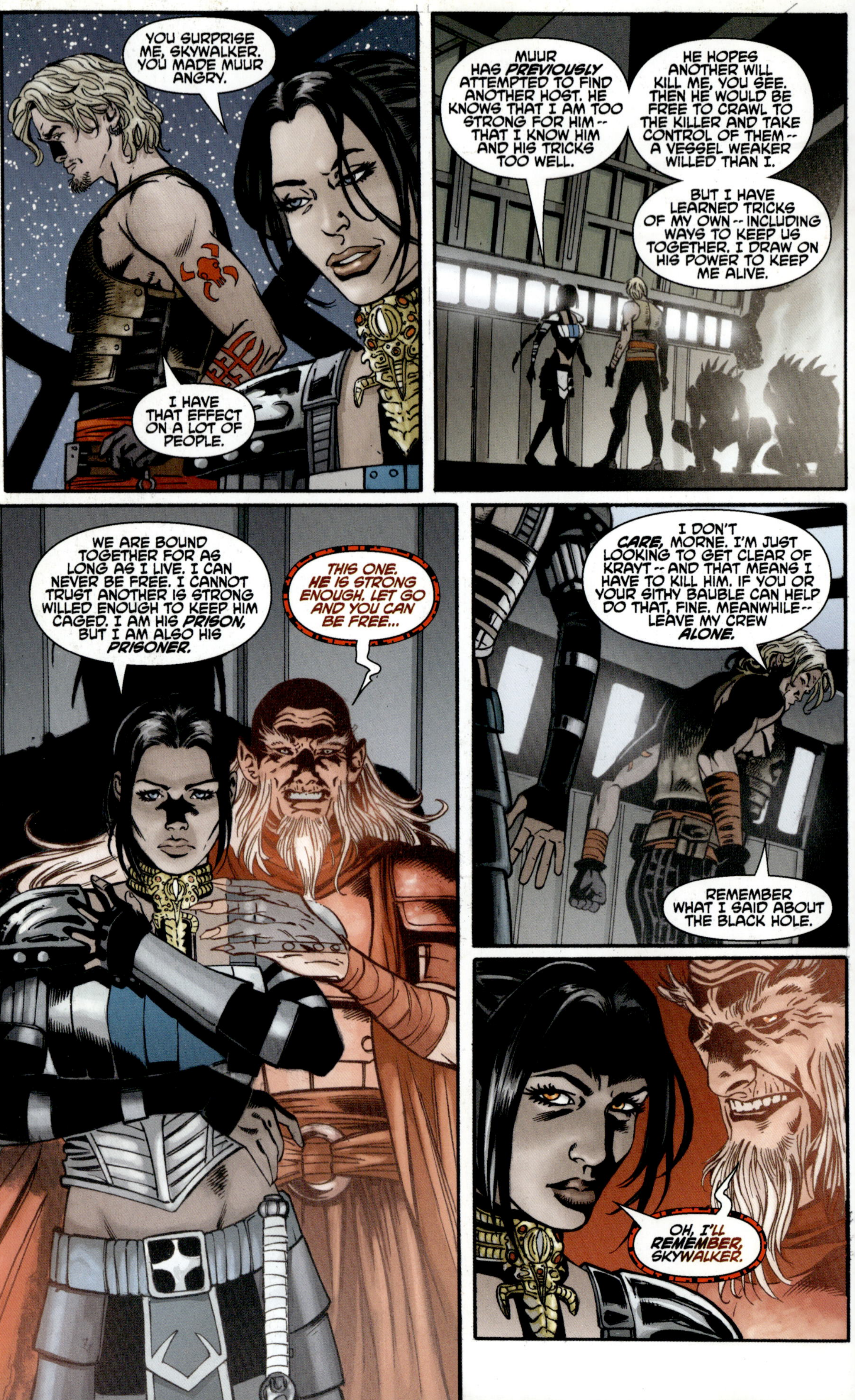
YOU SURPRISE ME, SKYWALKER. YOU MADE MUUR ANGRY.
I HAVE THAT EFFECT ON A LOT OF PEOPLE.
MUUR HAS *PREVIOUSLY* ATTEMPTED TO FIND ANOTHER HOST. HE KNOWS THAT I AM TOO STRONG FOR HIM -- THAT I KNOW HIM AND HIS TRICKS TOO WELL.
HE HOPES ANOTHER WILL KILL ME, YOU SEE. THEN HE WOULD BE FREE TO CRAWL TO THE KILLER AND TAKE CONTROL OF THEM -- A VESSEL WEAKER WILLED THAN I.
BUT I HAVE LEARNED TRICKS OF MY OWN -- INCLUDING WAYS TO KEEP US TOGETHER. I DRAW ON HIS POWER TO KEEP ME ALIVE.
WE ARE BOUND TOGETHER FOR AS LONG AS I LIVE. I CAN NEVER BE FREE. I CANNOT TRUST ANOTHER IS STRONG WILLED ENOUGH TO KEEP HIM CAGED. I AM HIS *PRISON,* BUT I AM ALSO HIS *PRISONER.*
THIS ONE. HE IS STRONG ENOUGH. LET GO AND YOU CAN BE FREE...
I DON'T *CARE,* MORNE. I'M JUST LOOKING TO GET CLEAR OF KRAYT -- AND THAT MEANS I HAVE TO KILL HIM. IF YOU OR YOUR SITHY BAUBLE CAN HELP DO THAT, FINE. MEANWHILE -- LEAVE MY CREW *ALONE.*
REMEMBER WHAT I SAID ABOUT THE BLACK HOLE.
OH, I'LL REMEMBER, SKYWALKER.

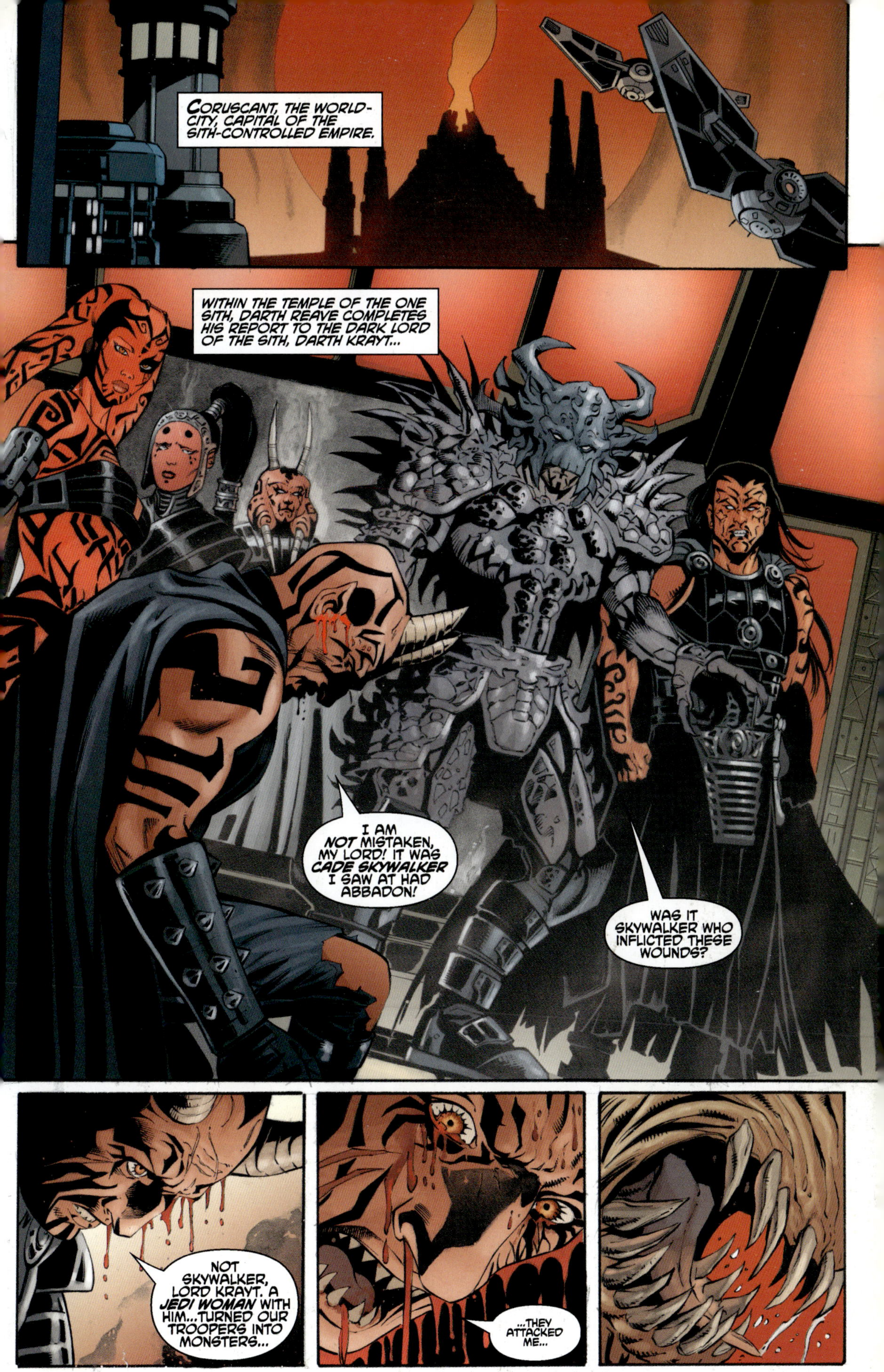
CORUSCANT, THE WORLD-CITY, CAPITAL OF THE SITH-CONTROLLED EMPIRE.
WITHIN THE TEMPLE OF THE ONE SITH, DARTH REAVE COMPLETES HIS REPORT TO THE DARK LORD OF THE SITH, DARTH KRAYT...
I AM NOT MISTAKEN, MY LORD! IT WAS CADE SKYWALKER I SAW AT HAD ABBADON!
WAS IT SKYWALKER WHO INFLICTED THESE WOUNDS?
NOT SKYWALKER, LORD KRAYT. A JEDI WOMAN WITH HIM...TURNED OUR TROOPERS INTO MONSTERS...
...THEY ATTACKED ME...

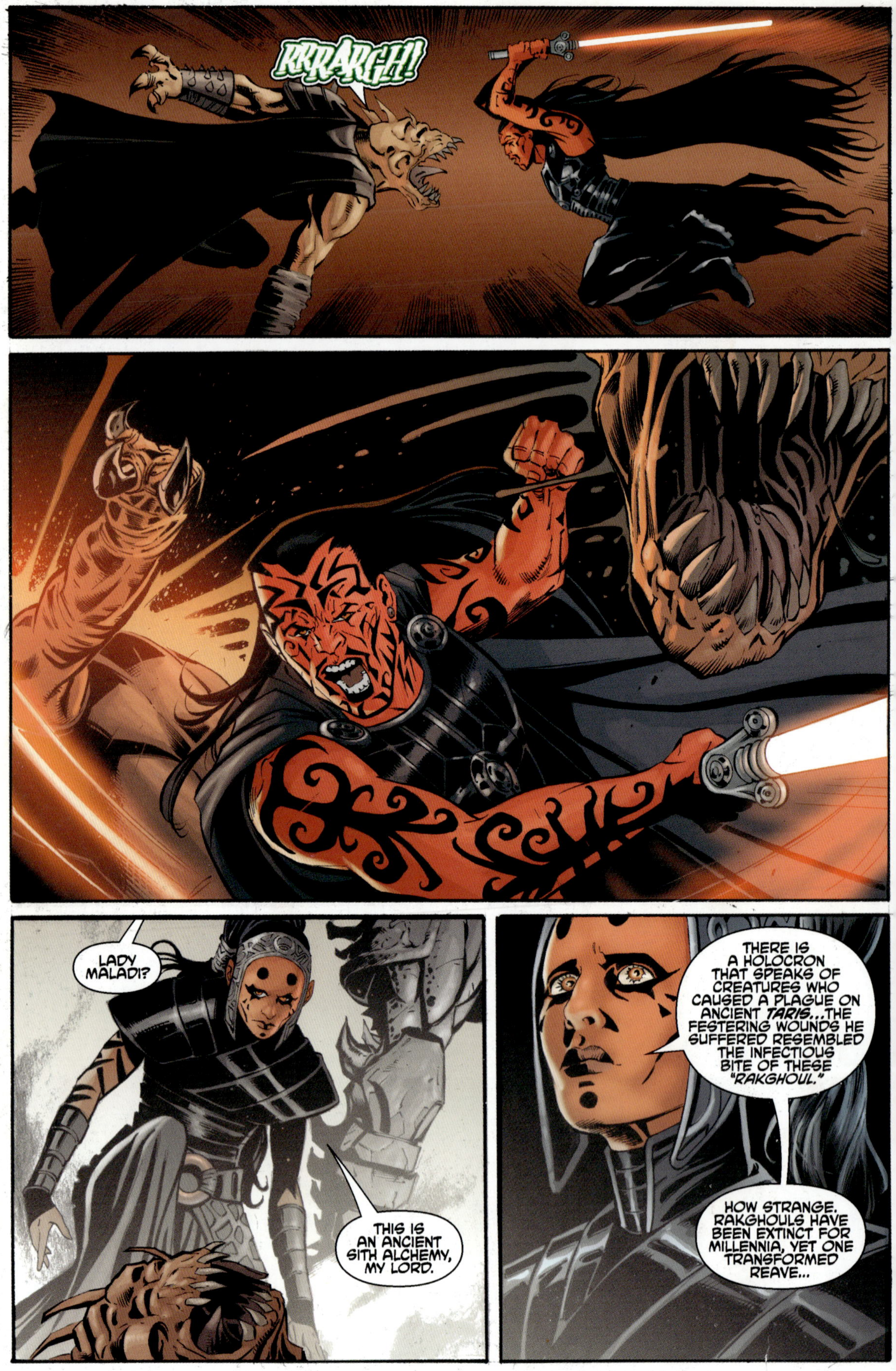

KRRARGH!
LADY MALADI?
THIS IS AN ANCIENT SITH ALCHEMY, MY LORD.
THERE IS A HOLOCRON THAT SPEAKS OF CREATURES WHO CAUSED A PLAGUE ON ANCIENT TARIS...THE FESTERING WOUNDS HE SUFFERED RESEMBLED THE INFECTIOUS BITE OF THESE "RAKGHOUL."
HOW STRANGE. RAKGHOULS HAVE BEEN EXTINCT FOR MILLENNIA, YET ONE TRANSFORMED REAVE...

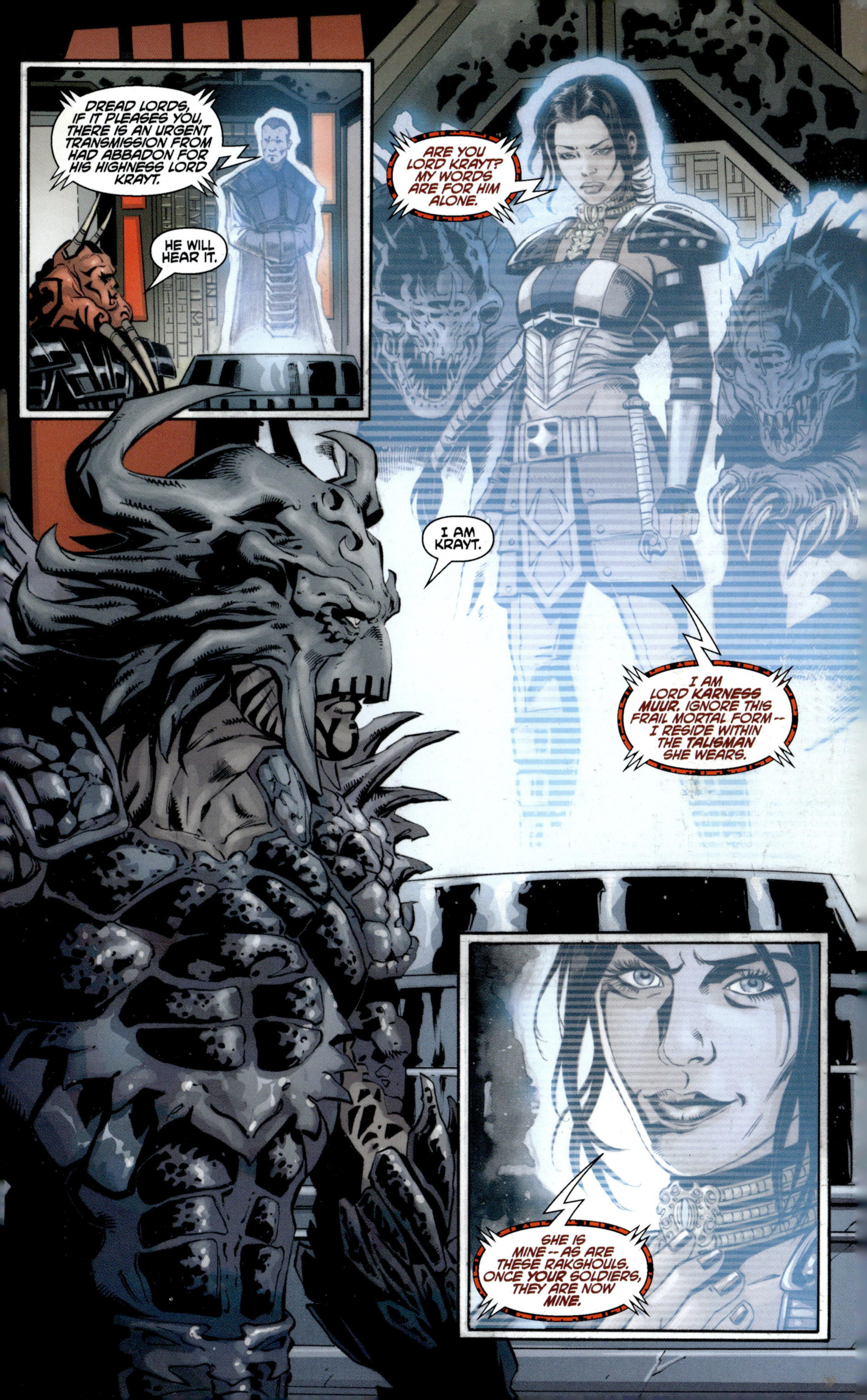
DREAD LORDS, IF IT PLEASES YOU, THERE IS AN URGENT TRANSMISSION FROM HAD ABBADON FOR HIS HIGHNESS LORD KRAYT.
HE WILL HEAR IT.
ARE YOU LORD KRAYT? MY WORDS ARE FOR HIM ALONE.
I AM KRAYT.
I AM LORD KARNESS MUUR. IGNORE THIS FRAIL MORTAL FORM -- I RESIDE WITHIN THE TALISMAN SHE WEARS.
SHE IS MINE -- AS ARE THESE RAKGHOULS. ONCE YOUR SOLDIERS, THEY ARE NOW MINE.

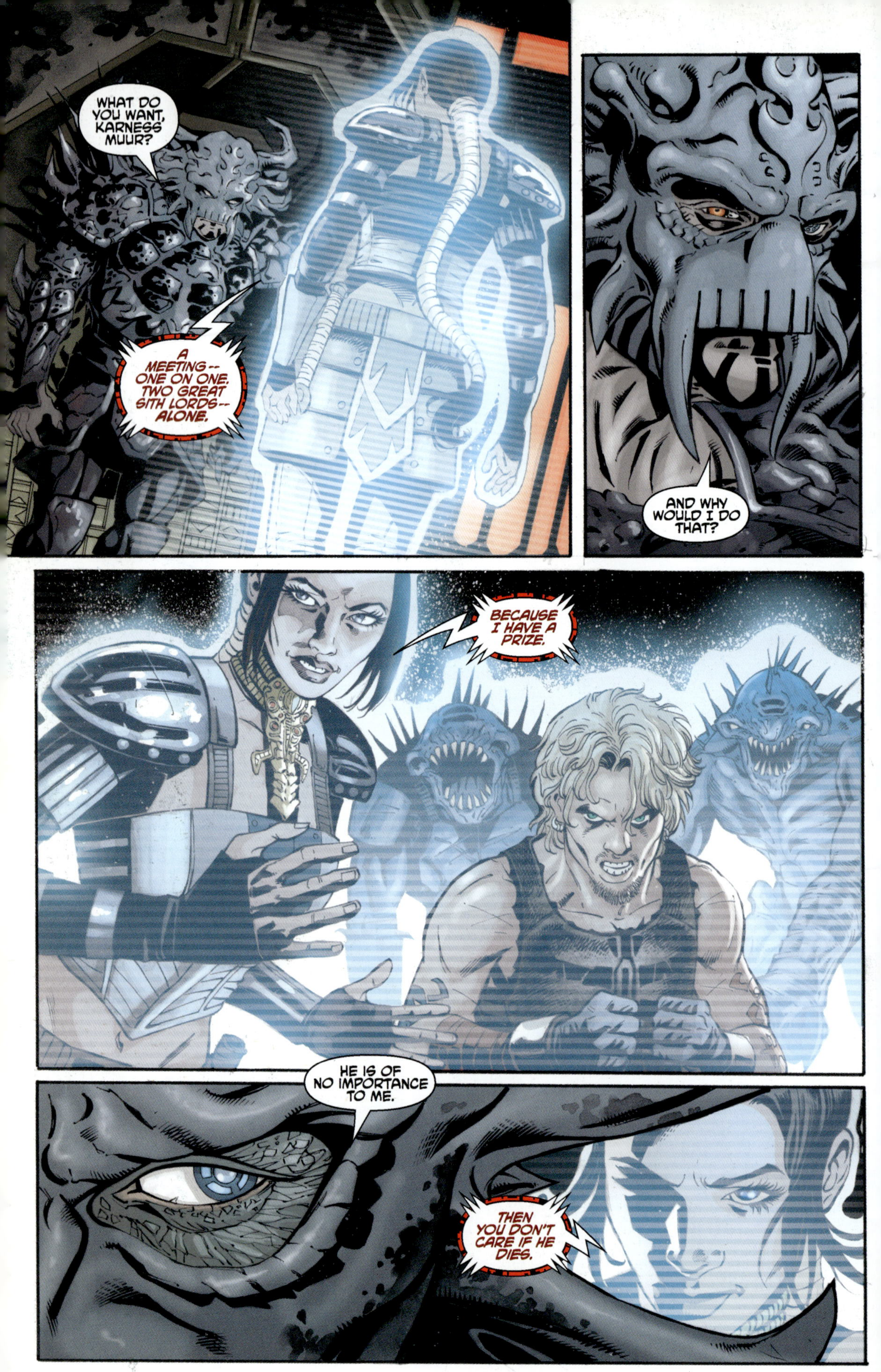
WHAT DO YOU WANT, KARNESS MUUR?
A MEETING-- ONE ON ONE. TWO GREAT SITH LORDS-- ALONE.
AND WHY WOULD I DO THAT?
BECAUSE I HAVE A PRIZE.
HE IS OF NO IMPORTANCE TO ME.
THEN YOU DON'T CARE IF HE DIES.

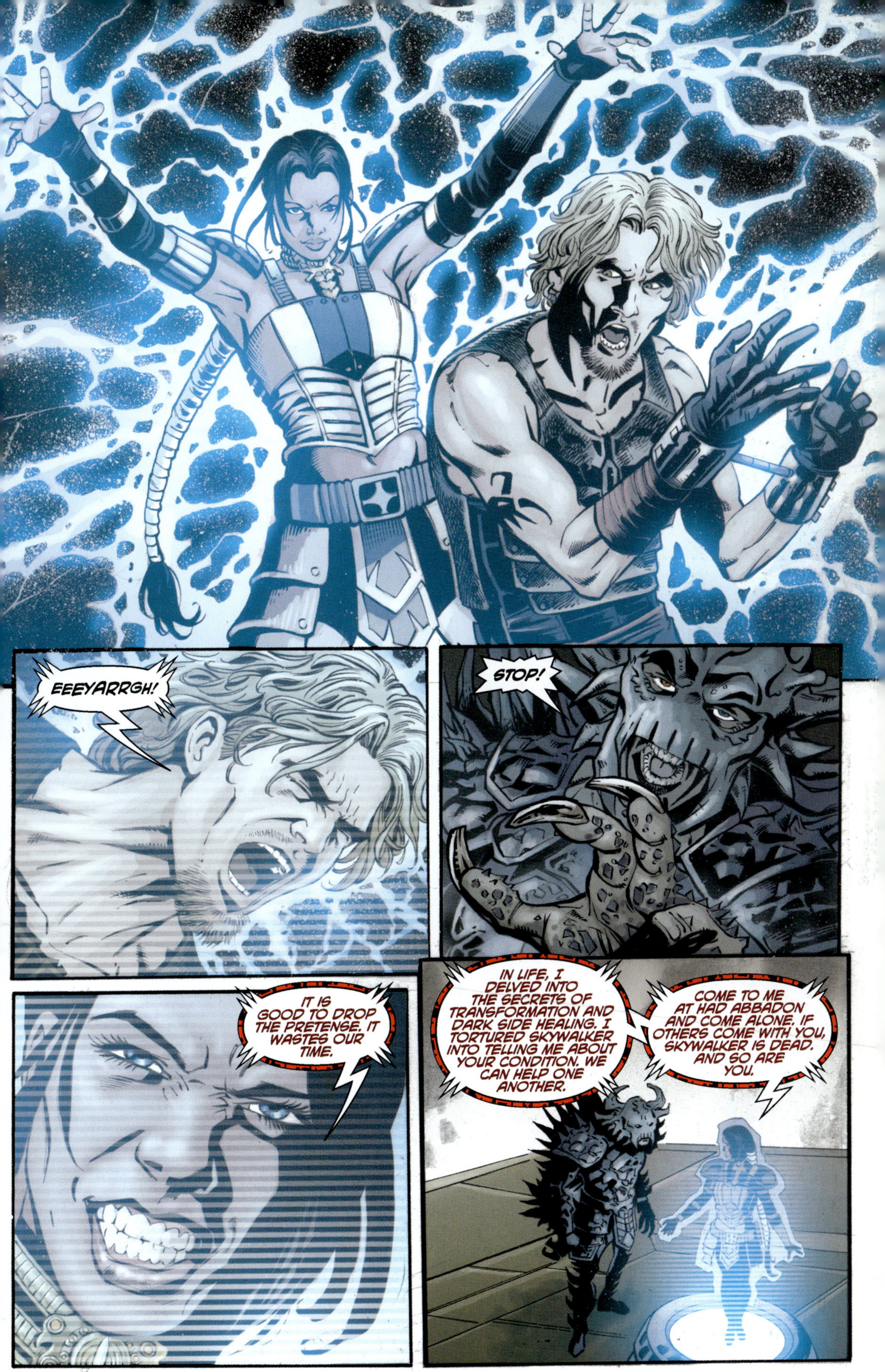
EEEYARRGH!
STOP!
IT IS GOOD TO DROP THE PRETENSE. IT WASTES OUR TIME.
IN LIFE, I DELVED INTO THE SECRETS OF TRANSFORMATION AND DARK SIDE HEALING. I TORTURED SKYWALKER INTO TELLING ME ABOUT YOUR CONDITION. WE CAN HELP ONE ANOTHER.
COME TO ME AT HAD ABBADON AND COME ALONE. IF OTHERS COME WITH YOU, SKYWALKER IS DEAD. AND SO ARE YOU.

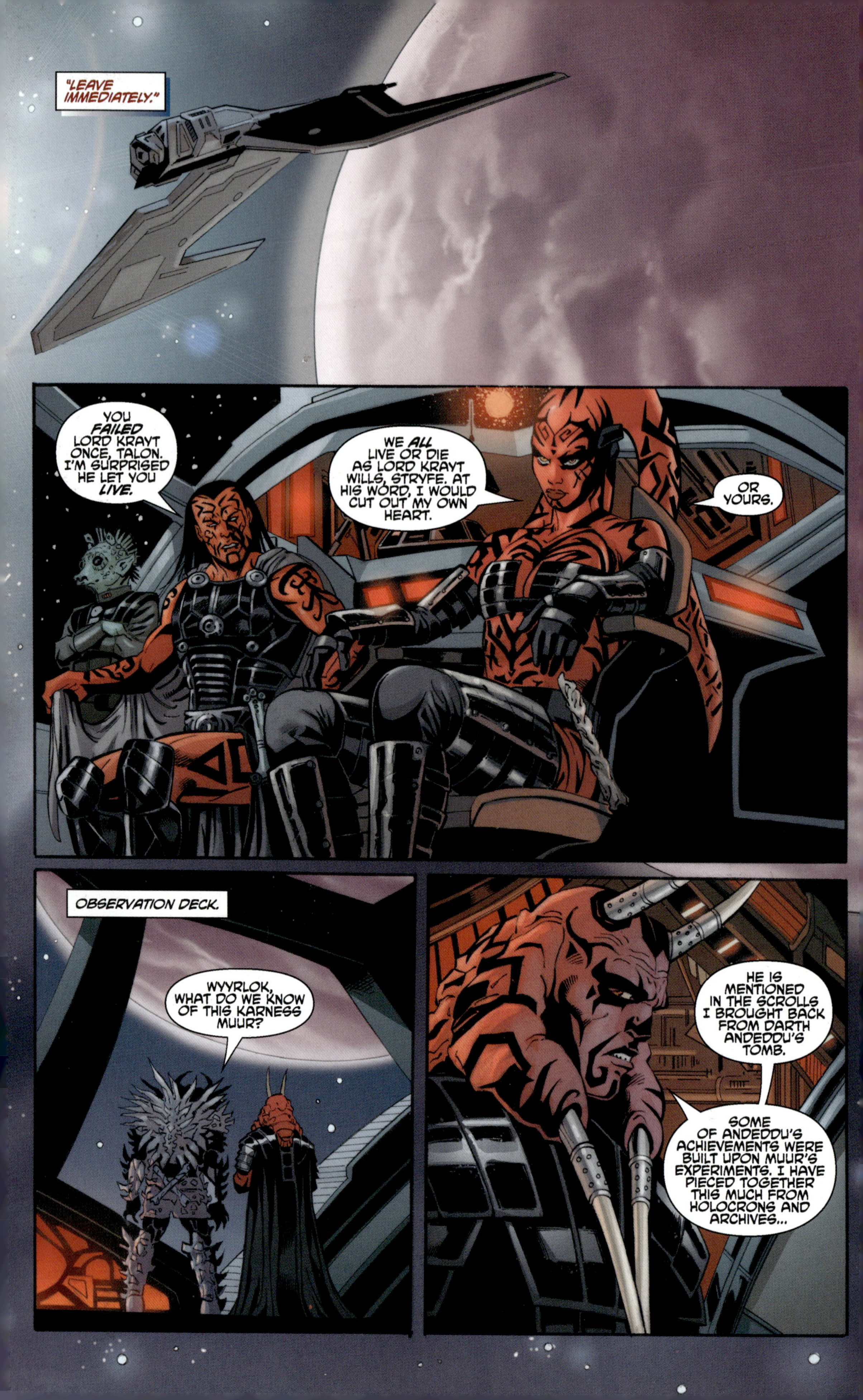
"LEAVE IMMEDIATELY."
YOU FAILED LORD KRAYT ONCE, TALON. I'M SURPRISED HE LET YOU LIVE.
WE ALL LIVE OR DIE AS LORD KRAYT WILLS, STRYFE. AT HIS WORD, I WOULD CUT OUT MY OWN HEART.
OR YOURS.
OBSERVATION DECK.
WYYRLOK, WHAT DO WE KNOW OF THIS KARNESS MUUR?
HE IS MENTIONED IN THE SCROLLS I BROUGHT BACK FROM DARTH ANDEDDU'S TOMB.
SOME OF ANDEDDU'S ACHIEVEMENTS WERE BUILT UPON MUUR'S EXPERIMENTS. I HAVE PIECED TOGETHER THIS MUCH FROM HOLOCRONS AND ARCHIVES...

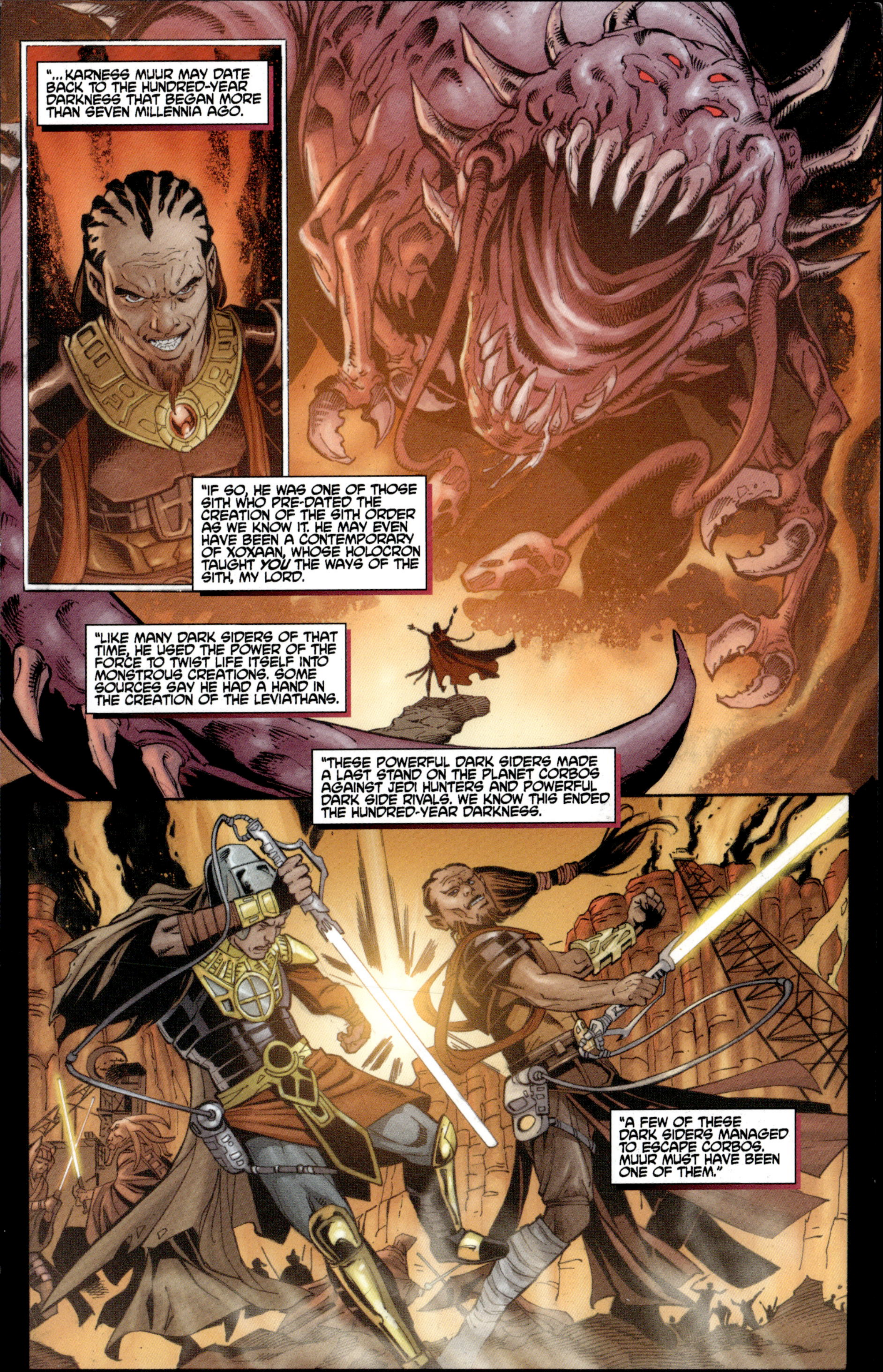
"...KARNESS MUUR MAY DATE BACK TO THE HUNDRED-YEAR DARKNESS THAT BEGAN MORE THAN SEVEN MILLENNIA AGO.
"IF SO, HE WAS ONE OF THOSE SITH WHO PRE-DATED THE CREATION OF THE SITH ORDER AS WE KNOW IT. HE MAY EVEN HAVE BEEN A CONTEMPORARY OF XOXAAN, WHOSE HOLOCRON TAUGHT *YOU* THE WAYS OF THE SITH, MY LORD.
"LIKE MANY DARK SIDERS OF THAT TIME, HE USED THE POWER OF THE FORCE TO TWIST LIFE ITSELF INTO MONSTROUS CREATIONS. SOME SOURCES SAY HE HAD A HAND IN THE CREATION OF THE LEVIATHANS.
"THESE POWERFUL DARK SIDERS MADE A LAST STAND ON THE PLANET CORBOS AGAINST JEDI HUNTERS AND POWERFUL DARK SIDE RIVALS. WE KNOW THIS ENDED THE HUNDRED-YEAR DARKNESS.
"A FEW OF THESE DARK SIDERS MANAGED TO ESCAPE CORBOS. MUUR MUST HAVE BEEN ONE OF THEM."

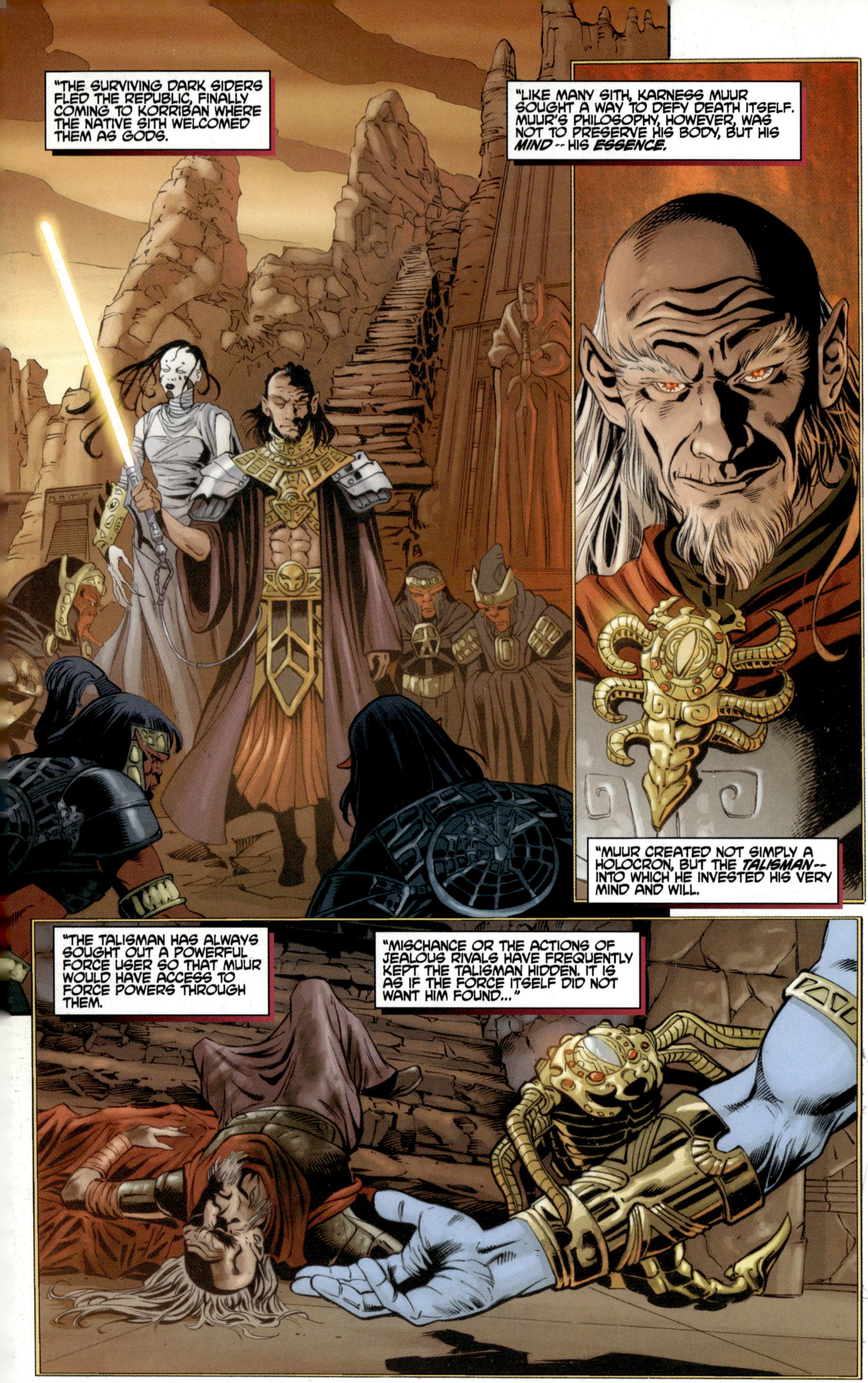
"THE SURVIVING DARK SIDERS FLED THE REPUBLIC, FINALLY COMING TO KORRIBAN WHERE THE NATIVE SITH WELCOMED THEM AS GODS.
"LIKE MANY SITH, KARNESS MUUR SOUGHT A WAY TO DEFY DEATH ITSELF. MUUR'S PHILOSOPHY, HOWEVER, WAS NOT TO PRESERVE HIS BODY, BUT HIS *MIND* -- HIS *ESSENCE.*
"MUUR CREATED NOT SIMPLY A HOLOCRON, BUT THE *TALISMAN*-- INTO WHICH HE INVESTED HIS VERY MIND AND WILL.
"THE TALISMAN HAS ALWAYS SOUGHT OUT A POWERFUL FORCE USER SO THAT MUUR WOULD HAVE ACCESS TO FORCE POWERS THROUGH THEM.
"MISCHANCE OR THE ACTIONS OF JEALOUS RIVALS HAVE FREQUENTLY KEPT THE TALISMAN HIDDEN. IT IS AS IF THE FORCE ITSELF DID NOT WANT HIM FOUND..."

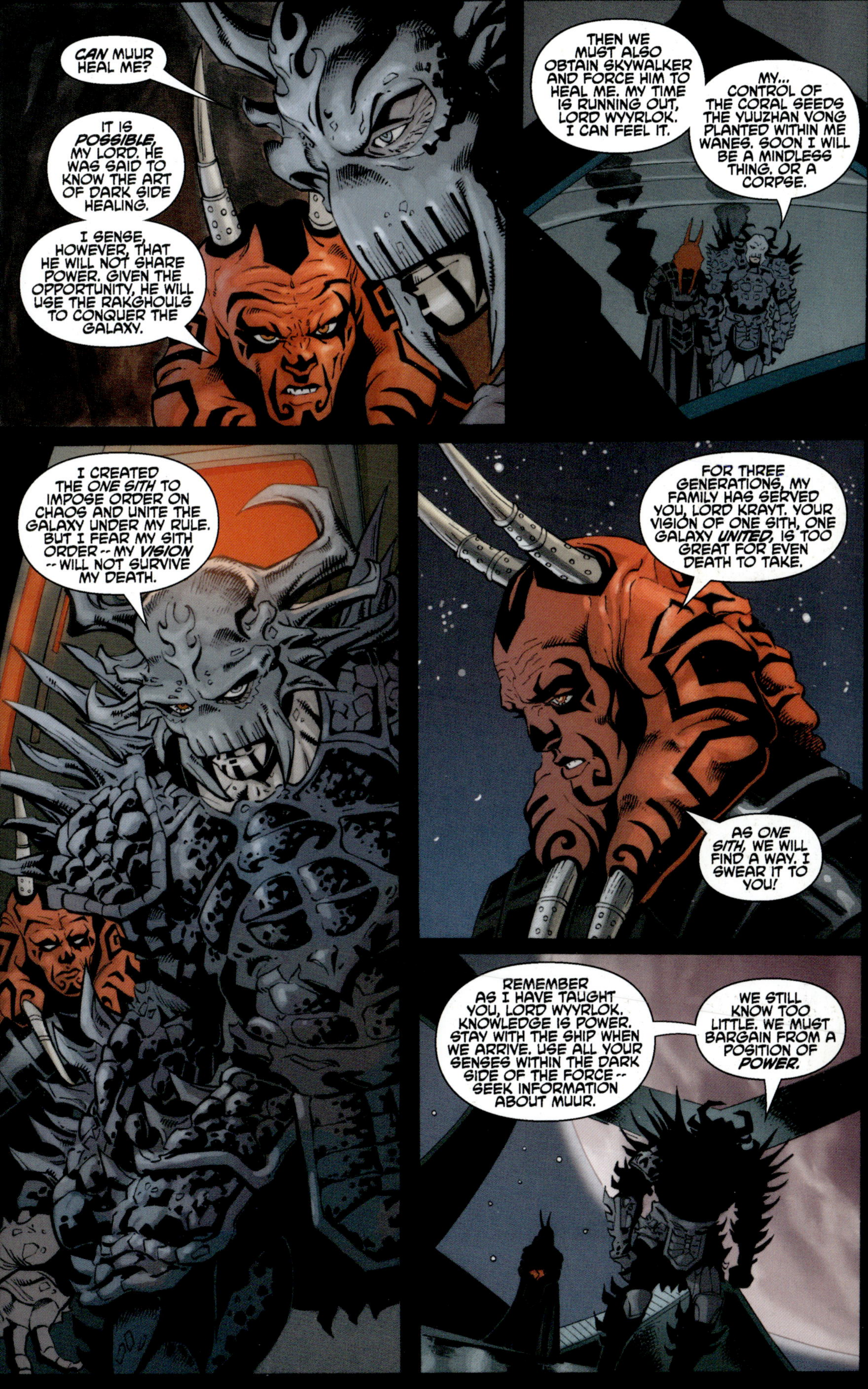
CAN MUUR HEAL ME?
IT IS POSSIBLE, MY LORD. HE WAS SAID TO KNOW THE ART OF DARK SIDE HEALING.
I SENSE, HOWEVER, THAT HE WILL NOT SHARE POWER. GIVEN THE OPPORTUNITY, HE WILL USE THE RAKGHOULS TO CONQUER THE GALAXY.
THEN WE MUST ALSO OBTAIN SKYWALKER AND FORCE HIM TO HEAL ME. MY TIME IS RUNNING OUT, LORD WYYRLOK. I CAN FEEL IT.
MY... CONTROL OF THE CORAL SEEDS THE YUUZHAN VONG PLANTED WITHIN ME WANES. SOON I WILL BE A MINDLESS THING, OR A CORPSE.
I CREATED THE ONE SITH TO IMPOSE ORDER ON CHAOS AND UNITE THE GALAXY UNDER MY RULE. BUT I FEAR MY SITH ORDER -- MY VISION -- WILL NOT SURVIVE MY DEATH.
FOR THREE GENERATIONS, MY FAMILY HAS SERVED YOU, LORD KRAYT. YOUR VISION OF ONE SITH, ONE GALAXY UNITED, IS TOO GREAT FOR EVEN DEATH TO TAKE.
AS ONE SITH, WE WILL FIND A WAY. I SWEAR IT TO YOU!
REMEMBER AS I HAVE TAUGHT YOU, LORD WYYRLOK. KNOWLEDGE IS POWER. STAY WITH THE SHIP WHEN WE ARRIVE. USE ALL YOUR SENSES WITHIN THE DARK SIDE OF THE FORCE -- SEEK INFORMATION ABOUT MUUR.
WE STILL KNOW TOO LITTLE. WE MUST BARGAIN FROM A POSITION OF POWER.

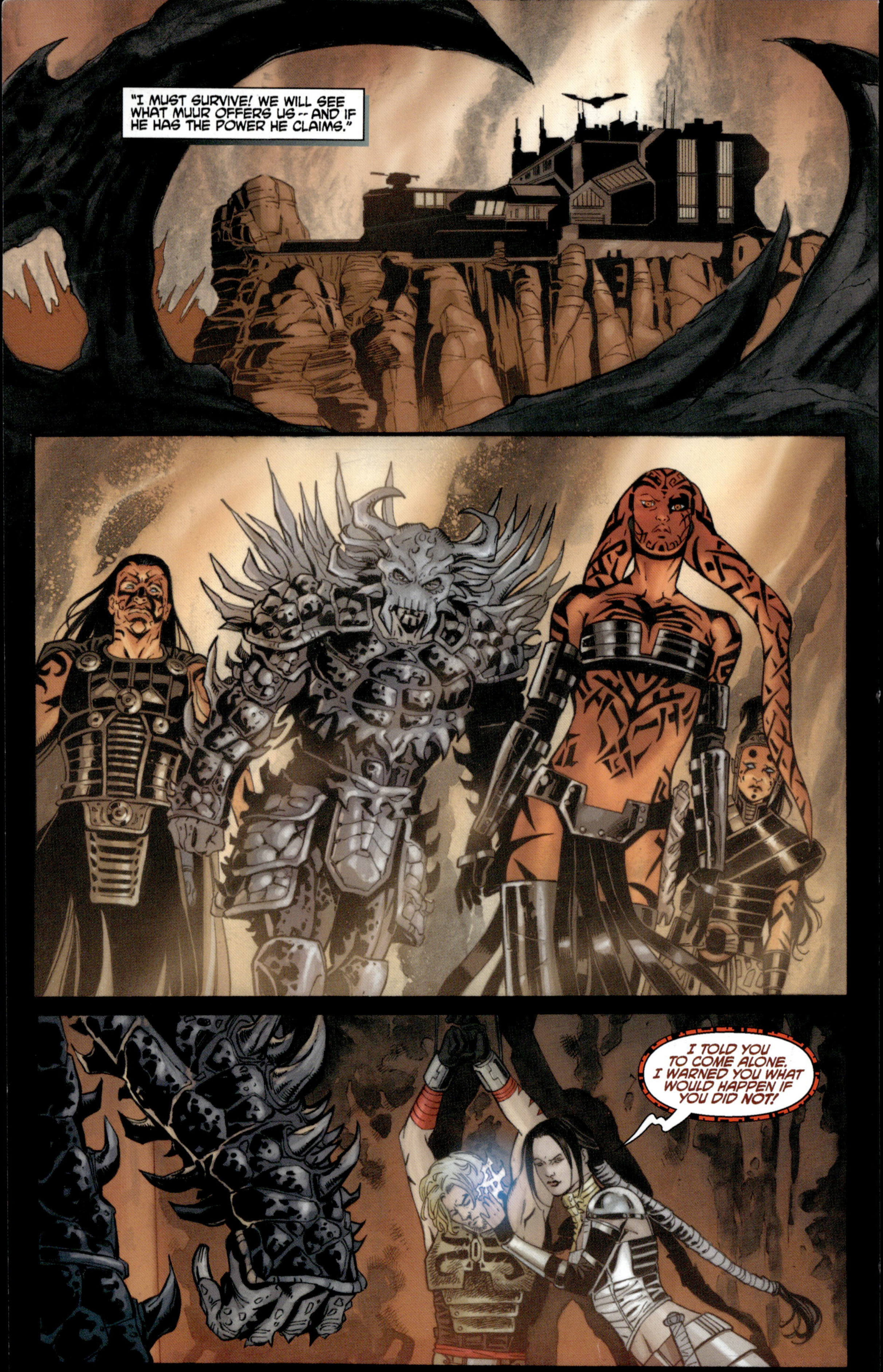
"I MUST SURVIVE! WE WILL SEE WHAT MUUR OFFERS US -- AND IF HE HAS THE POWER HE CLAIMS."
I TOLD YOU TO COME ALONE. I WARNED YOU WHAT WOULD HAPPEN IF YOU DID NOT!

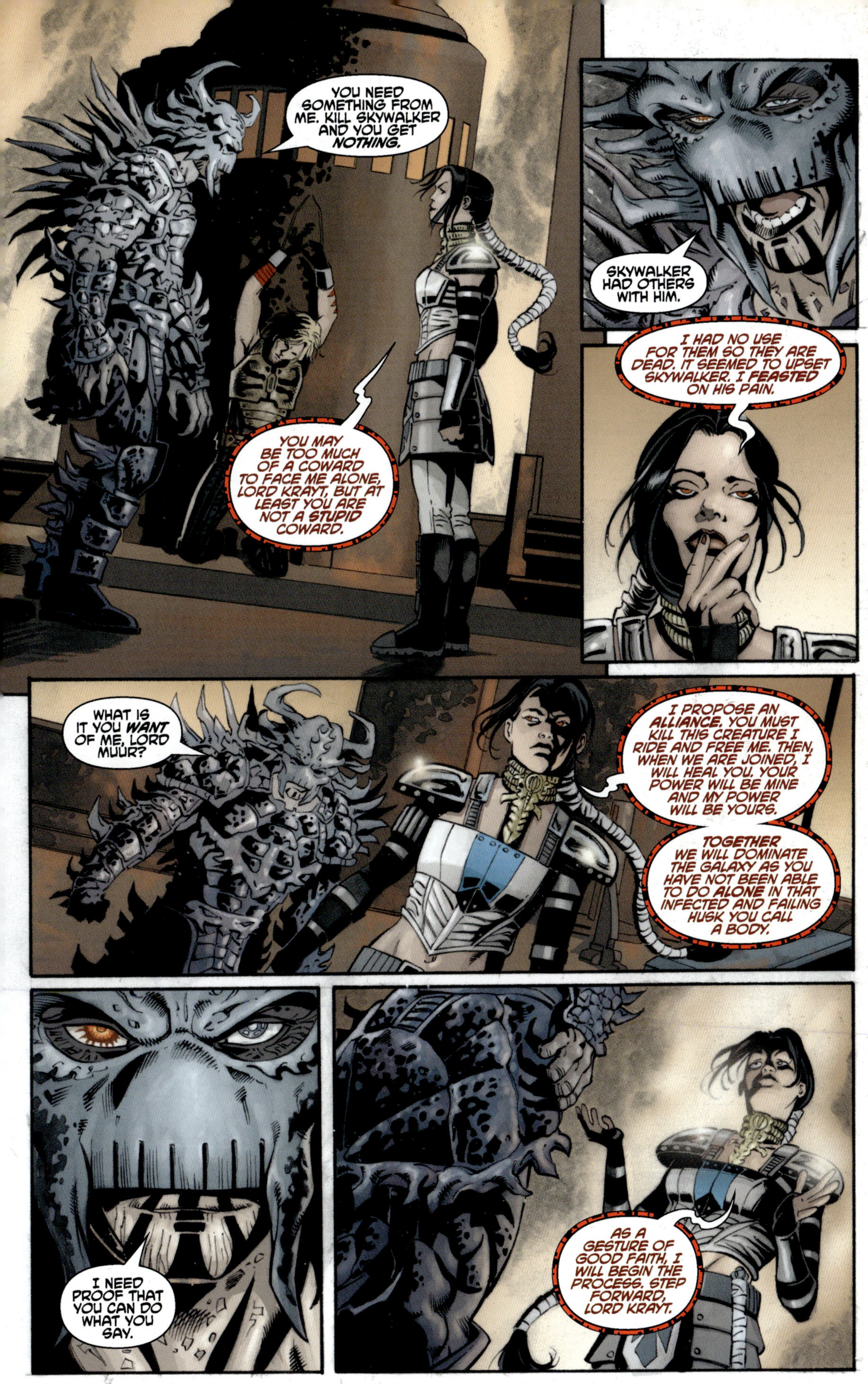

YOU NEED SOMETHING FROM ME. KILL SKYWALKER AND YOU GET NOTHING.
YOU MAY BE TOO MUCH OF A COWARD TO FACE ME ALONE, LORD KRAYT, BUT AT LEAST YOU ARE NOT A STUPID COWARD.
SKYWALKER HAD OTHERS WITH HIM.
I HAD NO USE FOR THEM SO THEY ARE DEAD. IT SEEMED TO UPSET SKYWALKER. I FEASTED ON HIS PAIN.
WHAT IS IT YOU WANT OF ME, LORD MUUR?
I PROPOSE AN ALLIANCE. YOU MUST KILL THIS CREATURE I RIDE AND FREE ME. THEN, WHEN WE ARE JOINED, I WILL HEAL YOU. YOUR POWER WILL BE MINE AND MY POWER WILL BE YOURS.
TOGETHER WE WILL DOMINATE THE GALAXY AS YOU HAVE NOT BEEN ABLE TO DO ALONE IN THAT INFECTED AND FAILING HUSK YOU CALL A BODY.
I NEED PROOF THAT YOU CAN DO WHAT YOU SAY.
AS A GESTURE OF GOOD FAITH, I WILL BEGIN THE PROCESS. STEP FORWARD, LORD KRAYT.

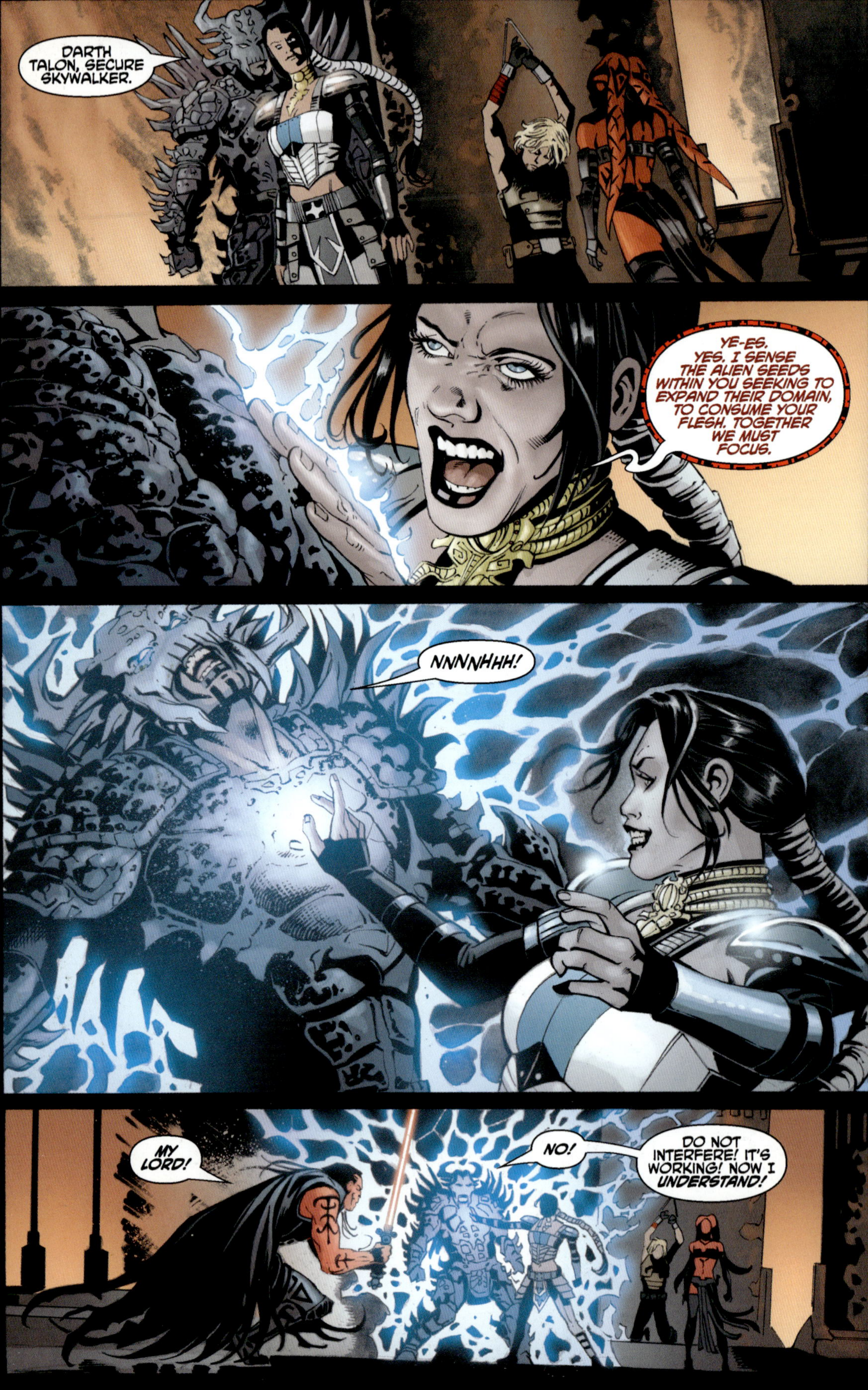
DARTH TALON, SECURE SKYWALKER.
YE-ES. YES. I SENSE THE ALIEN SEEDS WITHIN YOU SEEKING TO EXPAND THEIR DOMAIN, TO CONSUME YOUR FLESH. TOGETHER WE MUST FOCUS.
NNNNHHH!
MY LORD!
NO!
DO NOT INTERFERE! IT'S WORKING! NOW I UNDERSTAND!

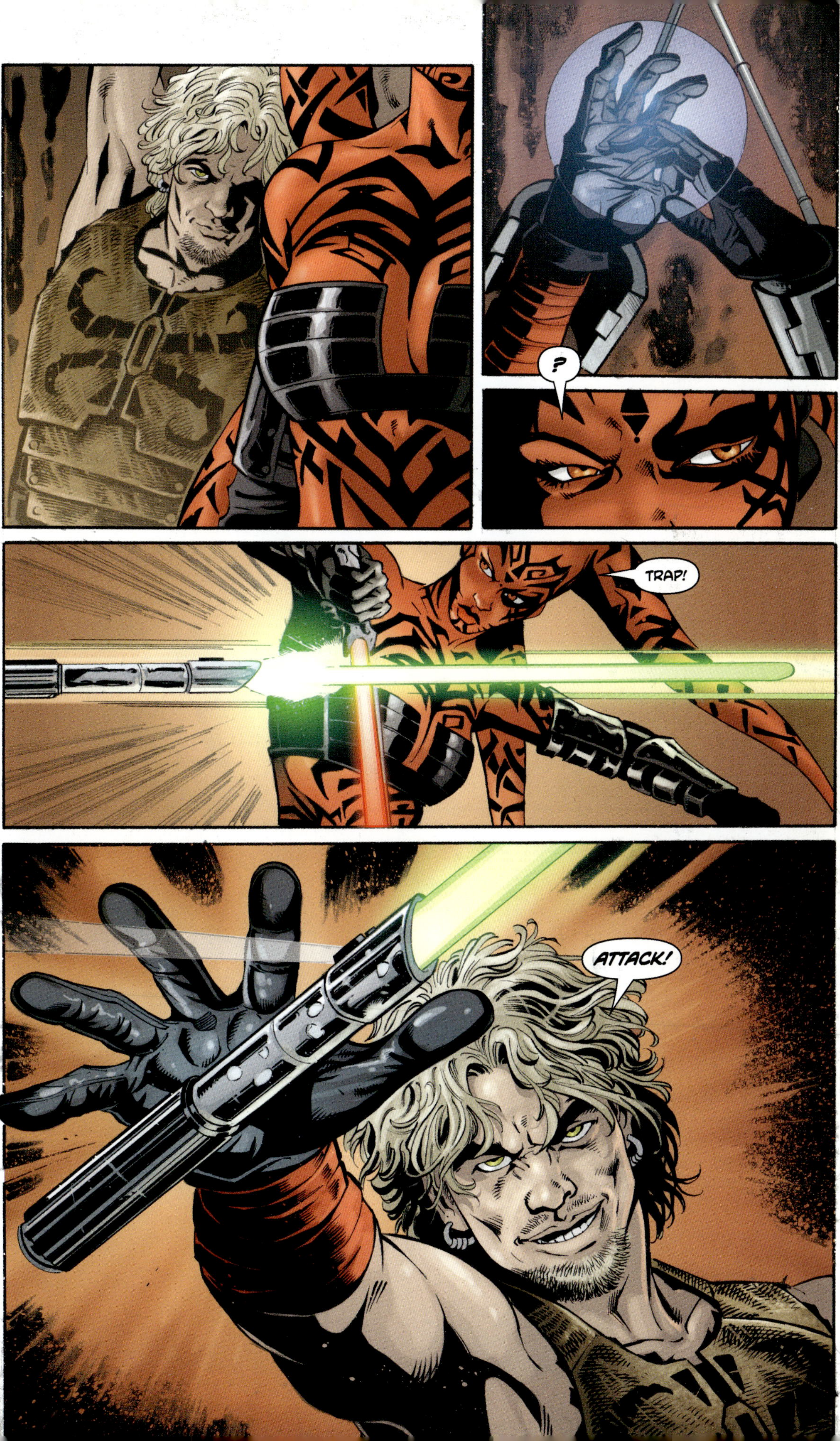
?
TRAP!
ATTACK!

YEAAAHHHGG!

CONTROL IS MINE!

DIE SITH!

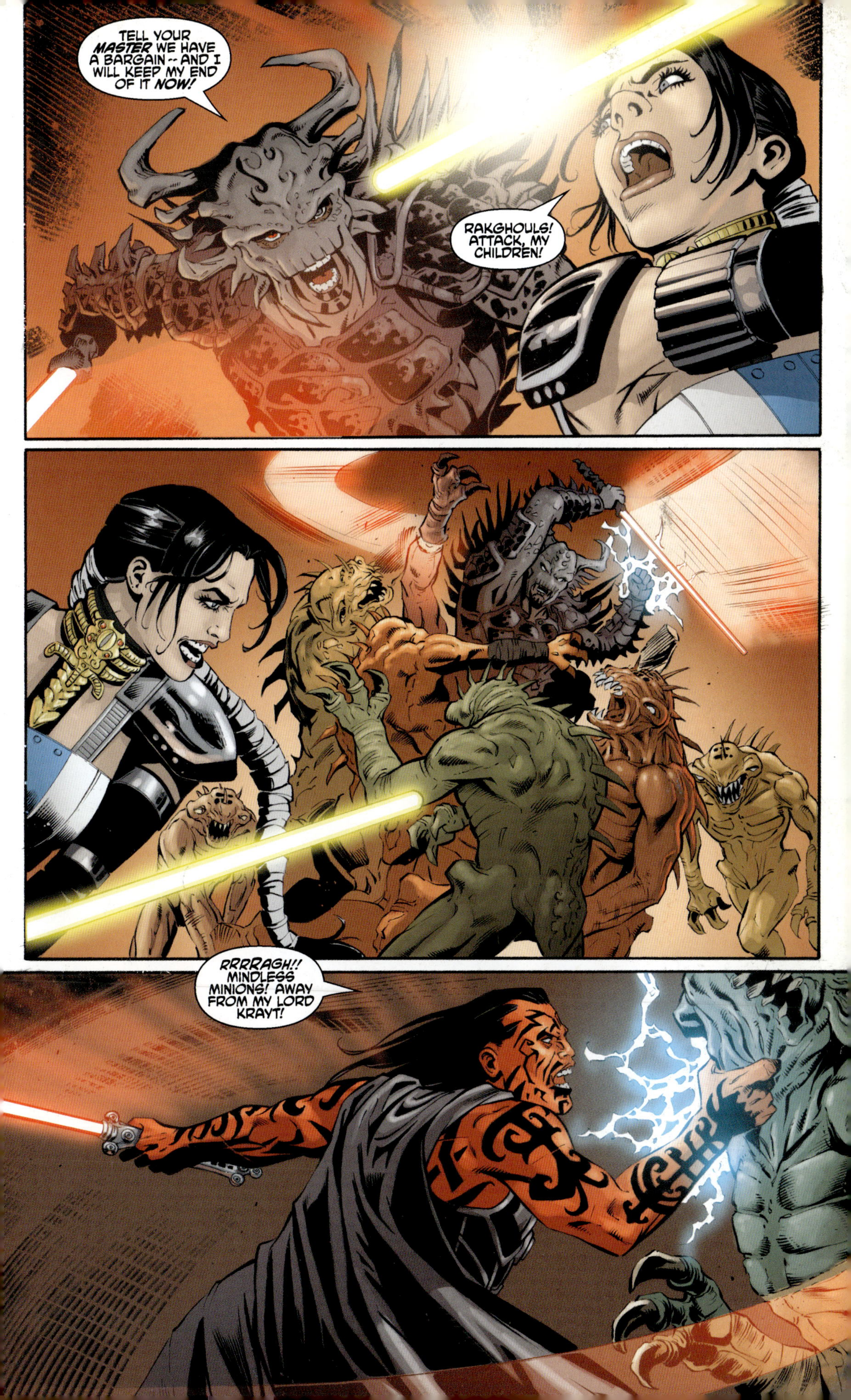
TELL YOUR MASTER WE HAVE A BARGAIN -- AND I WILL KEEP MY END OF IT NOW!
RAKGHOULS! ATTACK, MY CHILDREN!
RRRRAGH!! MINDLESS MINIONS! AWAY FROM MY LORD KRAYT!

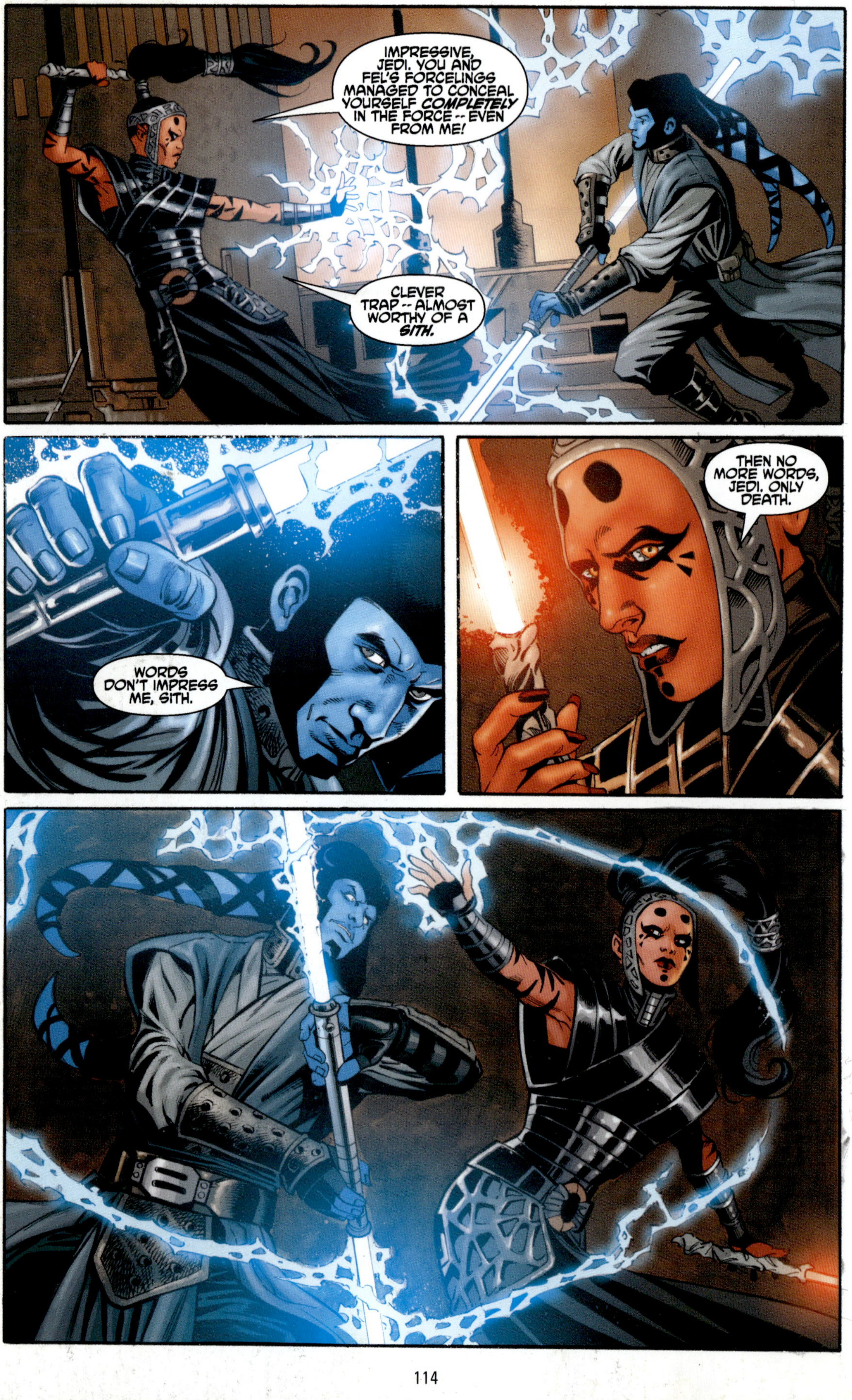
IMPRESSIVE, JEDI. YOU AND FEL'S FORCELINGS MANAGED TO CONCEAL YOURSELF *COMPLETELY* IN THE FORCE -- EVEN FROM ME!
CLEVER TRAP -- ALMOST WORTHY OF A *SITH.*
WORDS DON'T IMPRESS ME, SITH.
THEN NO MORE WORDS, JEDI. ONLY DEATH.

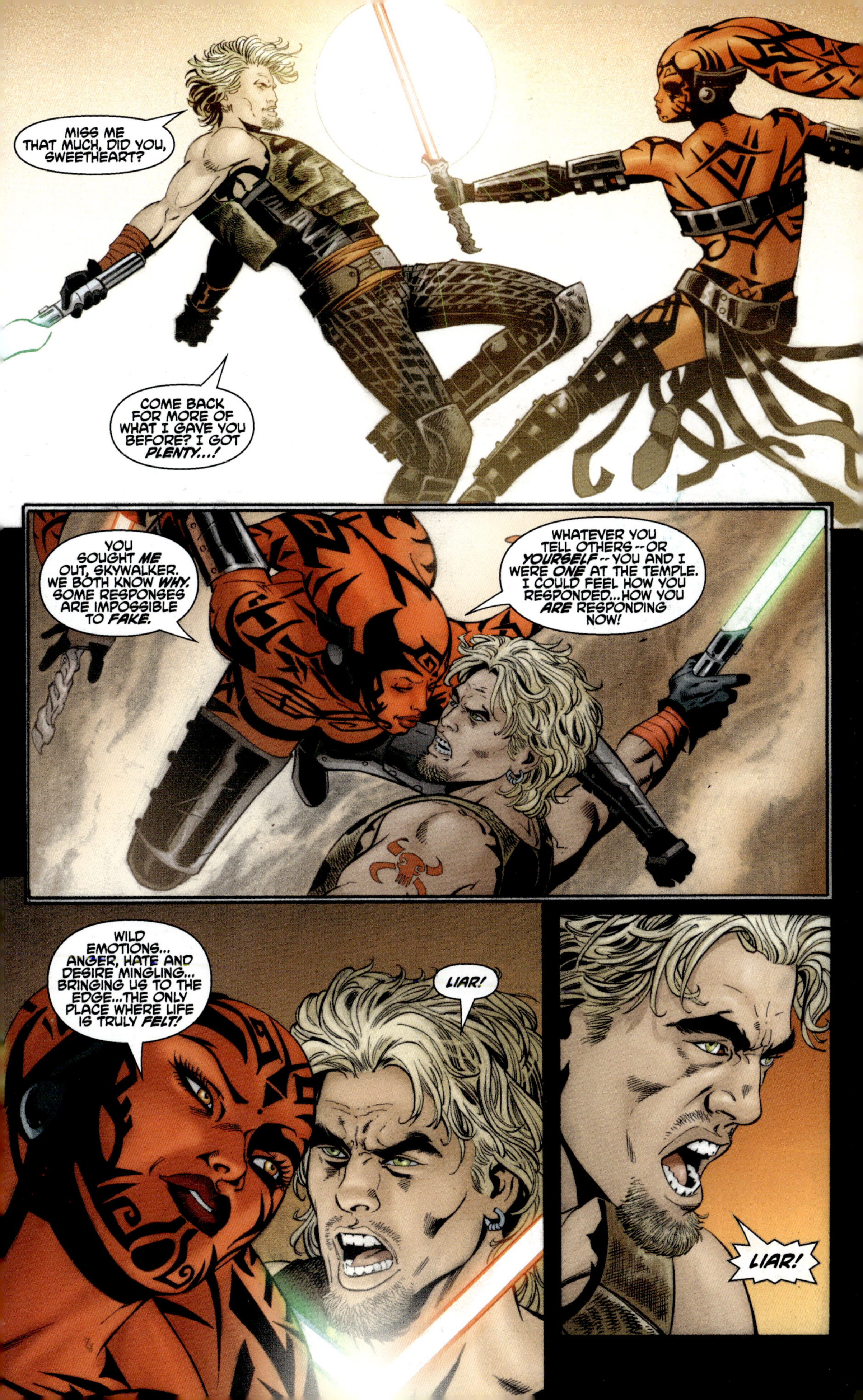
MISS ME THAT MUCH, DID YOU, SWEETHEART?
COME BACK FOR MORE OF WHAT I GAVE YOU BEFORE? I GOT PLENTY...!
YOU SOUGHT ME OUT, SKYWALKER. WE BOTH KNOW WHY. SOME RESPONSES ARE IMPOSSIBLE TO FAKE.
WHATEVER YOU TELL OTHERS--OR YOURSELF--YOU AND I WERE ONE AT THE TEMPLE. I COULD FEEL HOW YOU RESPONDED...HOW YOU ARE RESPONDING NOW!
WILD EMOTIONS... ANGER, HATE AND DESIRE MINGLING... BRINGING US TO THE EDGE...THE ONLY PLACE WHERE LIFE IS TRULY FELT!
LIAR!
LIAR!

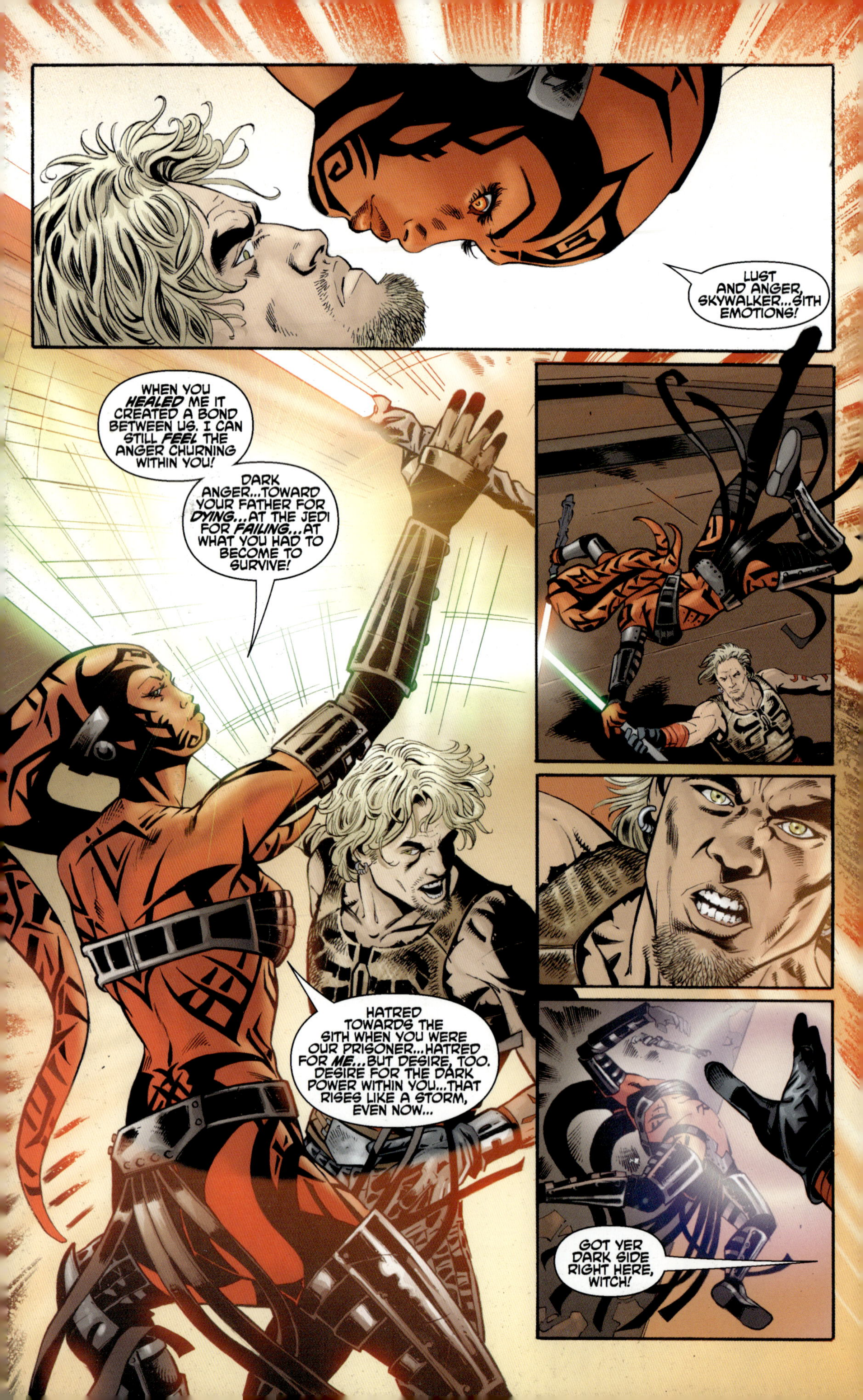
LUST AND ANGER, SKYWALKER...SITH EMOTIONS!
WHEN YOU HEALED ME IT CREATED A BOND BETWEEN US. I CAN STILL FEEL THE ANGER CHURNING WITHIN YOU!
DARK ANGER...TOWARD YOUR FATHER FOR DYING...AT THE JEDI FOR FAILING...AT WHAT YOU HAD TO BECOME TO SURVIVE!
HATRED TOWARDS THE SITH WHEN YOU WERE OUR PRISONER...HATRED FOR ME...BUT DESIRE, TOO. DESIRE FOR THE DARK POWER WITHIN YOU...THAT RISES LIKE A STORM, EVEN NOW...
GOT YER DARK SIDE RIGHT HERE, WITCH!

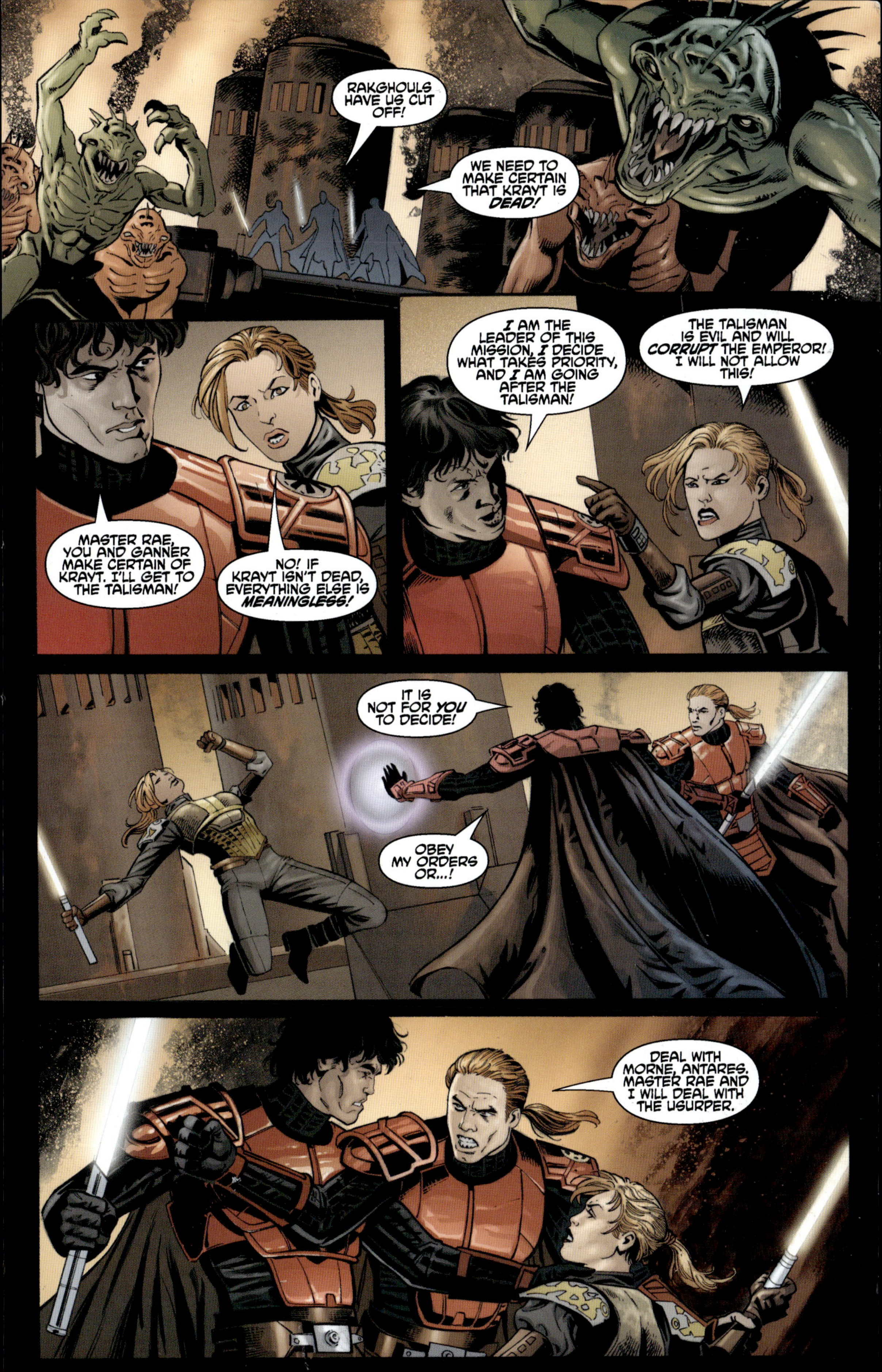
RAKGHOULS HAVE US CUT OFF!
WE NEED TO MAKE CERTAIN THAT KRAYT IS DEAD!
MASTER RAE, YOU AND GANNER MAKE CERTAIN OF KRAYT. I'LL GET TO THE TALISMAN!
NO! IF KRAYT ISN'T DEAD, EVERYTHING ELSE IS MEANINGLESS!
I AM THE LEADER OF THIS MISSION, I DECIDE WHAT TAKES PRIORITY, AND I AM GOING AFTER THE TALISMAN!
THE TALISMAN IS EVIL AND WILL CORRUPT THE EMPEROR! I WILL NOT ALLOW THIS!
IT IS NOT FOR YOU TO DECIDE!
OBEY MY ORDERS OR...!
DEAL WITH MORNE, ANTARES. MASTER RAE AND I WILL DEAL WITH THE USURPER.

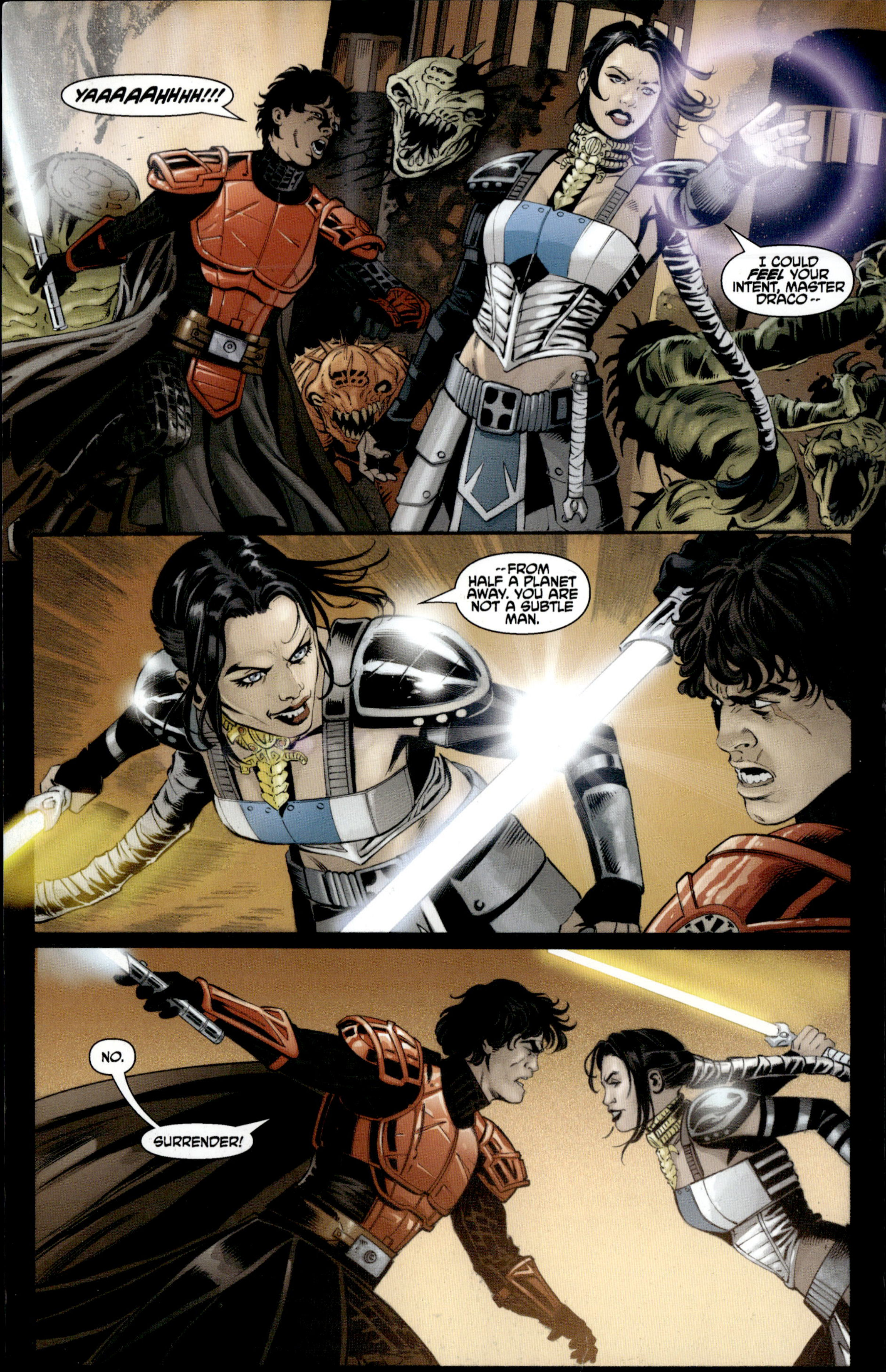
YAAAAAHHHH!!!
I COULD FEEL YOUR INTENT, MASTER DRACO--
--FROM HALF A PLANET AWAY. YOU ARE NOT A SUBTLE MAN.
NO.
SURRENDER!

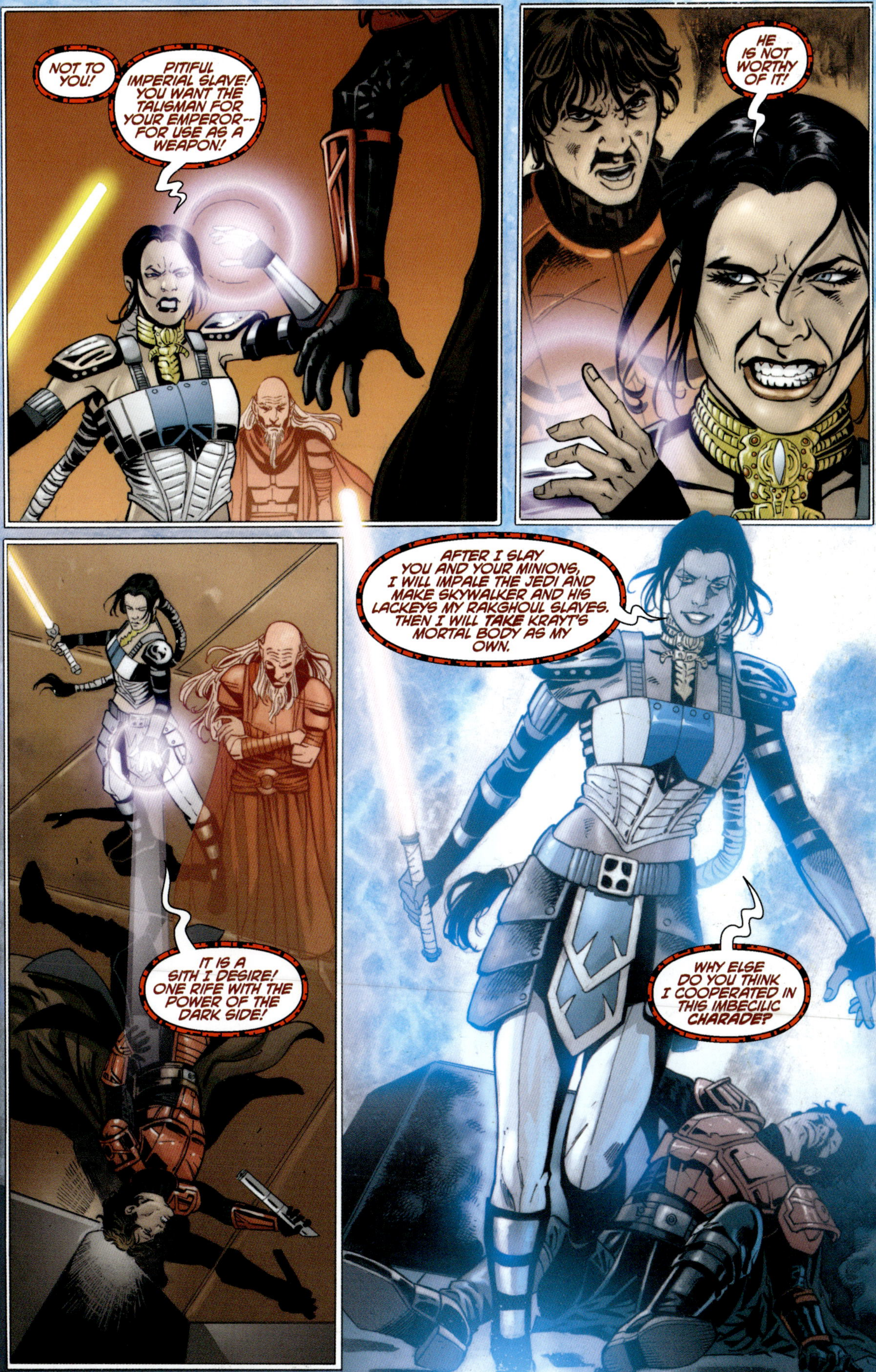
NOT TO YOU!
PITIFUL IMPERIAL SLAVE! YOU WANT THE TALISMAN FOR YOUR EMPEROR-- FOR USE AS A WEAPON!
HE IS NOT WORTHY OF IT!
IT IS A SITH I DESIRE! ONE RIFE WITH THE POWER OF THE DARK SIDE!
AFTER I SLAY YOU AND YOUR MINIONS, I WILL IMPALE THE JEDI AND MAKE SKYWALKER AND HIS LACKEYS MY RAKGHOUL SLAVES. THEN I WILL TAKE KRAYT'S MORTAL BODY AS MY OWN.
WHY ELSE DO YOU THINK I COOPERATED IN THIS IMBECILIC CHARADE?

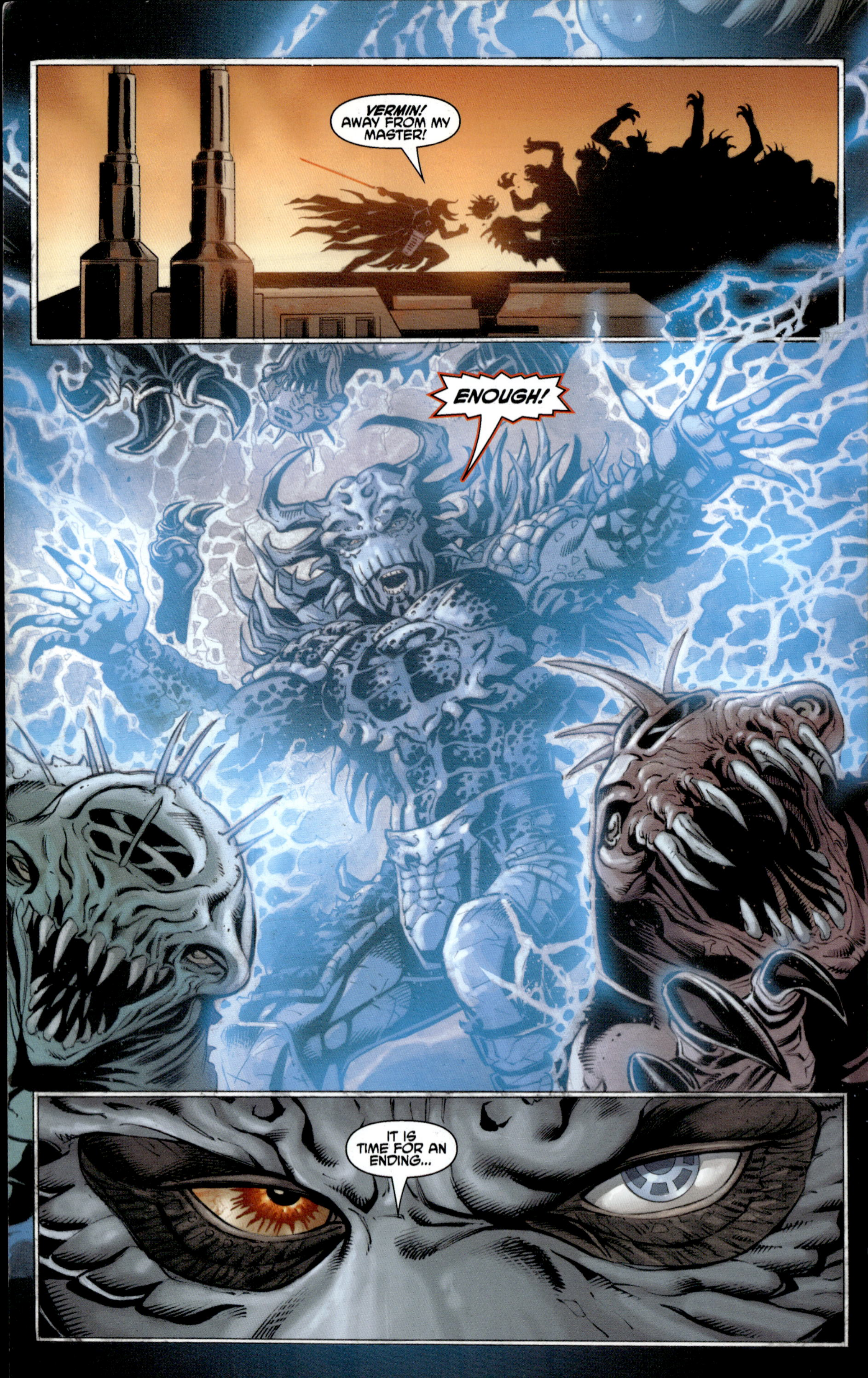
VERMIN! AWAY FROM MY MASTER!
ENOUGH!
IT IS TIME FOR AN ENDING...

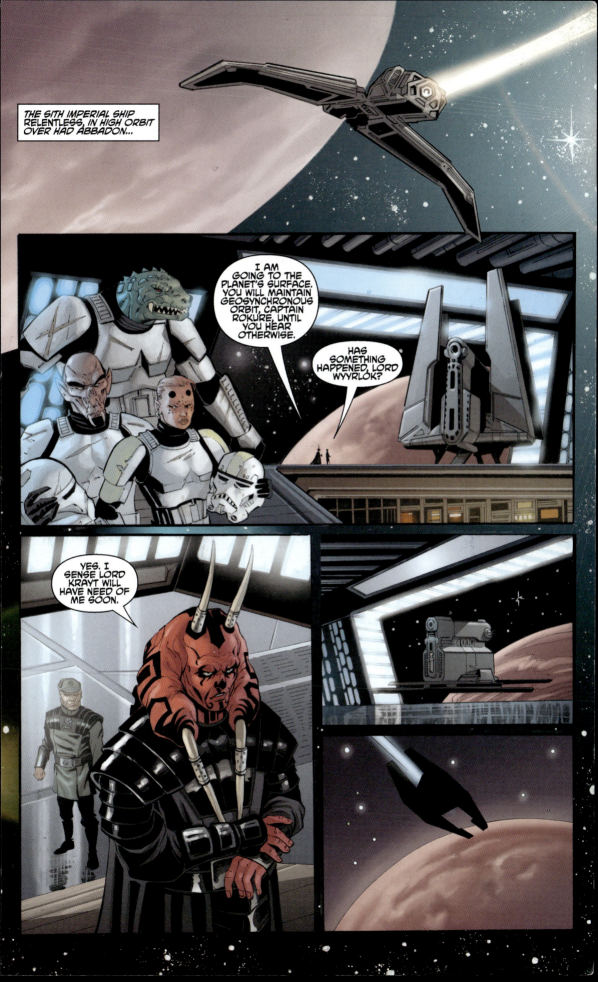

THE SITH IMPERIAL SHIP RELENTLESS, IN HIGH ORBIT OVER HAD ABBADON...

I AM GOING TO THE PLANET'S SURFACE. YOU WILL MAINTAIN GEOSYNCHRONOUS ORBIT, CAPTAIN ROKURE, UNTIL YOU HEAR OTHERWISE.

HAS SOMETHING HAPPENED, LORD WYYRLOK?

YES. I SENSE LORD KRAYT WILL HAVE NEED OF ME SOON.

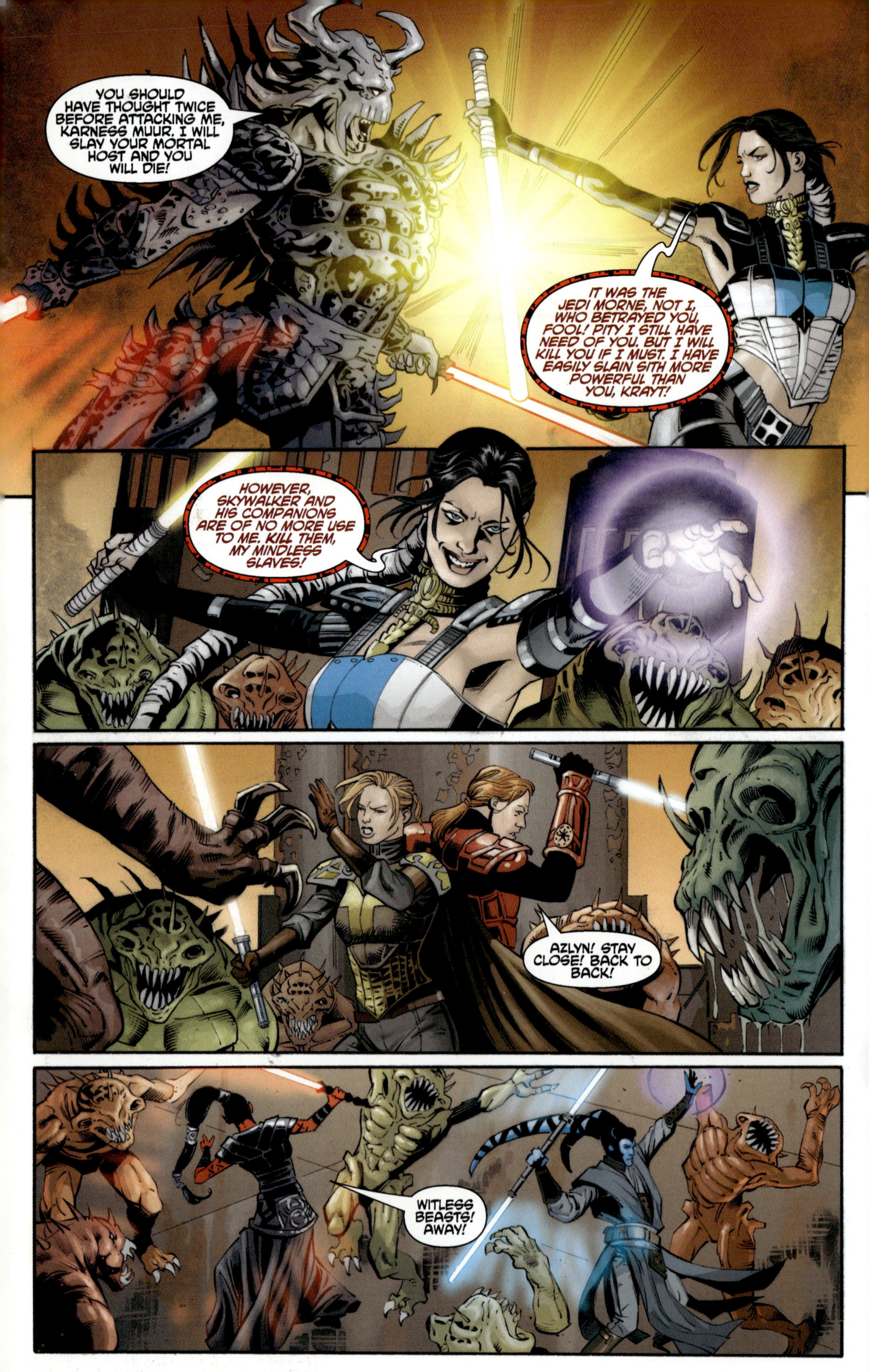
YOU SHOULD HAVE THOUGHT TWICE BEFORE ATTACKING ME, KARNESS MUUR. I WILL SLAY YOUR MORTAL HOST AND YOU WILL DIE!
IT WAS THE JEDI MORNE, NOT I, WHO BETRAYED YOU, FOOL! PITY I STILL HAVE NEED OF YOU. BUT I WILL KILL YOU IF I MUST. I HAVE EASILY SLAIN SITH MORE POWERFUL THAN YOU, KRAYT!
HOWEVER, SKYWALKER AND HIS COMPANIONS ARE OF NO MORE USE TO ME. KILL THEM, MY MINDLESS SLAVES!
AZLYN! STAY CLOSE! BACK TO BACK!
WITLESS BEASTS! AWAY!

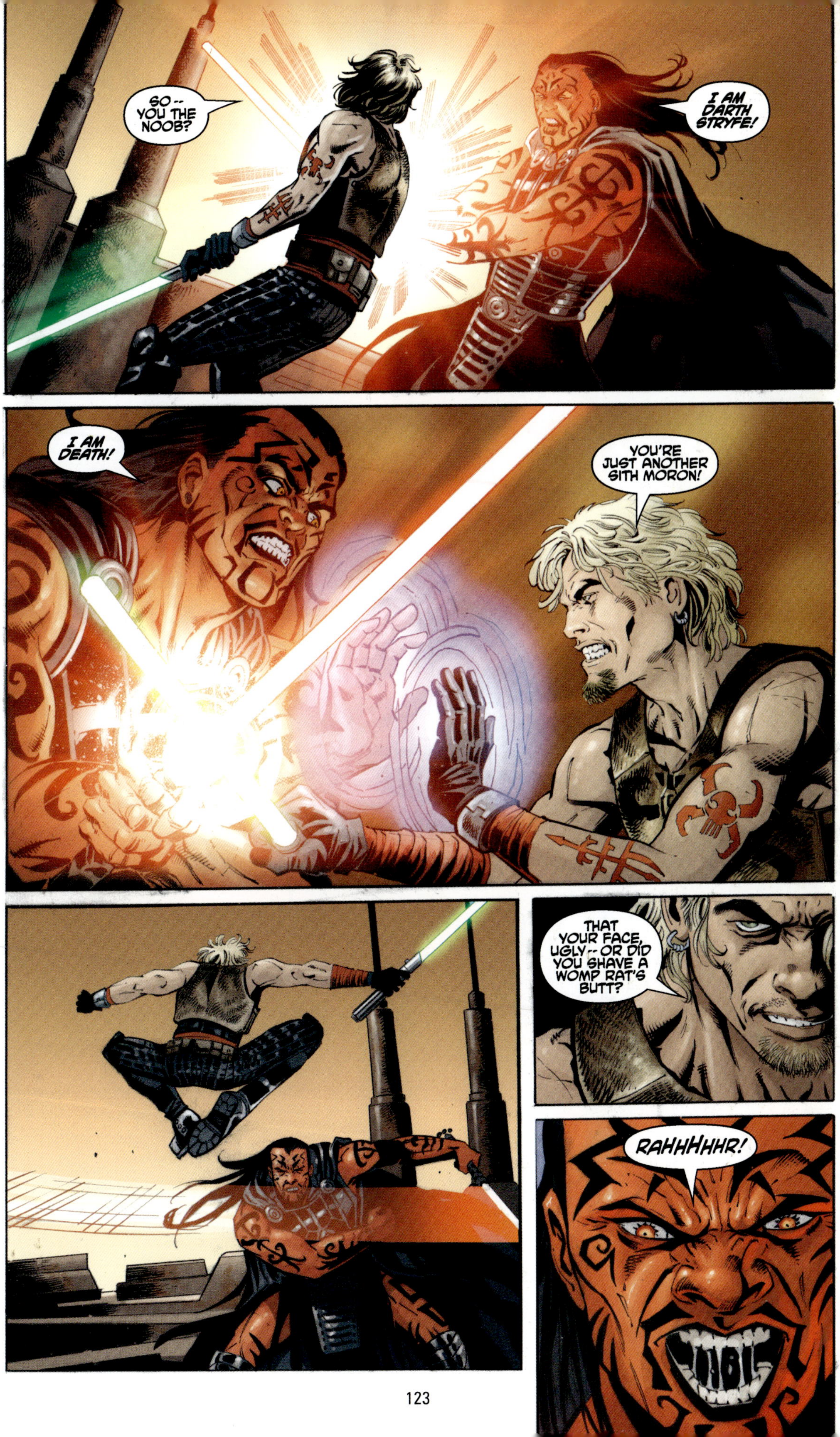
SO-- YOU THE NOOB?
I AM DARTH STRYFE!
I AM DEATH!
YOU'RE JUST ANOTHER SITH MORON!
THAT YOUR FACE, UGLY--OR DID YOU SHAVE A WOMP RAT'S BUTT?
RAHHHHHR!

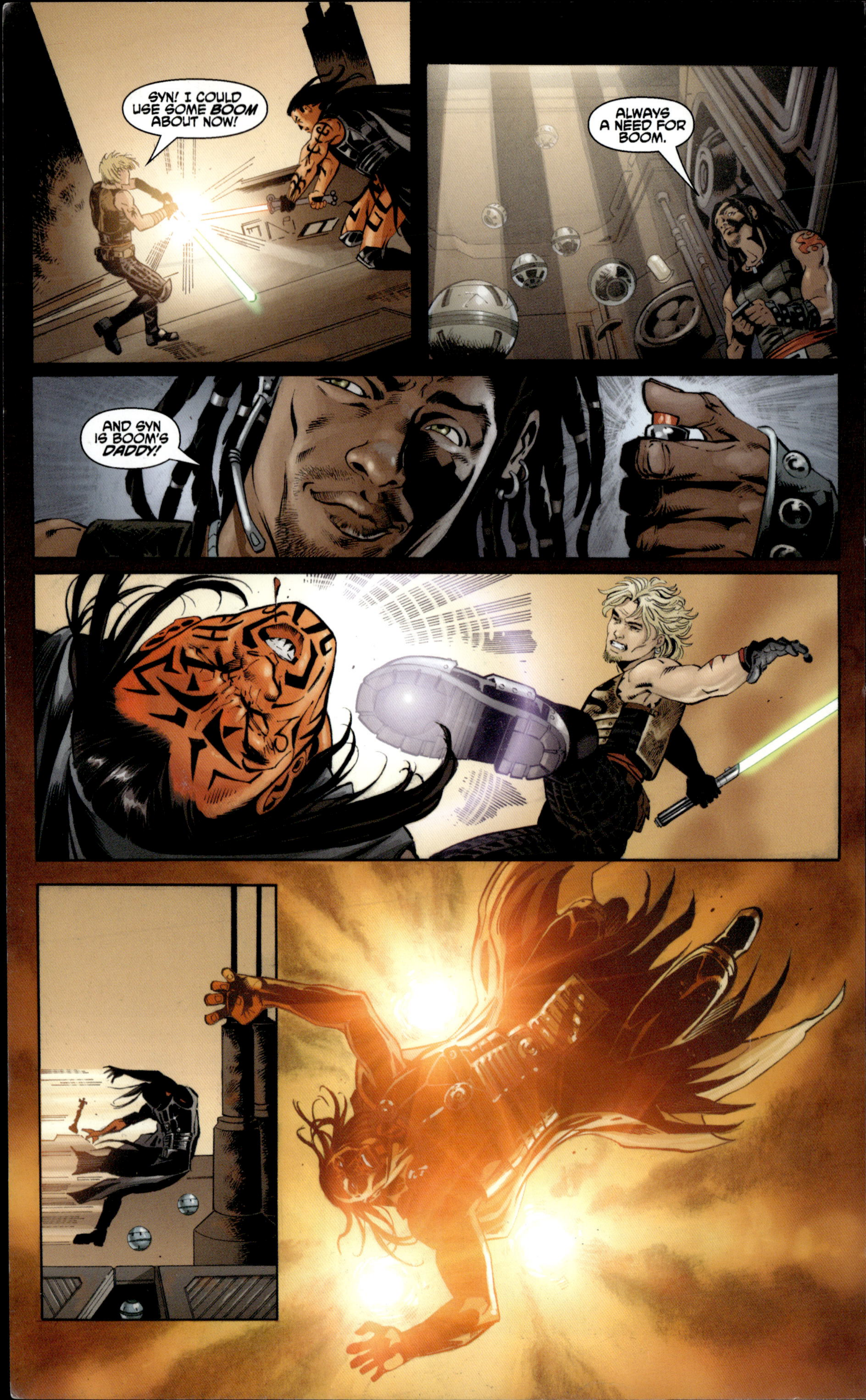
SYN! I COULD USE SOME BOOM ABOUT NOW!
ALWAYS A NEED FOR BOOM.
AND SYN IS BOOM'S DADDY!

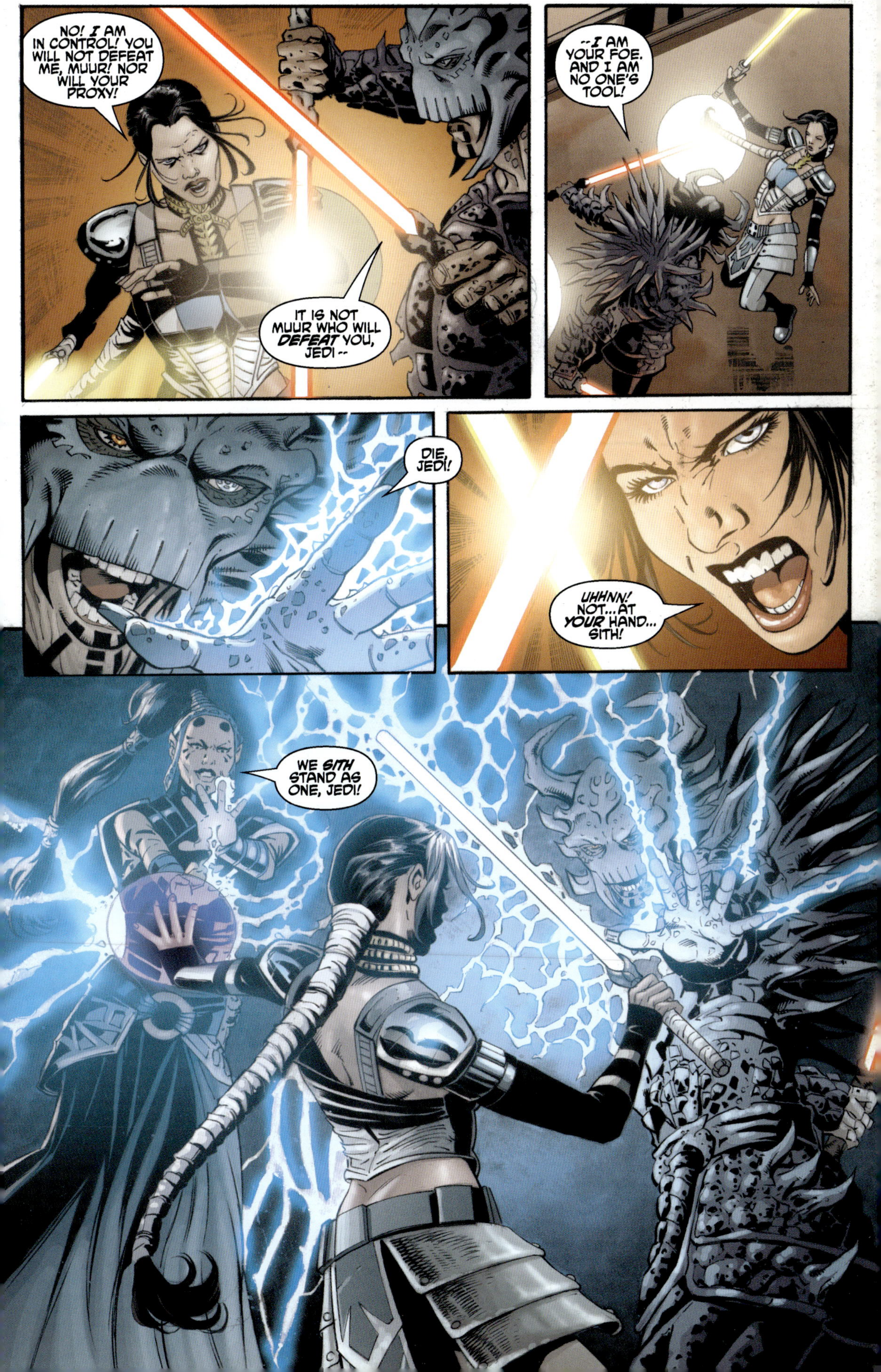
NO! I AM IN CONTROL! YOU WILL NOT DEFEAT ME, MUUR! NOR WILL YOUR PROXY!
IT IS NOT MUUR WHO WILL DEFEAT YOU, JEDI --
--I AM YOUR FOE. AND I AM NO ONE'S TOOL!
DIE, JEDI!
UHHNN! NOT...AT YOUR HAND... SITH!
WE SITH STAND AS ONE, JEDI!

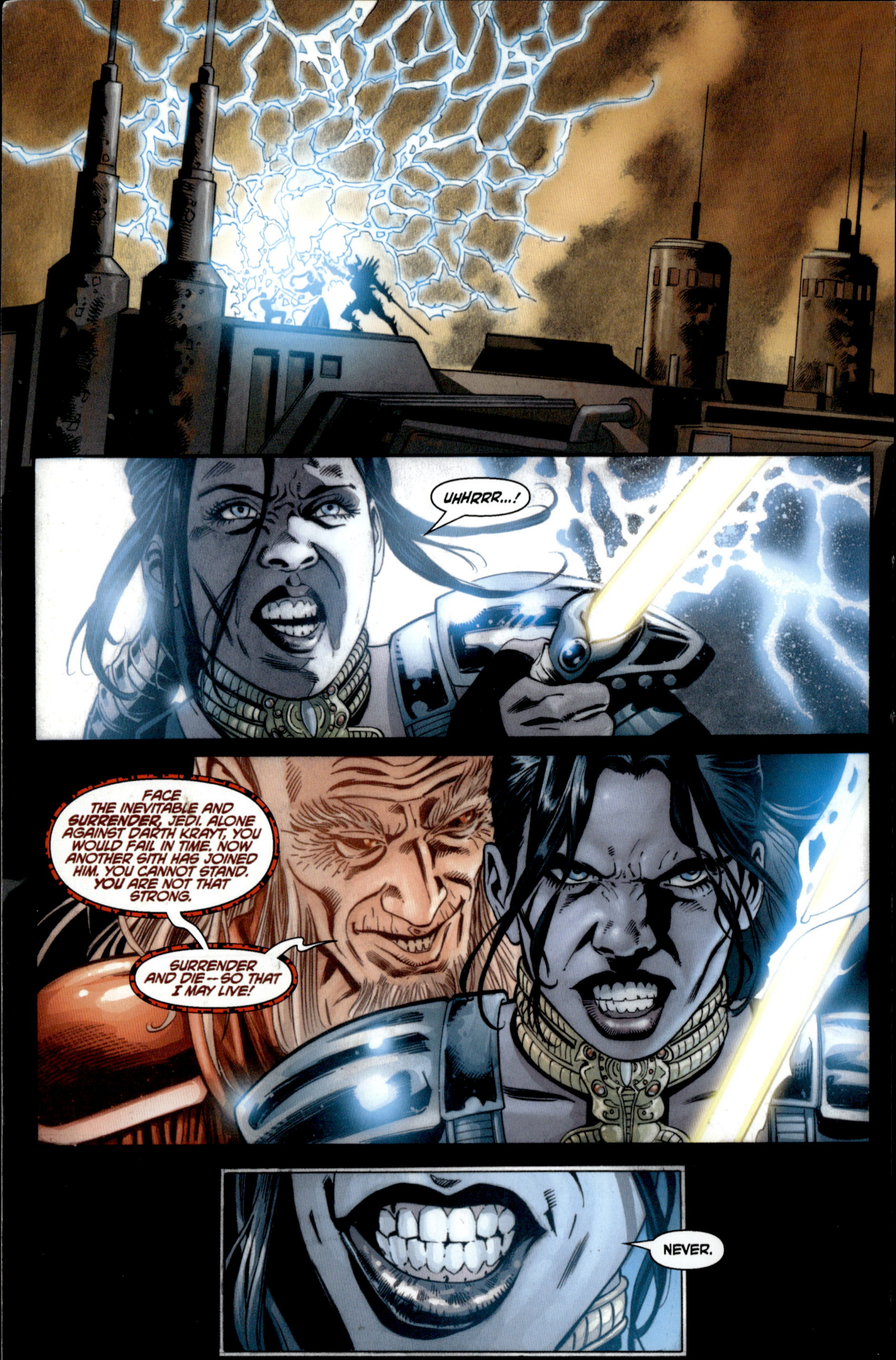
UHHRRR...!
FACE THE INEVITABLE AND SURRENDER, JEDI. ALONE AGAINST DARTH KRAYT, YOU WOULD FAIL IN TIME. NOW ANOTHER SITH HAS JOINED HIM. YOU CANNOT STAND. YOU ARE NOT THAT STRONG.
SURRENDER AND DIE--SO THAT I MAY LIVE!
NEVER.

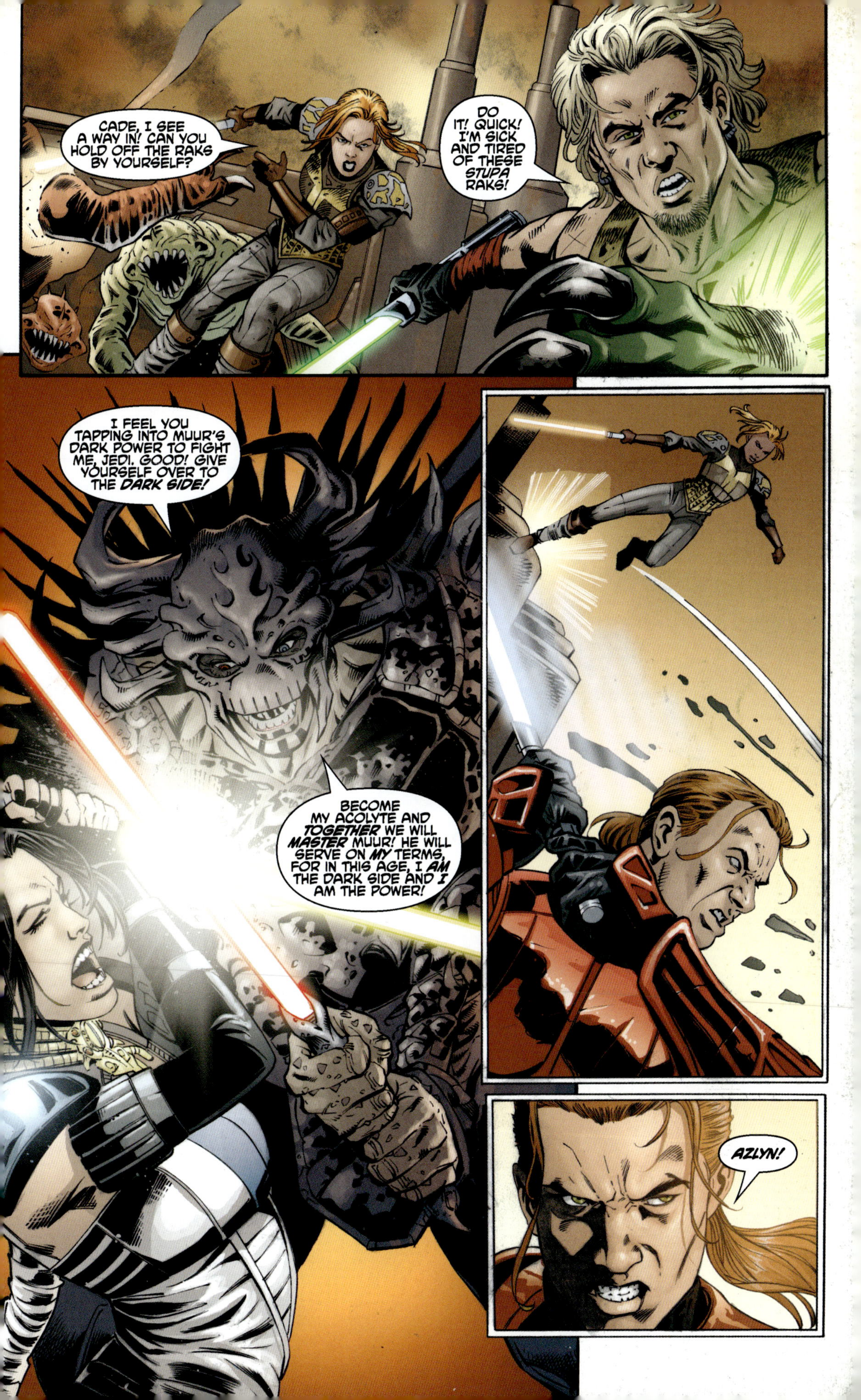
CADE, I SEE A WAY IN! CAN YOU HOLD OFF THE RAKS BY YOURSELF?
DO IT! QUICK! I'M SICK AND TIRED OF THESE STUPA RAKS!
I FEEL YOU TAPPING INTO MUUR'S DARK POWER TO FIGHT ME, JEDI. GOOD! GIVE YOURSELF OVER TO THE DARK SIDE!
BECOME MY ACOLYTE AND TOGETHER WE WILL MASTER MUUR! HE WILL SERVE ON MY TERMS, FOR IN THIS AGE, I AM THE DARK SIDE AND I AM THE POWER!
AZLYN!

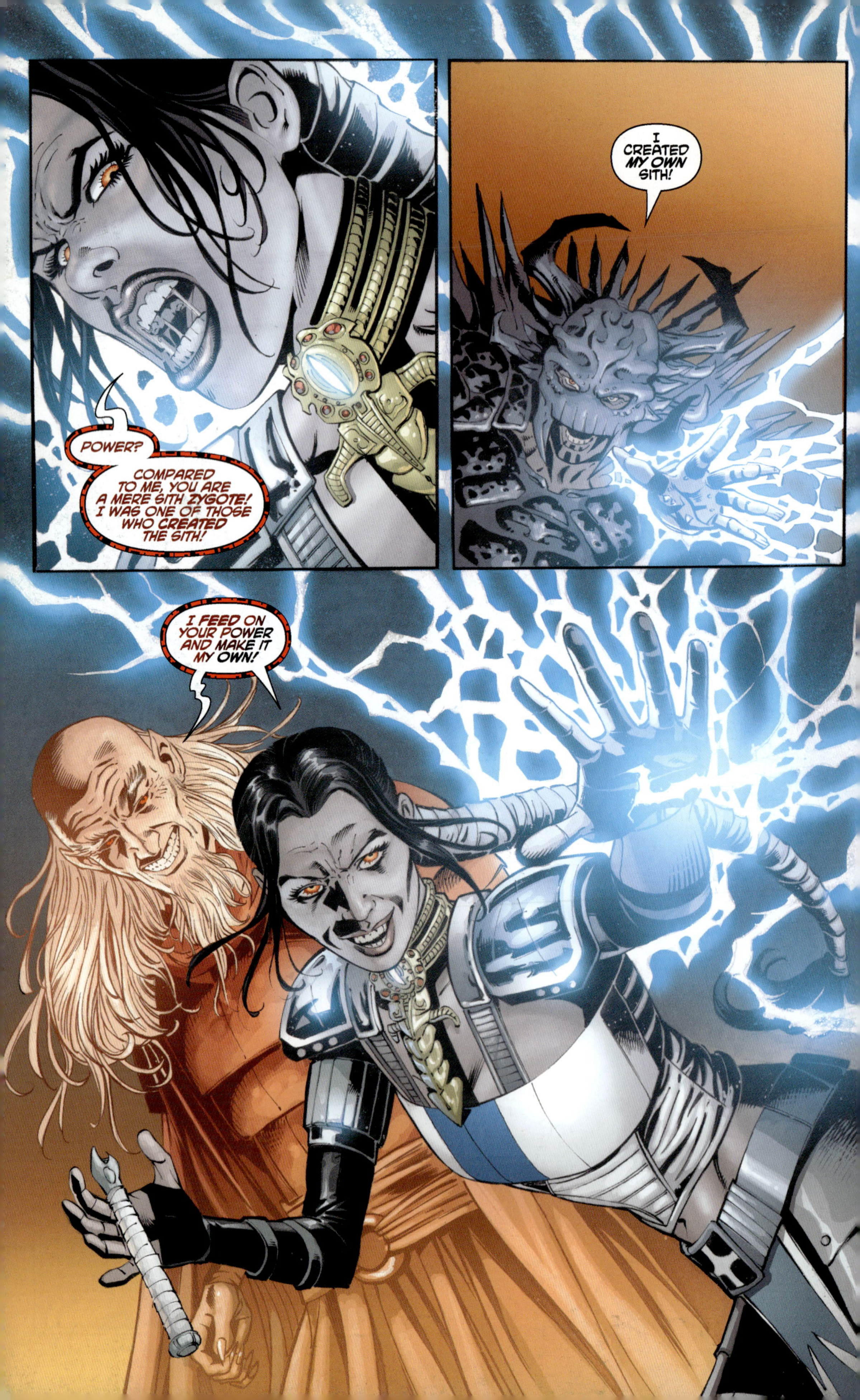
POWER?
COMPARED TO ME, YOU ARE A MERE SITH ZYGOTE! I WAS ONE OF THOSE WHO CREATED THE SITH!
I CREATED MY OWN SITH!
I FEED ON YOUR POWER AND MAKE IT MY OWN!

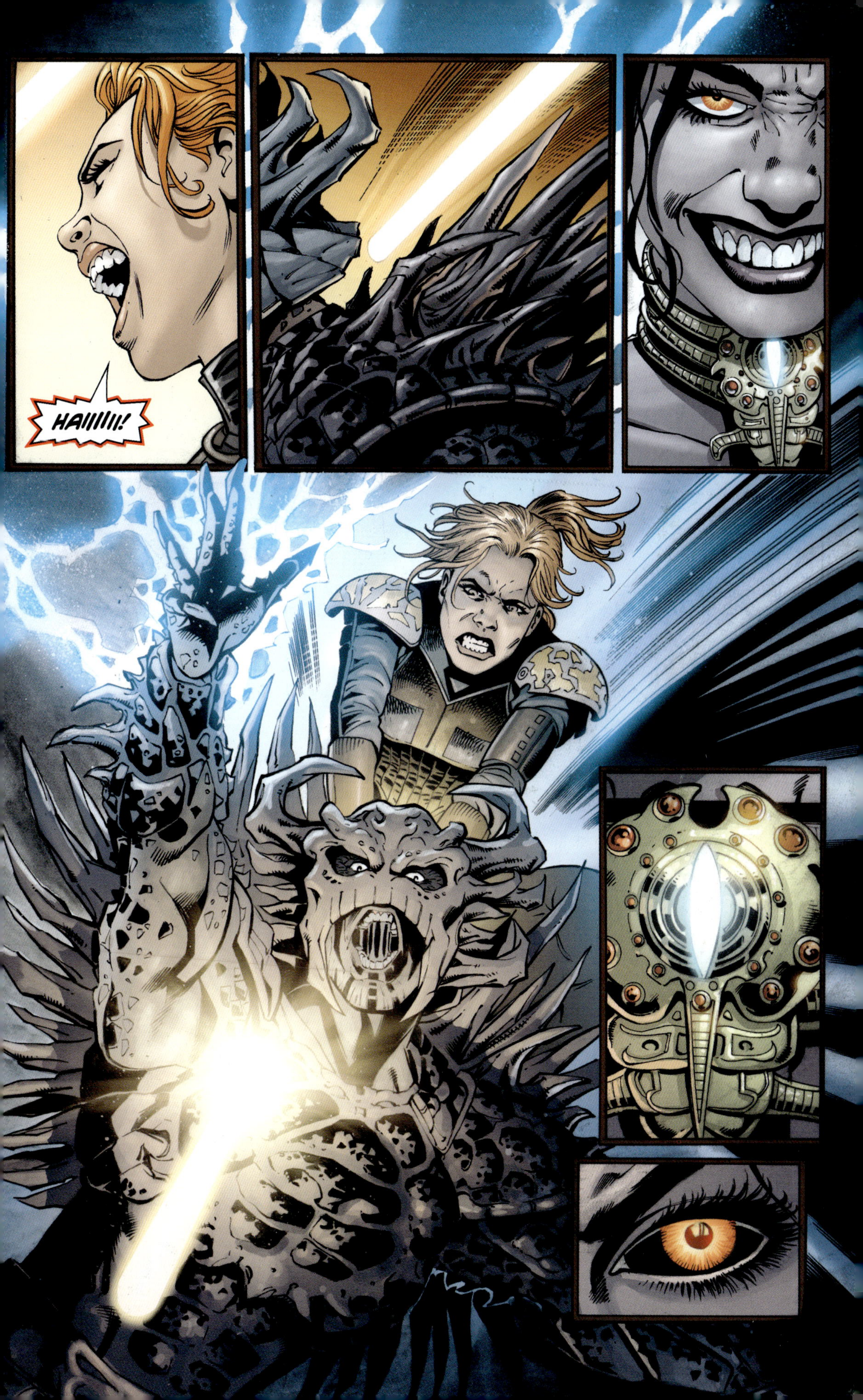
HAIIIIII!

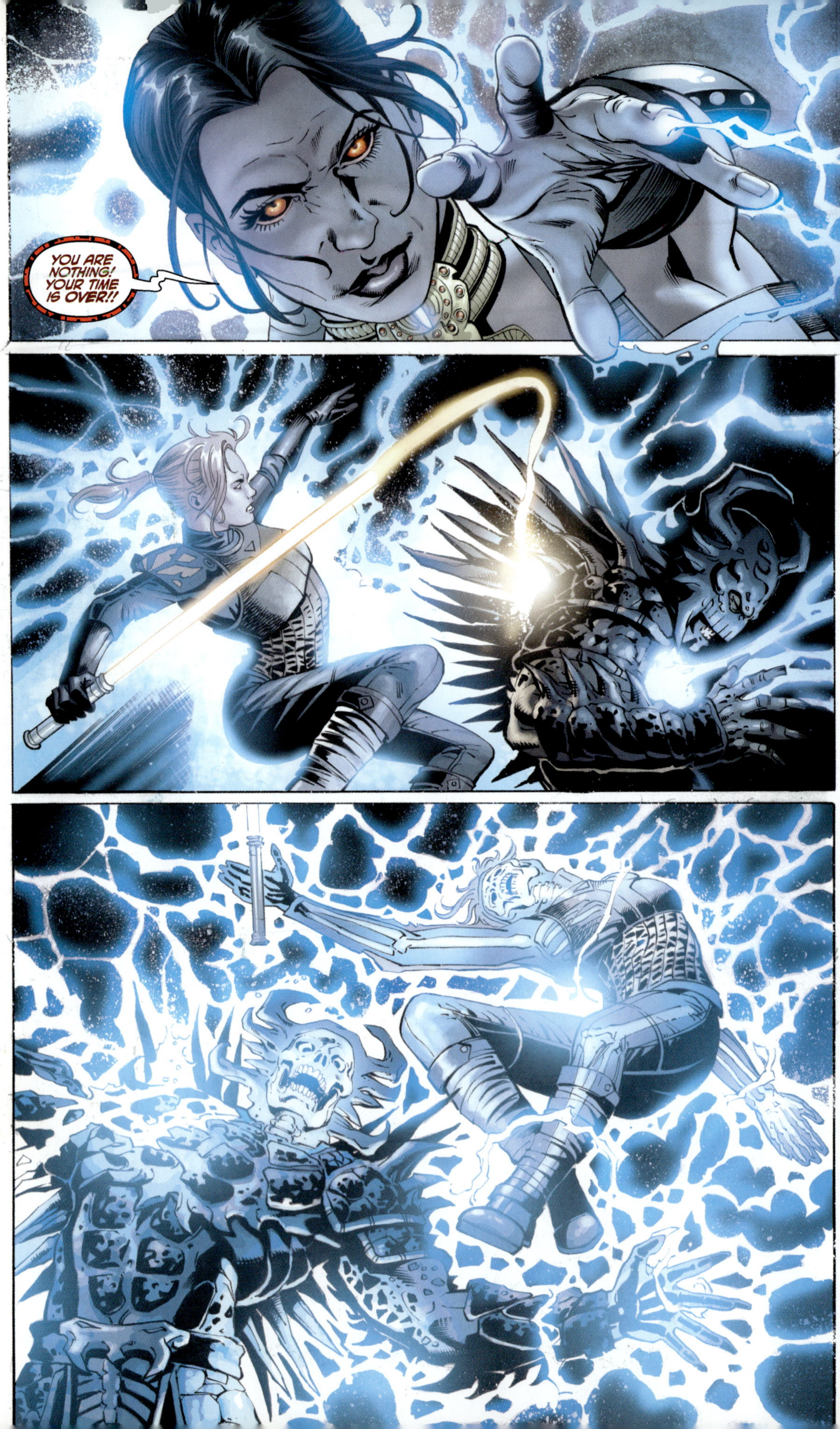
YOU ARE NOTHING! YOUR TIME IS OVER!!

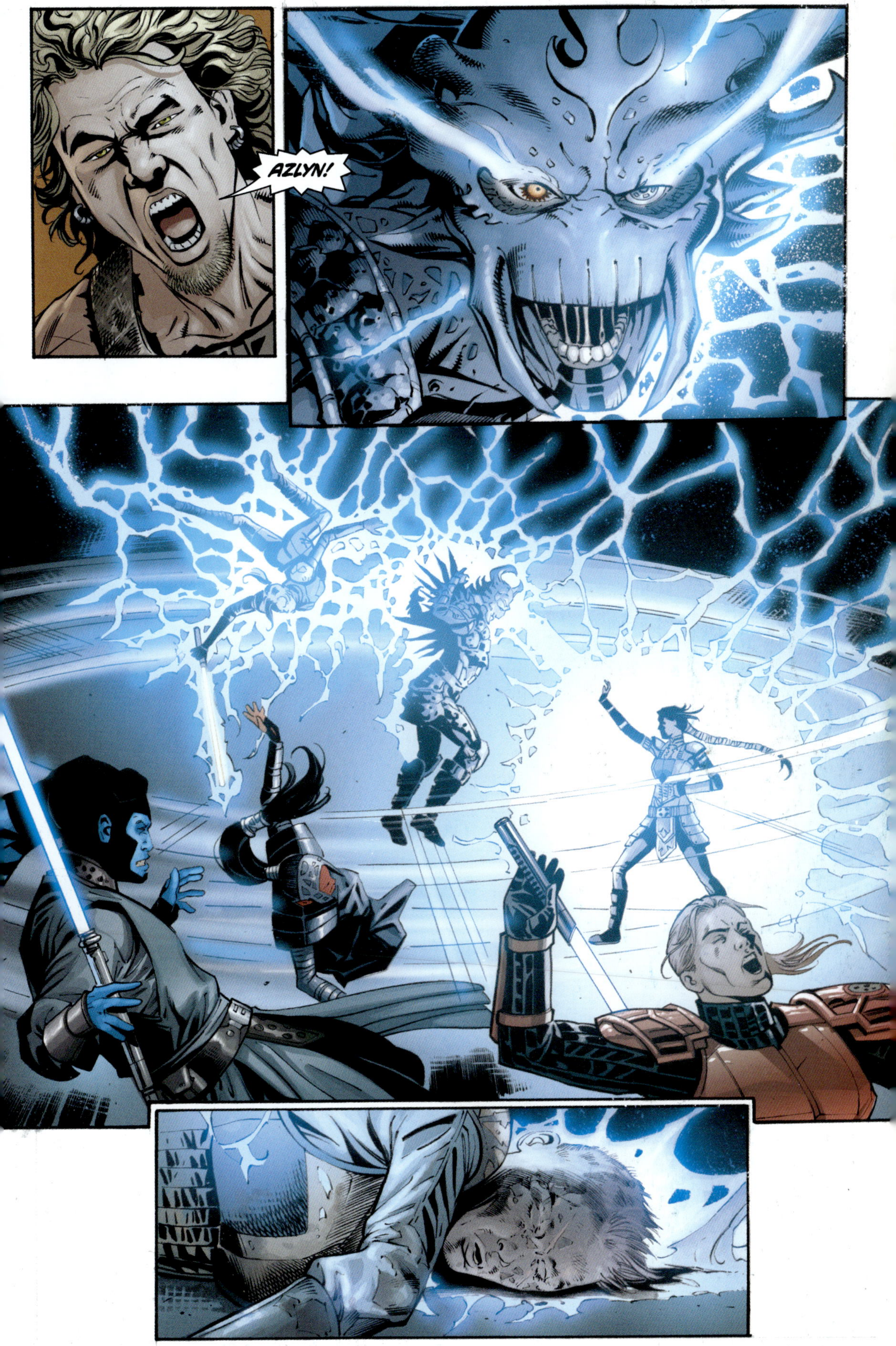
AZLYN!

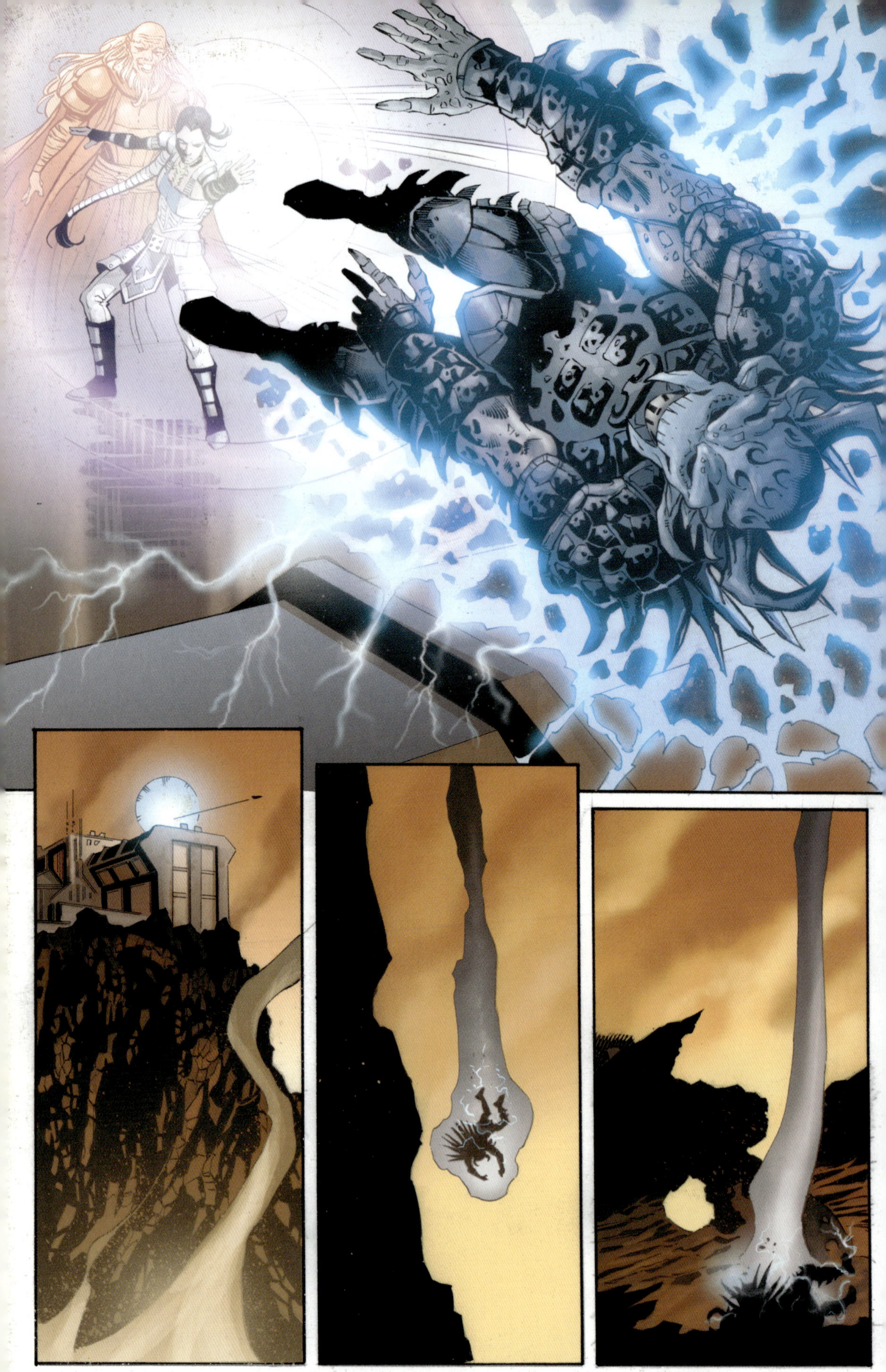

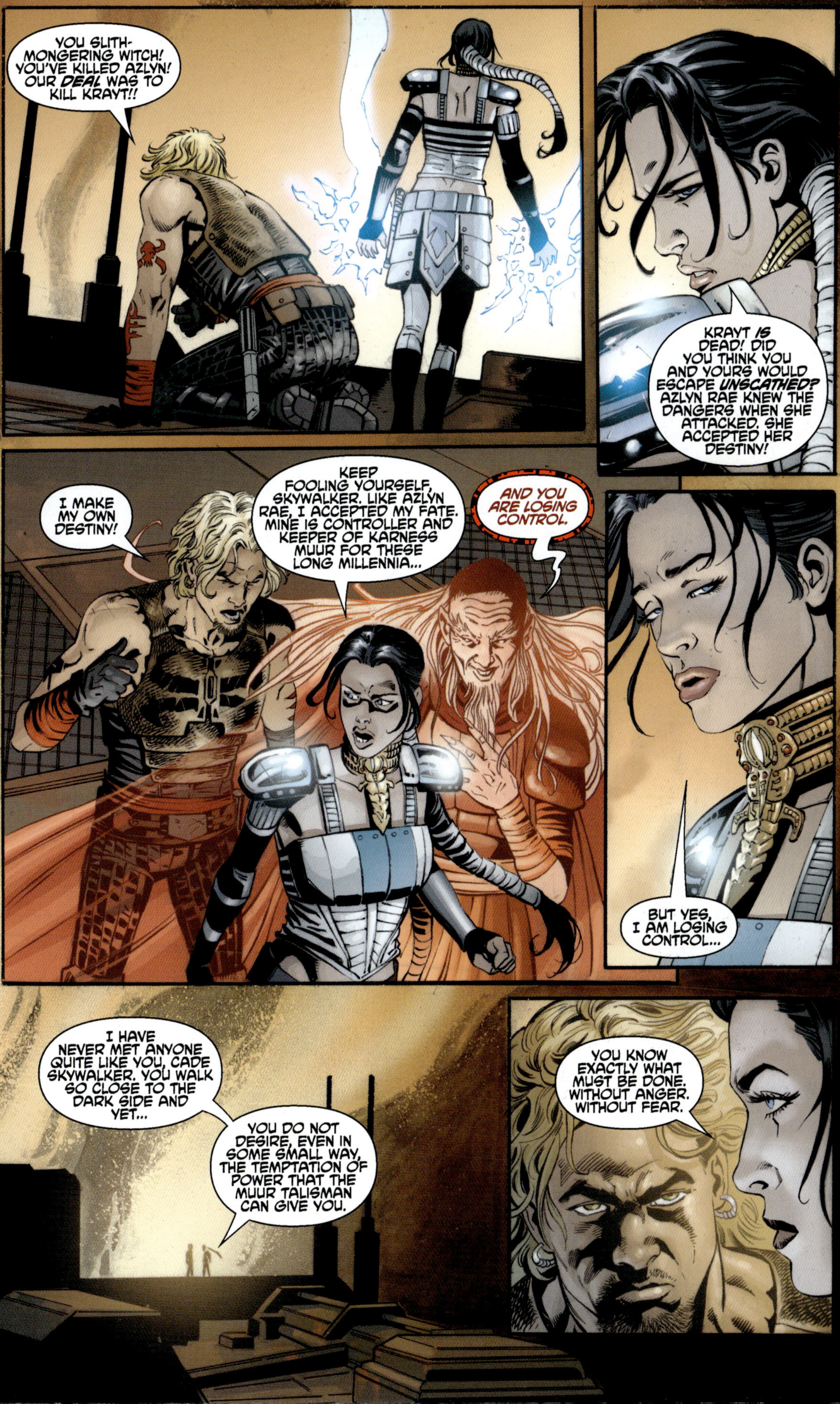
YOU SLITH-MONGERING WITCH! YOU'VE KILLED AZLYN! OUR DEAL WAS TO KILL KRAYT!!
KRAYT IS DEAD! DID YOU THINK YOU AND YOURS WOULD ESCAPE UNSCATHED? AZLYN RAE KNEW THE DANGERS WHEN SHE ATTACKED. SHE ACCEPTED HER DESTINY!
I MAKE MY OWN DESTINY!
KEEP FOOLING YOURSELF, SKYWALKER. LIKE AZLYN RAE, I ACCEPTED MY FATE. MINE IS CONTROLLER AND KEEPER OF KARNESS MUUR FOR THESE LONG MILLENNIA...
AND YOU ARE LOSING CONTROL.
BUT YES, I AM LOSING CONTROL...
I HAVE NEVER MET ANYONE QUITE LIKE YOU, CADE SKYWALKER. YOU WALK SO CLOSE TO THE DARK SIDE AND YET...
YOU DO NOT DESIRE, EVEN IN SOME SMALL WAY, THE TEMPTATION OF POWER THAT THE MUUR TALISMAN CAN GIVE YOU.
YOU KNOW EXACTLY WHAT MUST BE DONE. WITHOUT ANGER. WITHOUT FEAR.

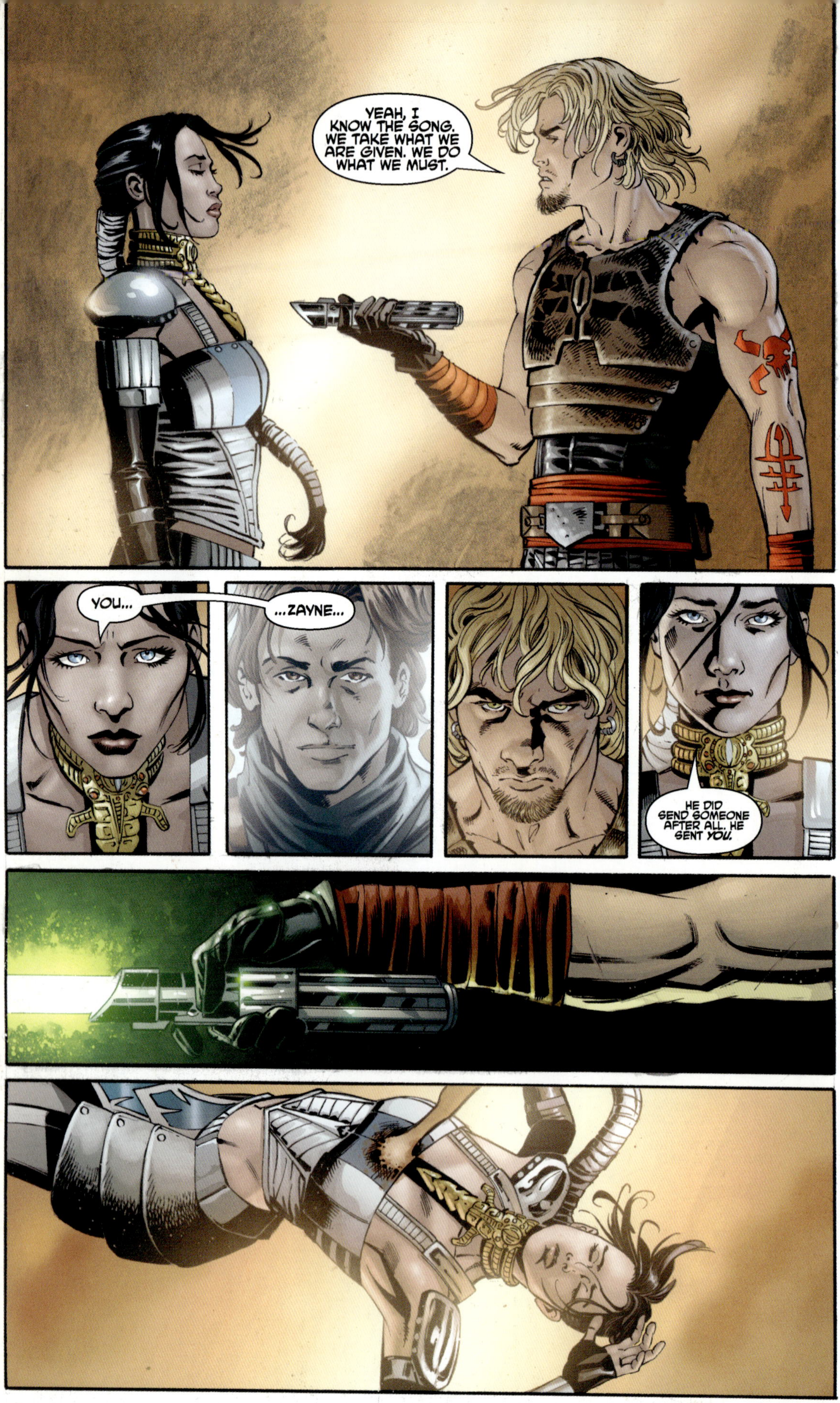
YEAH, I KNOW THE SONG. WE TAKE WHAT WE ARE GIVEN. WE DO WHAT WE MUST.
YOU...
...ZAYNE...
HE DID SEND SOMEONE AFTER ALL. HE SENT *YOU.*

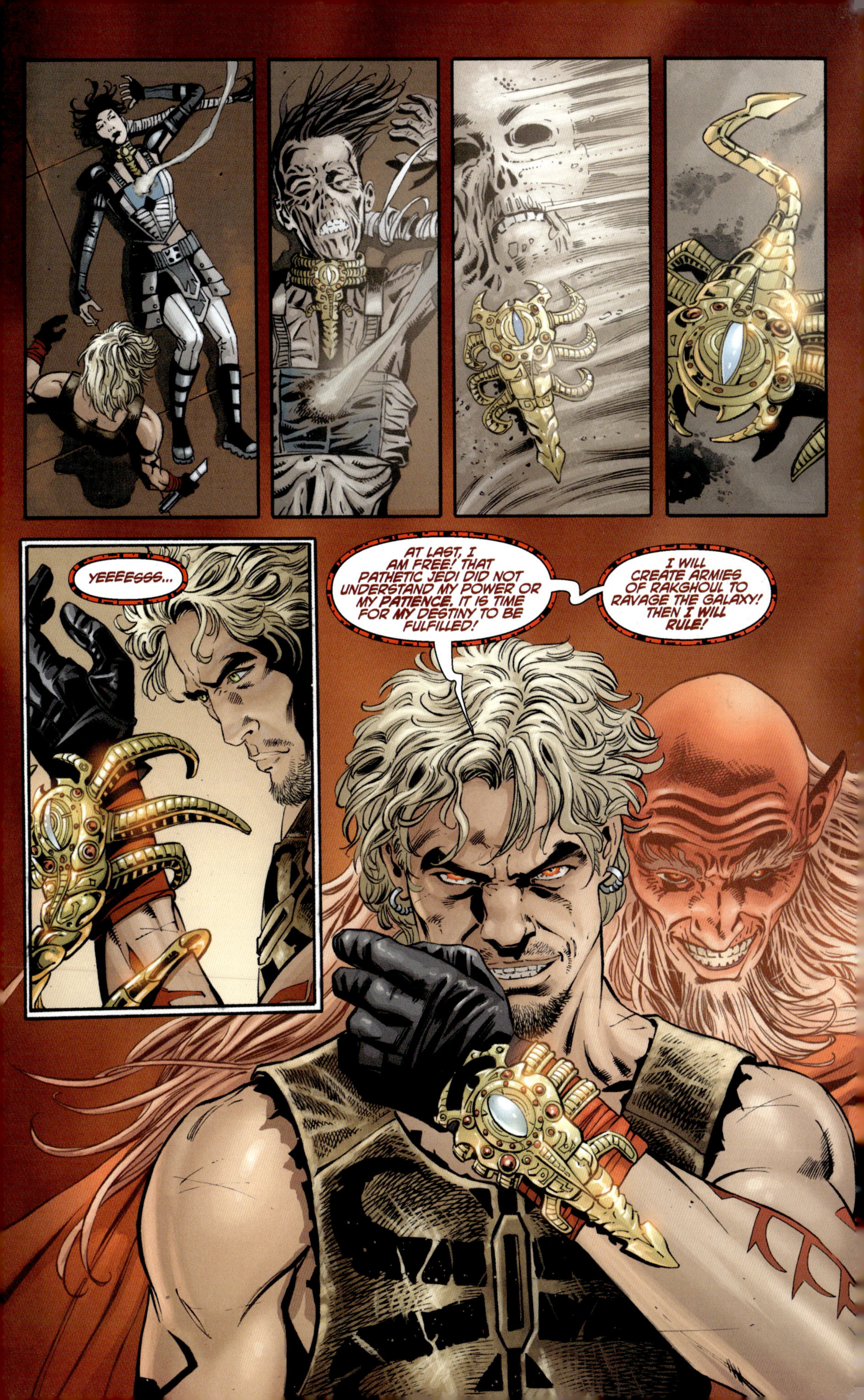
YEEEESSS...
AT LAST, I AM FREE! THAT PATHETIC JEDI DID NOT UNDERSTAND MY POWER OR MY PATIENCE. IT IS TIME FOR MY DESTINY TO BE FULFILLED!
I WILL CREATE ARMIES OF RAKGHOUL TO RAVAGE THE GALAXY! THEN I WILL RULE!

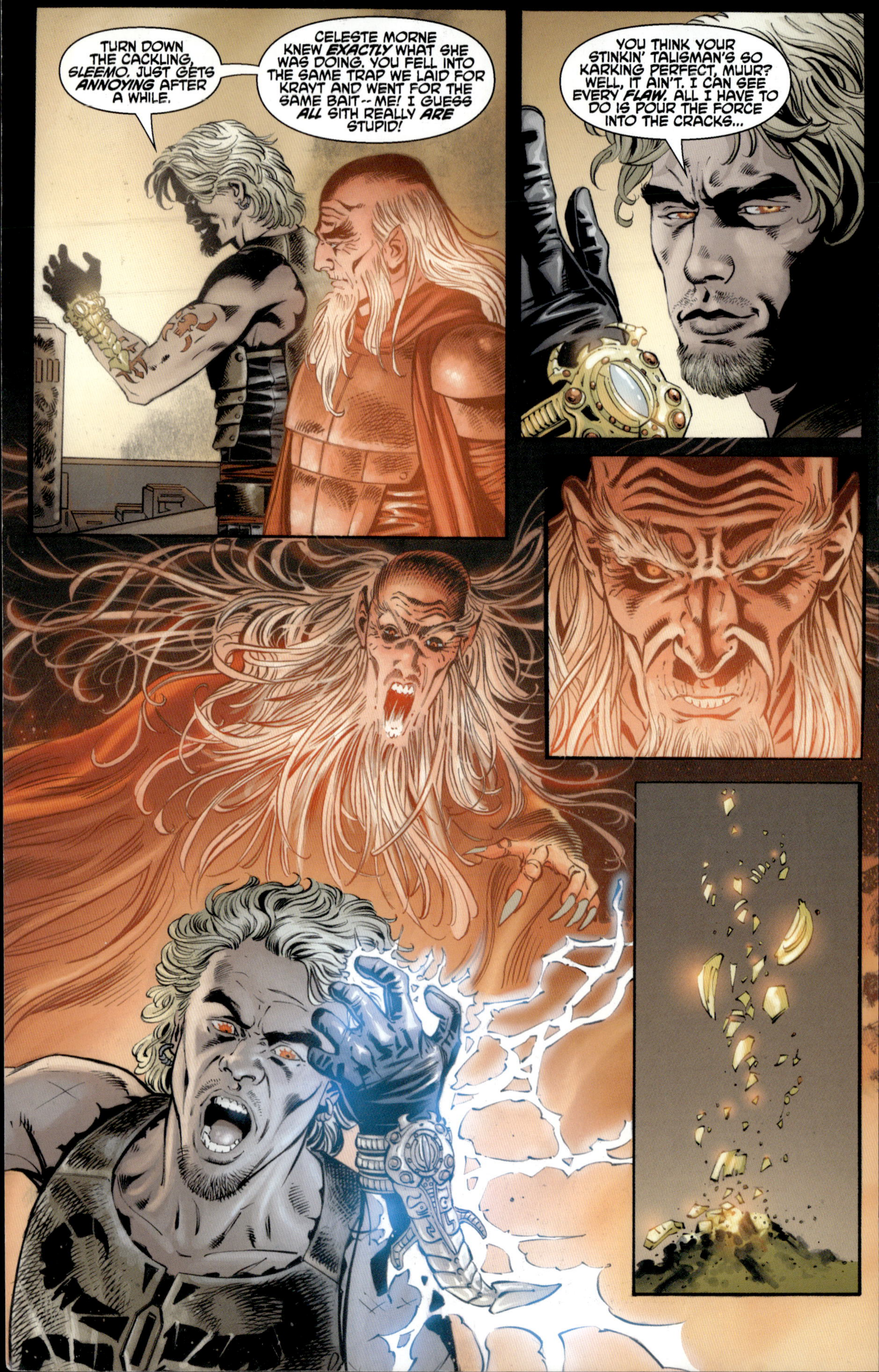
TURN DOWN THE CACKLING, SLEEMO. JUST GETS ANNOYING AFTER A WHILE.
CELESTE MORNE KNEW EXACTLY WHAT SHE WAS DOING. YOU FELL INTO THE SAME TRAP WE LAID FOR KRAYT AND WENT FOR THE SAME BAIT-- ME! I GUESS ALL SITH REALLY ARE STUPID!
YOU THINK YOUR STINKIN' TALISMAN'S SO KARKING PERFECT, MUUR? WELL, IT AIN'T. I CAN SEE EVERY FLAW. ALL I HAVE TO DO IS POUR THE FORCE INTO THE CRACKS...

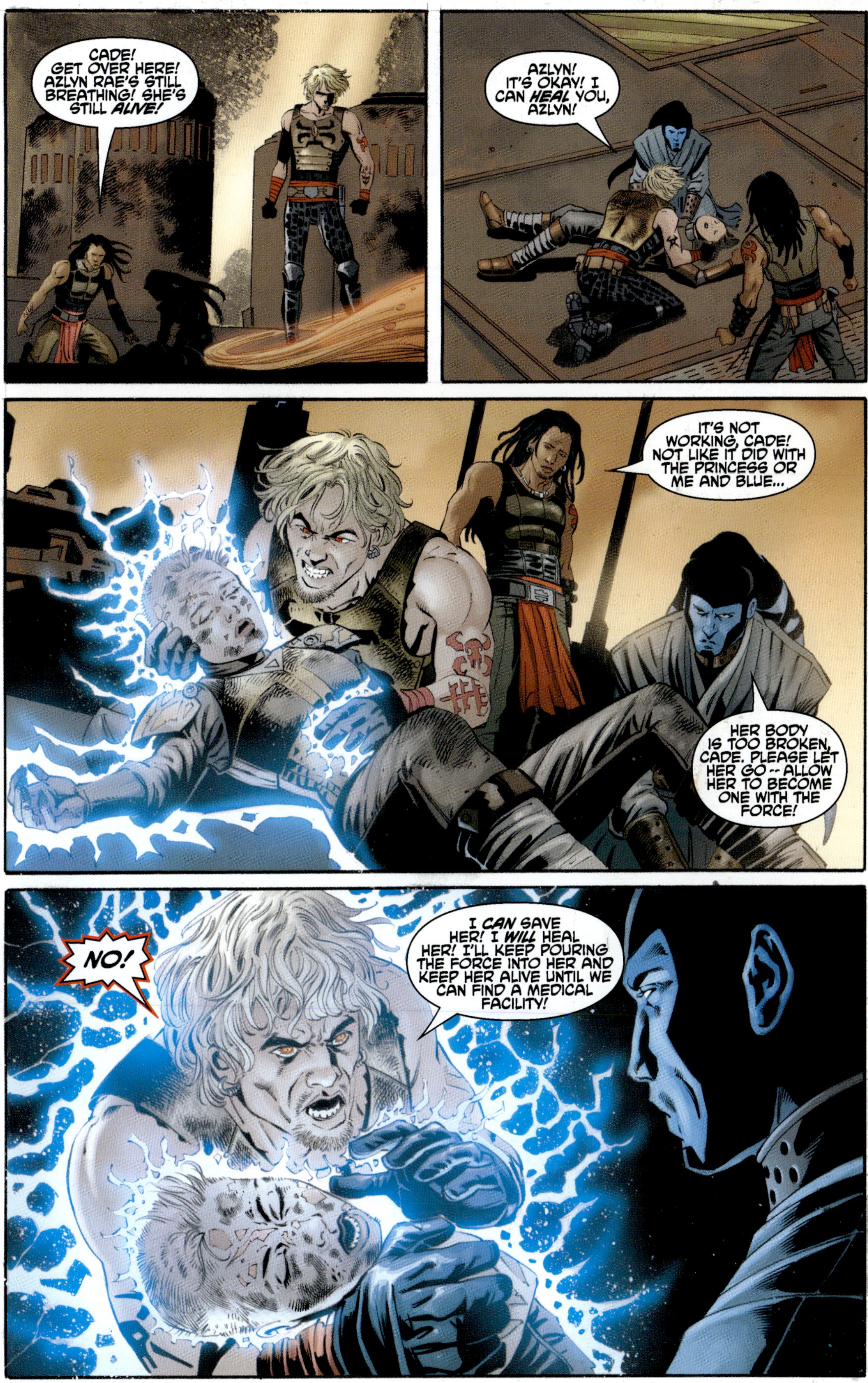
CADE! GET OVER HERE! AZLYN RAE'S STILL BREATHING! SHE'S STILL ALIVE!
AZLYN! IT'S OKAY! I CAN HEAL YOU, AZLYN!
IT'S NOT WORKING, CADE! NOT LIKE IT DID WITH THE PRINCESS OR ME AND BLUE...
HER BODY IS TOO BROKEN, CADE. PLEASE LET HER GO -- ALLOW HER TO BECOME ONE WITH THE FORCE!
NO!
I CAN SAVE HER! I WILL HEAL HER! I'LL KEEP POURING THE FORCE INTO HER AND KEEP HER ALIVE UNTIL WE CAN FIND A MEDICAL FACILITY!

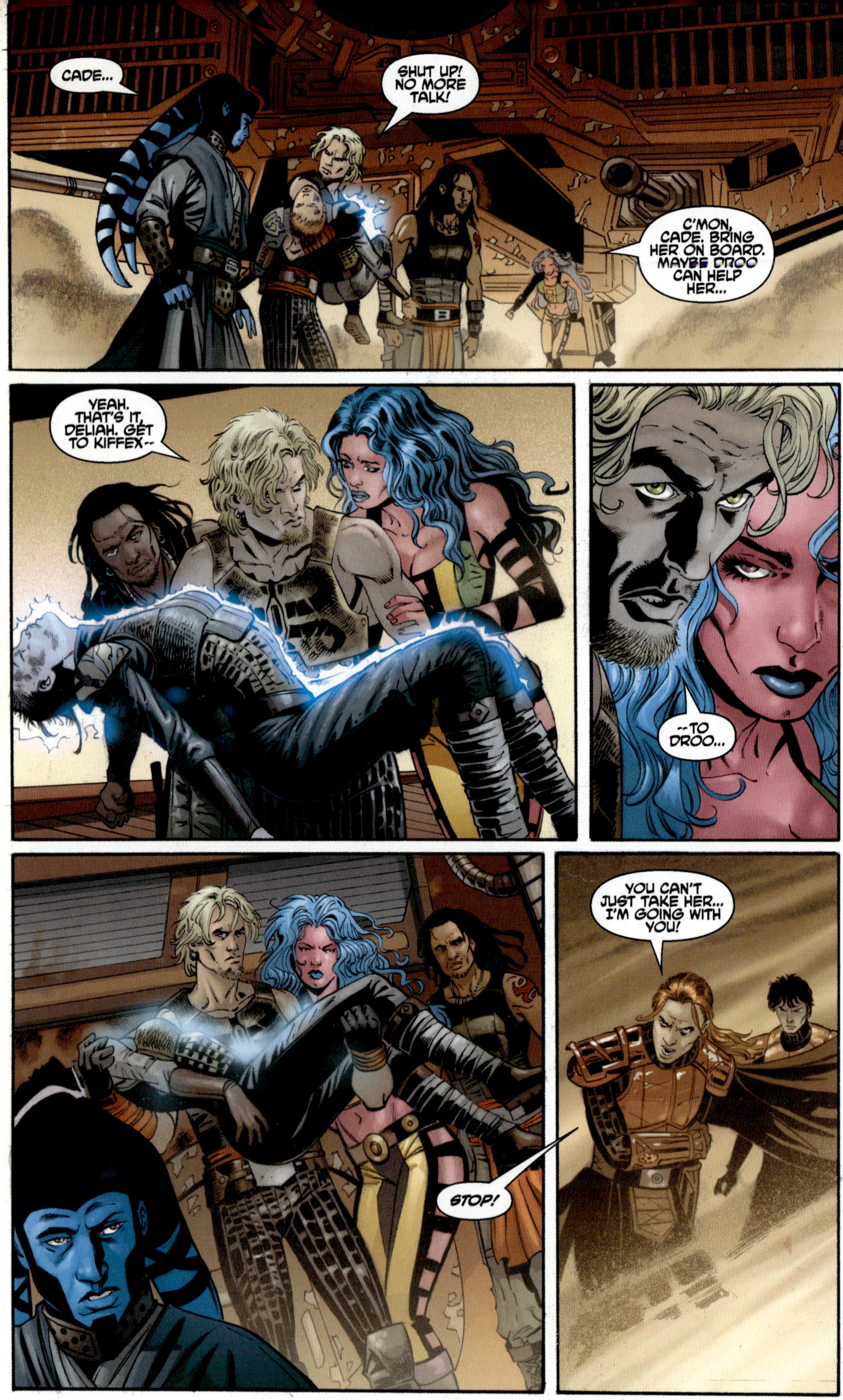
CADE...
SHUT UP! NO MORE TALK!
C'MON, CADE. BRING HER ON BOARD. MAYBE DROO CAN HELP HER...
YEAH. THAT'S IT, DELIAH. GET TO KIFFEX--
--TO DROO...
STOP!
YOU CAN'T JUST TAKE HER... I'M GOING WITH YOU!

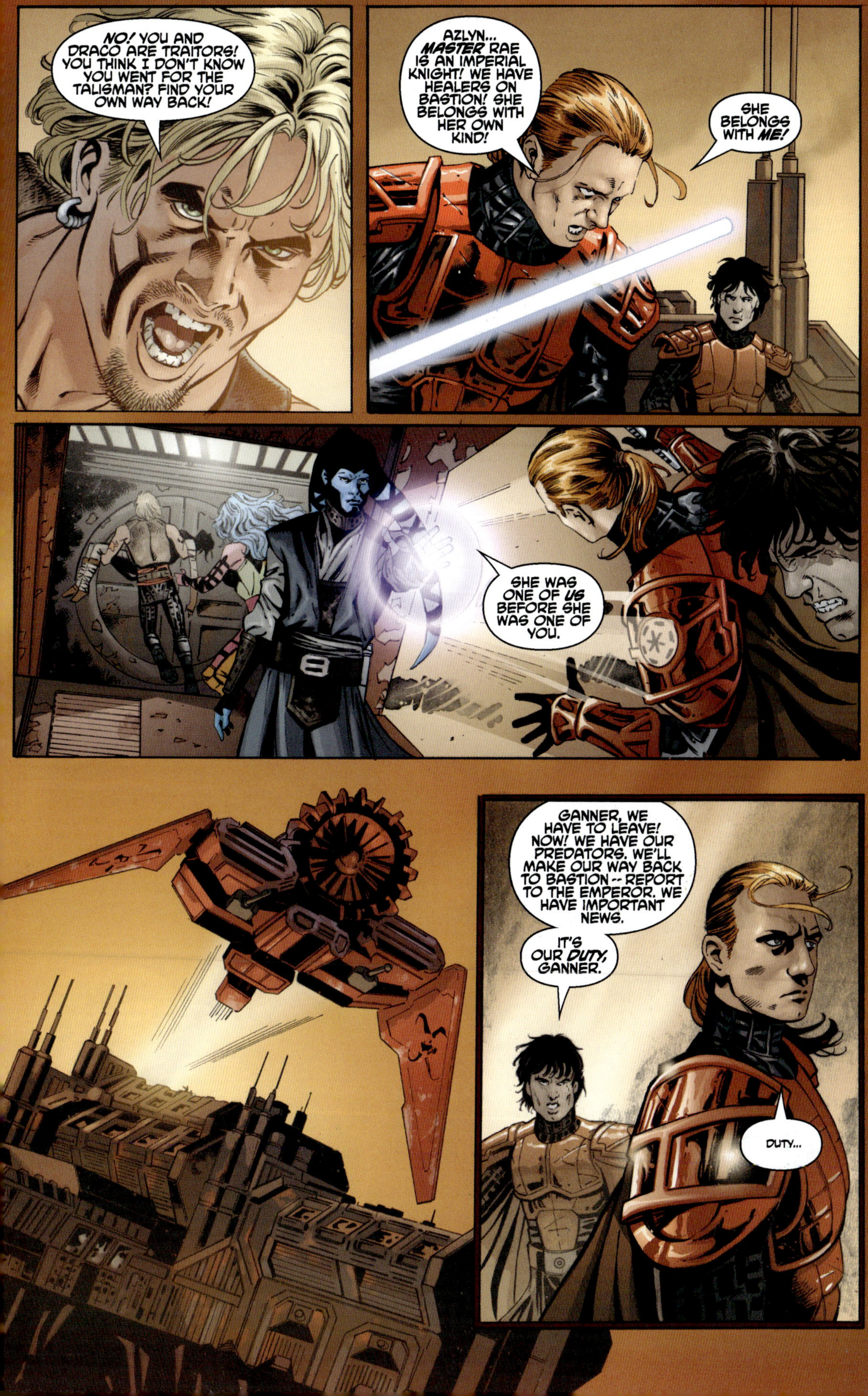
NO! YOU AND DRACO ARE TRAITORS! YOU THINK I DON'T KNOW YOU WENT FOR THE TALISMAN? FIND YOUR OWN WAY BACK!
AZLYN... MASTER RAE IS AN IMPERIAL KNIGHT! WE HAVE HEALERS ON BASTION! SHE BELONGS WITH HER OWN KIND!
SHE BELONGS WITH ME!
SHE WAS ONE OF US BEFORE SHE WAS ONE OF YOU.
GANNER, WE HAVE TO LEAVE! NOW! WE HAVE OUR PREDATORS. WE'LL MAKE OUR WAY BACK TO BASTION -- REPORT TO THE EMPEROR. WE HAVE IMPORTANT NEWS.
IT'S OUR DUTY, GANNER.
DUTY...

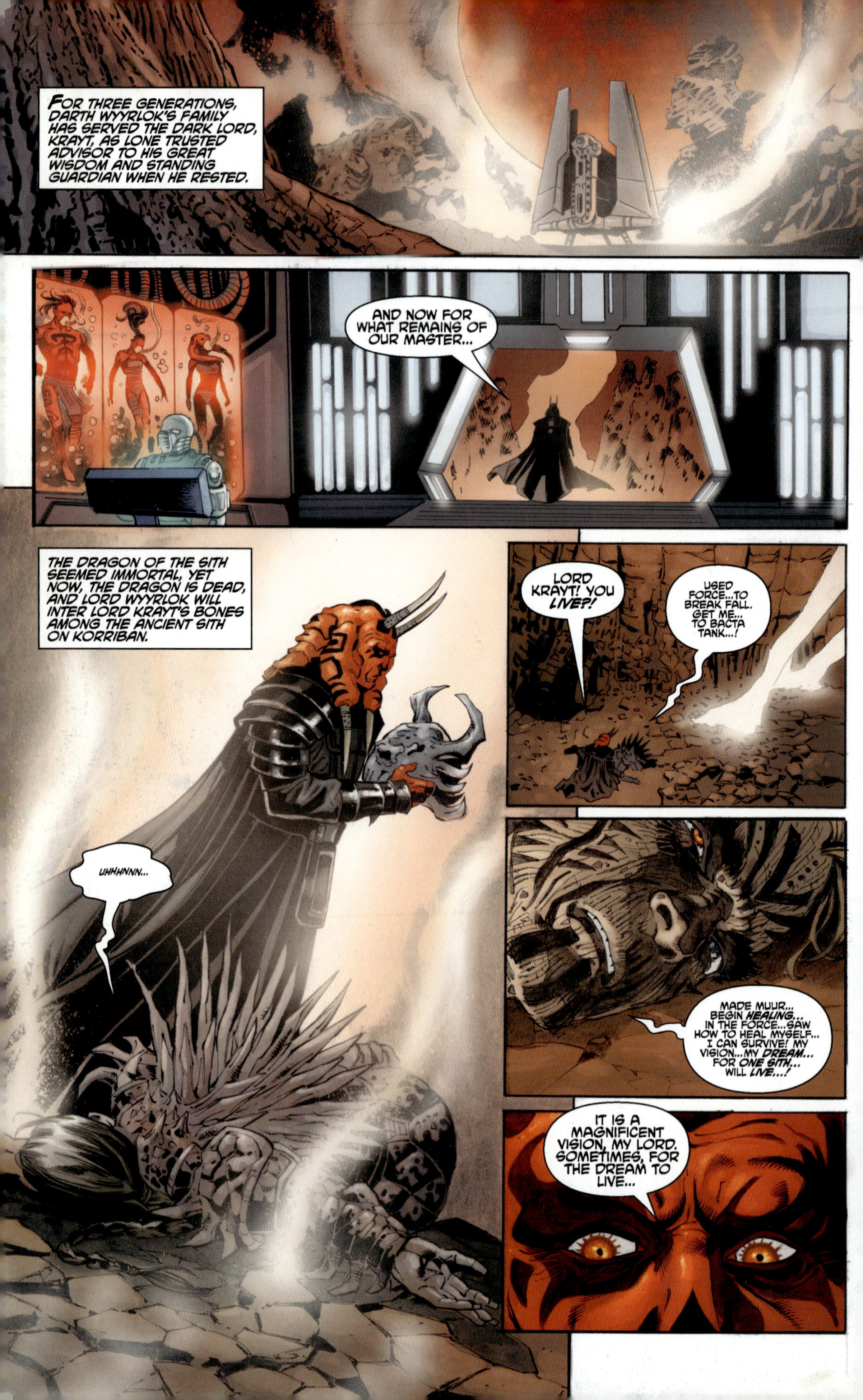

FOR THREE GENERATIONS, DARTH WYYRLOK'S FAMILY HAS SERVED THE DARK LORD, KRAYT, AS LONE TRUSTED ADVISOR TO HIS GREAT WISDOM AND STANDING GUARDIAN WHEN HE RESTED.
AND NOW FOR WHAT REMAINS OF OUR MASTER...
THE DRAGON OF THE SITH SEEMED IMMORTAL, YET NOW, THE DRAGON IS DEAD, AND LORD WYYRLOK WILL INTER LORD KRAYT'S BONES AMONG THE ANCIENT SITH ON KORRIBAN.
UHHHNNN...
LORD KRAYT! YOU LIVE?!
USED FORCE...TO BREAK FALL. GET ME... TO BACTA TANK...!
MADE MUUR... BEGIN HEALING... IN THE FORCE...SAW HOW TO HEAL MYSELF... I CAN SURVIVE! MY VISION...MY DREAM... FOR ONE SITH... WILL LIVE...!
IT IS A MAGNIFICENT VISION, MY LORD. SOMETIMES, FOR THE DREAM TO LIVE...

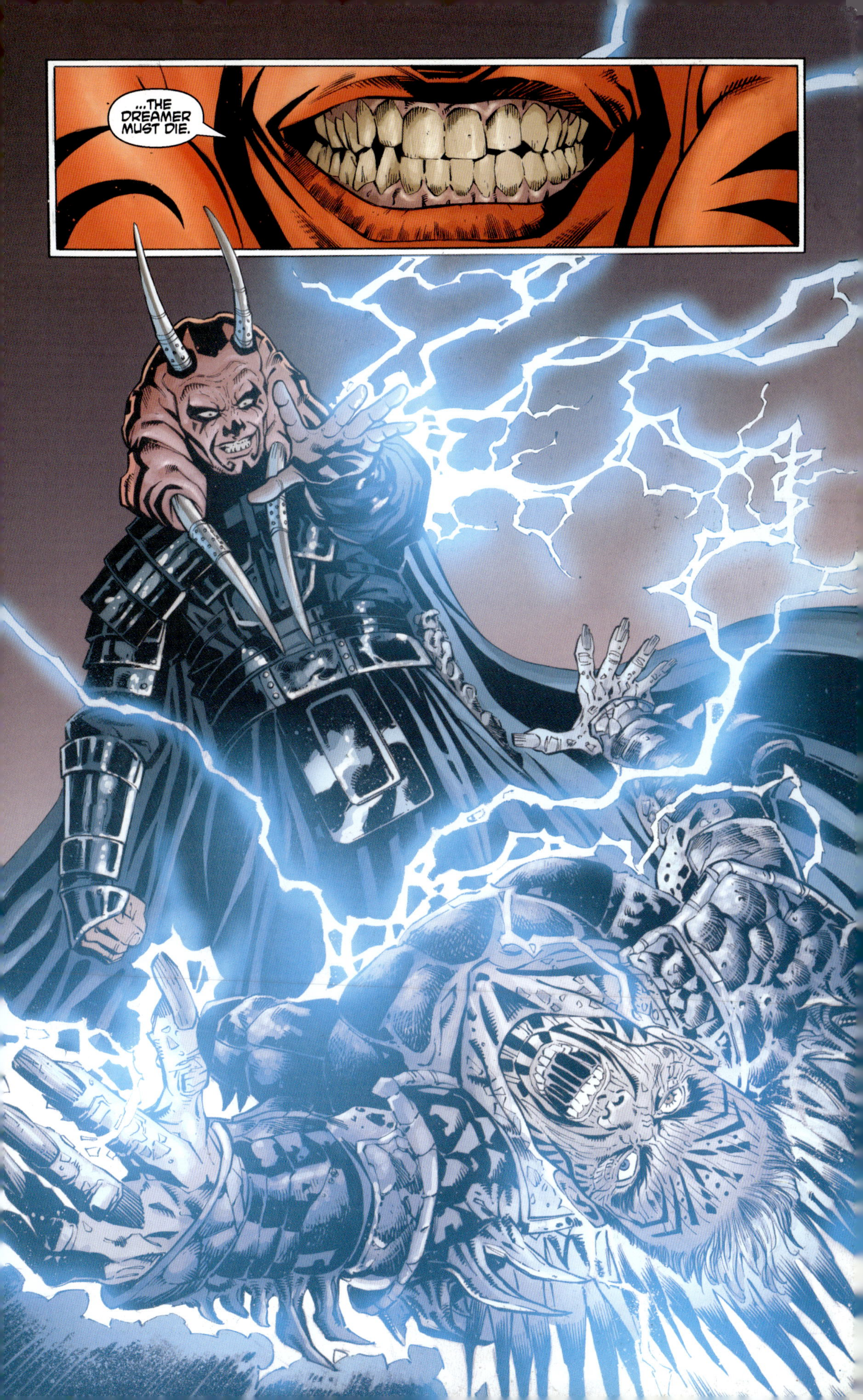
...THE DREAMER MUST DIE.

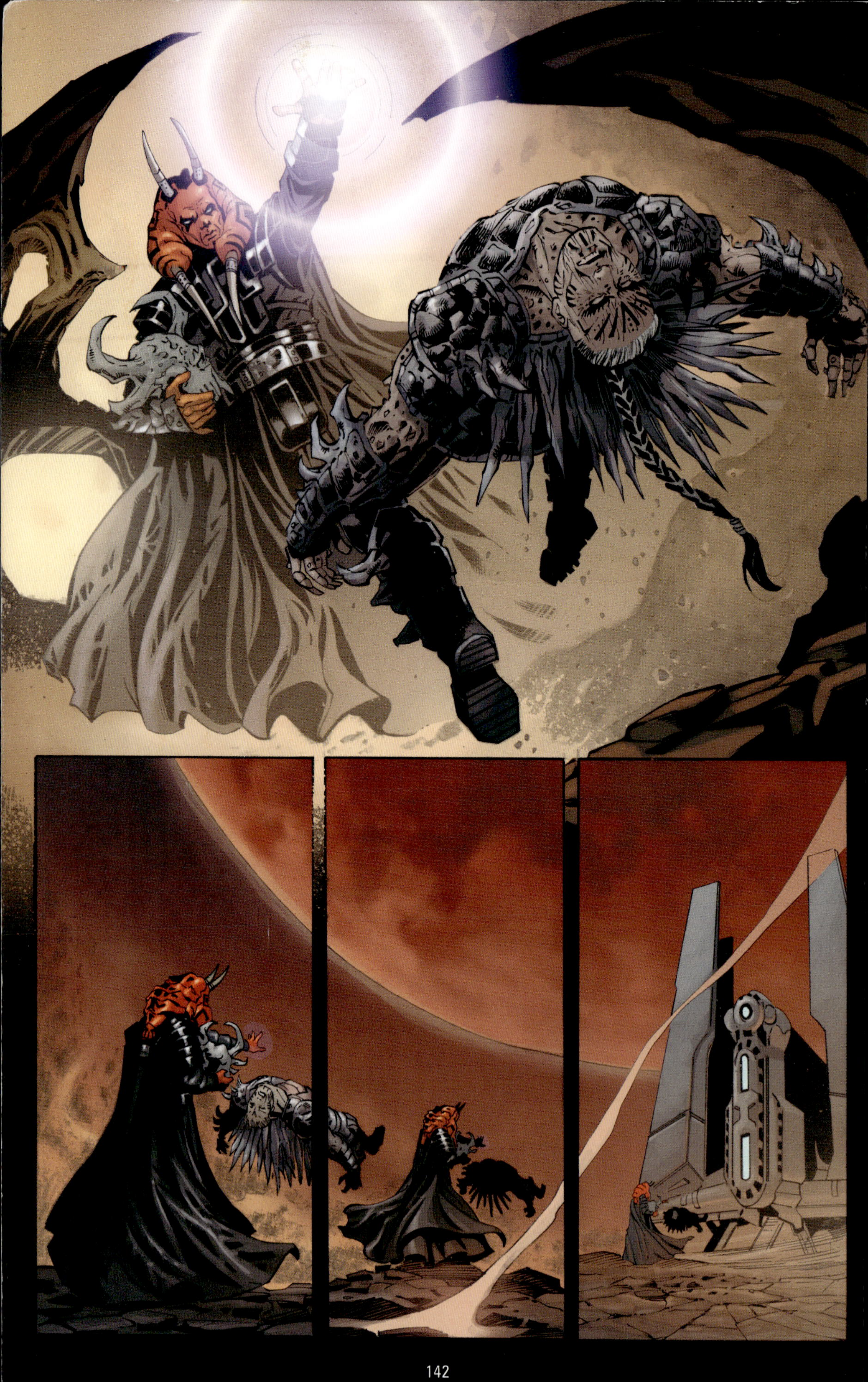

MIKE RICHARDSON president and publisher NEIL HANKERSON executive vice president TOM WEDDLE chief financial officer RANDY STRADLEY vice president of publishing MICHAEL MARTENS vice president of business development ANITA NELSON vice president of marketing, sales, and licensing DAVID SCROGGY vice president of product development DALE LAFOUNTAIN vice president of information technology DARLENE VOGEL director of purchasing KEN LIZZI general counsel DAVEY ESTRADA editorial director SCOTT ALLIE senior managing editor CHRIS WARNER senior books editor, Dark Horse Books ROB SIMPSON senior books editor, M Press DIANA SCHUTZ executive editor CARY GRAZZINI director of design and production LIA RIBACCHI art director CARA NIECE director of scheduling

PAST > > > > > > > PRESENT > > > > > > > FUTURE

STAR WARS® VECTOR

An event with repercussions for every era and every hero in the *Star Wars* galaxy begins here! For anyone who never knew where to start with *Star Wars* comics, *Vector* is the perfect introduction to the entire *Star Wars* line! For any serious *Star Wars* fan, *Vector* is a must-see event with major happenings throughout the most important moments of the galaxy's history!

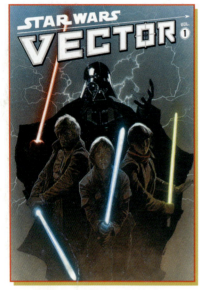

VOLUME ONE
(*Knights of the Old Republic* Vol. 5; *Dark Times* Vol. 3)
ISBN 978-1-59582-226-0 | $17.95

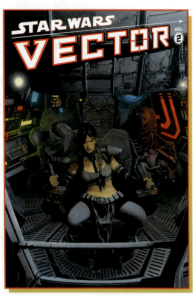

VOLUME TWO
(*Rebellion* Vol. 4; *Legacy* Vol. 6)
ISBN 978-1-59582-227-7 | $17.95

KNIGHTS OF THE OLD REPUBLIC
Volume One: Commencement
ISBN 978-1-59307-640-5 | $18.95

Volume Two: Flashpoint
ISBN 978-1-59307-761-7 | $18.95

Volume Three: Days of Fear, Nights of Anger
ISBN 978-1-59307-867-6 | $18.95

Volume Four: Daze of Hate, Knights of Suffering
ISBN 978-1-59582-208-6 | $18.95

REBELLION
Volume One: My Brother, My Enemy
ISBN 978-1-59307-711-2 | $14.95

Volume Two: The Ahakista Gambit
ISBN 978-1-59307-890-4 | $17.95

Volume Three: Small Victories
ISBN 978-1-59582-166-9 | $12.95

LEGACY
Volume One: Broken
ISBN 978-1-59307-716-7 | $17.95

Volume Two: Shards
ISBN 978-1-59307-879-9 | $19.95

Volume Three: Claws of the Dragon
ISBN 978-1-59307-946-8 | $17.95

Volume Four: Alliance
ISBN 978-1-59582-223-9 | $15.95

Volume Five: The Hidden Temple
ISBN 978-1-59582-224-6 | $15.95

DARK TIMES
Volume One: The Path to Nowhere
ISBN 978-1-59307-792-1 | $17.95

Volume Two: Parallels
ISBN 978-1-59307-945-1 | $17.95

www.darkhorse.com
**AVAILABLE AT YOUR LOCAL COMICS SHOP OR BOOKSTORE.
TO FIND A COMICS SHOP IN YOUR AREA, CALL 1-888-266-4226**
For more information or to order direct: On the web: darkhorse.com
E-mail: mailorder@darkhorse.com • Phone: 1-800-862-0052 Mon.–Fri.
9 A.M. to 5 P.M. Pacific Time. STAR WARS © 2004–2008 Lucasfilm Ltd. & ™ (BL8005)

DARK HORSE BOOKS